A Short History of Shanghai

A Short History of Shanghai

BEING AN ACCOUNT OF THE GROWTH AND DEVELOPMENT OF THE INTERNATIONAL SETTLEMENT

BY

F. L. HAWKS POTT, D.D.

Author of *A Sketch of Chinese History*

*With Seven Illustrations
and One Map*

SHANGHAI

KELLY & WALSH, LIMITED

AND AT HONGKONG & SINGAPORE

MCMXXVIII

PRINTED AT THE PRESS OF KELLY & WALSH, LTD., SHANGHAI, CHINA.

To E. G. P.

WHO LIKE THE AUTHOR HAS WITNESSED THE DEVELOP-
MENT OF THE UNIQUE SETTLEMENT FOR OVER
FORTY YEARS, AND WHO BY HER VALU-
ABLE CO-OPERATION HAS MADE HIS
TASK MORE ENJOYABLE, THIS
BOOK IS GRATEFULLY
DEDICATED.

PREFACE.

When the author first undertook to write this brief history of the International Settlement of Shanghai, he failed to realize the difficulty of the task. Messrs. George Lanning and Samuel Couling gathered a large amount of material concerning the early days, but no one continued what they began, and therefore a good deal of spade work became necessary.

Many books have been consulted. a list of which is published at the end of the volume, and the columns of the *North-China Herald* have proved invaluable.

Another difficulty presented itself in regard to the public for which he was writing. He tried to bear in mind that it was for a larger public than for the residents of Shanghai. Many incidents might be of interest to those who live in the Settlement but would not be of much importance to the public at large. By some, probably, the criticism will be raised that the book lacks local colour, while others will perhaps object that too much reference has been made to matters that are of no concern to the rest of the world. It was hard to please the tastes of both classes.

As the book developed several things became apparent. It was evident that the history of Shanghai was difficult to condense, and that there was room for a bigger volume than this. There are so many details that it would have been easier to have depicted it on a larger canvas.

One also realized that in order to understand what has happened in Shanghai, considerable reference to Chinese contemporary history was necessary, and there was always a temptation to wander away from what was strictly the history of Shanghai to that of China.

It is hardly possible that the book is entirely free from inaccuracies, especially as much of it is derived from second-hand sources, and the author will consider it a favour to have mistakes pointed out.

He wishes to acknowledge his indebtedness to a large number of friends, both foreign and Chinese, for their assistance, especially Mr. Isaac Mason, (who read the manuscript and made many valuable suggestions), Lady Annie de Sausmarez, Mr. J. C. Shengle, Dr. C. Noel Davis, Dr. H. Chatley, Mr. C. Harpur, Mr. O. M. Green, Mr. R. Y. F. Sun, Mr. A. F. Ollerdessen, Mr. E. T. Byrne, and to his Secretary, Mr. K. L. Dzung, who supplied him with interesting information from Chinese sources, otherwise difficult to obtain.

Appreciating the large amount of work done by previous writers, he is content if the book is useful in carrying the story a stage further, and proves of some value to future historians as well as to the general public.

F. L. H. P.

St. John's University,

Shanghai, December, 1928.

CONTENTS.

LIST OF ILLUSTRATIONS.

MAP.

A Short History of Shanghai

A Short History of Shanghai

CHAPTER I.

SHANGHAI
BEFORE ITS OPENING TO FOREIGN TRADE.

First Impressions When a traveller arrives in Shanghai to-day he is struck by the fact that to all intents and purposes he might be in a large European city.

The tall buildings, the well paved streets, the large hotels and clubs, the parks and bridges, the stream of automobiles, the trams and buses, the numerous foreign shops, and, at night, the brilliant electric lighting,—all are things he is accustomed to in the homeland. Of course there is much that is different; the crowds of Chinese in the streets, the imposing Sikh policemen, the ricshas and the wheelbarrows, and the Chinese shops with their ornate gilding and picturesque signboards.

Shanghai is a very cosmopolitan place, a meeting-ground for people from all countries, a great and a unique city, one of the most remarkable in the world.

When the stranger is told that the land now occupied by the International Settlement and the French Concession was originally a low mud bank with scattered Chinese hamlets, he is surprised and astonished at the marvellous growth that has taken place between 1843 and 1927, a period of about eighty-five years.

The Old Native City Before the advent of the foreigner to the shores of China, the old city of Shanghai had existed for many years. It is situated in latitude 31° 41′ 15″ North, longitude 121° 29′ East, in the province of Kiangsu, on the left, or west, bank of the Whangpoo, about twelve miles from the point where that river empties itself into the estuary of the Yangtze. Into the Whangpoo, a short distance to the north, flows the Soochow Creek, a waterway connecting Shanghai with the cities of the hinterland.

It was built on delta land formed in ancient days by the silt from the Yangtze River.

Just when the city was first founded it is impossible to say, but it is mentioned in history 2,150 years ago. Judging from its old name "Hu," it probably first came into importance as a fishing town. Owing to its excellent anchorage, it was destined to become a commercial port, and in A.D. 1280 it was re-named Shanghai, meaning "above the sea," or "Upper Sea." From the fact that there is another place some distance below the present city, called "Hsia Hai" or "Lower Sea," it is supposed that originally there may have been two arms of the sea, extending inland, one known as the "Lower Sea," and the other as the "Upper Sea," and that Shanghai derived its name through being built on the "Upper Sea." [1]

On account of the depredations of Japanese pirates, permission was obtained to enclose it with a wall in A.D. 1554. This wall was removed after the Revolution of 1911, and the moat which originally surrounded it was filled up, making it difficult for the stranger to tell now where the old native city begins.

Shanghai from the historical point of view is insignificant compared with other large Chinese cities.

One of the most famous local sites is the temple Ching An Ssu, close by the Bubbling Well, about three miles from The Bund of the modern Settlement. This well is known as the sixth spring of importance in the

---

[1] Some interesting information in regard to old Shanghai may be found in "Some Notes on the History and Folk Lore of Old Shanghai" by Rev. A. P. Parker, D.D., *Journal of the North-China Branch of the Royal Asiatic Society,* Vol. XLVII (1916), pp. 87-88.

country. Its "bubbling," which appears mysterious to visitors, is caused by the formation of marsh and carbonic acid gas. Near the temple is held every year in the spring what is known as the Bamboo Fair. It comes at the time of the birthday of Buddha. Articles made of bamboo and other commodities are on sale for several days and vast crowds of purchasers and sightseers gather in the same way as at a country fair.

Another notable site is that of the Lunghua, or "Dragon Flower," Pagoda, which dates from the later Han Dynasty, A.D. 221, or, according to another account, from the Tang Dynasty, A.D. 800.

One other historic place, Siccawei, might be mentioned, although it belongs to a much later period. The correct spelling of the name in the Shanghai dialect would be Zi-ka-wei, and from this Siccawei has been derived. The Chinese characters mean, "the residence of the family Zi." Here was born in 1562, Hsü Kwang-ch'i, or as he was afterwards called Paul Hsü (Hsü is the mandarin pronunciation of Zi). He was one of the first of the high Chinese officials to enter the Christian Church, being pupil, convert, and friend of the great Jesuit missionary Matteo Ricci. He was a great scholar and the author of several important works, among them being a tract written in 1616 in defence of the Christian Religion. His family property was afterwards acquired by the Jesuits and became the site of the large work now carried on at Siccawei. His grave may be seen at Siccawei at the south-west corner of the Church of St. Ignatius.

Shanghai passed through many vicissitudes. Between the fourteenth and eighteenth centuries there were more than forty periods of public distress, some of them due to floods, probably caused by typhoons, and others to the incursions of the Japanese pirates, who for many years harried the coasts of China.

First Attempts to Open up Commerce with China Owing to the difficulties under which trade was carried on in the factories[1] or trading posts at Canton, several attempts were made by British merchants to open up new points of access.

In 1832 the East India Company despatched the ship "Lord Amherst" from Macao on a commercial mission in charge of Mr. Hugh Hamilton Lindsay with the Rev. Charles Gutzlaff as interpreter. Wherever he called along the coast, Mr. Lindsay met a series of rebuffs. After failing to gain admittance into Amoy, Foochow, and Ningpo, he proceeded to Shanghai. The officials of that port had been notified of his coming and were prepared to oppose his entrance into the harbour. He managed, however, to obtain an interview with the Taotai, the official in charge of trade, in the temple of the Queen of Heaven.

Although received with scant courtesy, he was able to present his petition. He was told, however, that the right of trade could only be allowed at Canton and was advised to return there as soon as possible. Trade with Shanghai being impossible, Mr. Lindsay left for Corea.

Reasons for the Unwillingness to Trade When we consider that a certain amount of trade had always been carried on between China and Western countries by the overland route through Central Asia, it seems strange that so many obstacles were put in the way of trade by the new sea routes.

The obstinate attitude of the Chinese Government was due to many causes. Undoubtedly the piratical incursions of the Portuguese traders along the coast injured the reputation of Western traders, and gave some excuse for regarding them as barbarians. The real

---

[1] Factories were establishments of factors or agents for carrying on business in China.

reason, however, for the strong opposition was that these merchants from the West were demanding the privilege of trade as a right to which they were entitled, and asked that commercially and diplomatically they should be treated on terms of equality.

Furthermore, the trade of the overland routes had been very limited in scope, while that by the sea route was carried on on a much larger scale. In those days China regarded imports as an evil and thought that the purchase of foreign goods resulted in the outflow of money and in the consequent impoverishment of the country.[1]

Although in his report, *Proceedings on a Voyage to the Northern Ports of China in the Ship "Lord Amherst,"* Mr. Lindsay described Shanghai as an excellent *entrepôt* for commerce, the East India Company did not seem to appreciate its possibilities. Even after the monopoly of trade of that Company ceased in 1834, Shanghai was not deemed of much importance in the minds of British merchants.

For a time it seemed as if one of the Chusan Islands[2] might be destined to be the centre of British trade in East China rather than Shanghai, but after the signing of the Treaty of Nanking, these islands were evacuated.

The Battle of Woosung
During the first war between China and Great Britain, 1840-1843, in order to bring hostilities to a close, the British decided to invade the North, so as to strike a blow at the Central Government. A British fleet commanded by Vice-Admiral Sir William Parker, with a military force of 4,000 men under Sir Henry Gough, was despatched for

---

[1] This view is also expressed in Dr. Sun Yat-sen's modern lectures, known as *San Min Chu I* or *Three Principles*.

[2] These islands were occupied by the British during the first war between Great Britain and China.

this purpose.   Amoy, Ningpo, and Chapoo were taken in
succession, and on June 13th, 1842, the expedition reached
Woosung and found itself at the outer gate of Shanghai.

The Chinese authorities had neglected to make adequate preparations, but when they realized that Shanghai
was to be attacked, they did what they could to strengthen
its defences and to block the mouth of the Yangtze against
the British fleet.   The forts at Woosung on both sides of
the Whangpoo were rebuilt and enlarged.   Earthworks,
following the course of the Yangtze, were constructed on
the Woosung side, having an extreme length of three and
a third miles, between the Woosung Creek and the town
of Paoshan.   A large number of more or less ancient
guns was collected to arm the forts.   These guns were
ten feet long and had an inner tube of wrought metal
round which the outer covering had been run.   Among
them were 16- and 24-pounders.   Some were of brass and
were mounted in such a way that they could traverse on
a pivot, but were without any device by which they could
be elevated or lowered.

As to the native troops engaged, although some
Tartars and regular troops had been hurried to the place,
the larger proportion was inefficient, composed of recruits
hastily gathered from the towns and villages.   There were
thirty armed vessels, some of which were junks provided
with paddle wheels revolved by coolies somewhat in the
same way as they work the water wheels for irrigating the
fields.   Boats worked in this way could travel about three
miles an hour.

The British fleet, sailing in unknown waters, ap-
proached Shanghai slowly.

On the morning of June 16th, at 6 o'clock, the men-of-
war, being sailing vessels, were towed into position
by the steamers, so as to face the Chinese lines at the
short distance of 500 yards or less.   While this manœuvre

was being carried out, the Chinese began hostilities and as a result of their first volley several of the British ships were hulled, three men being killed and others severely wounded. As soon as the ships were in position, however, the British gunners showed their superiority over the untrained, undisciplined, and badly equipped enemy. The junks were easily put to flight, and although the land forces put up a brave resistance, they were completely overwhelmed and compelled to abandon the forts.

When the British landed and advanced to Paoshan, the Chinese troops in possession of the city retreated towards Soochow.

Viceroy Niu, in command of the Chinese forces, gives the following quaint account of the fray: "Cannon balls innumerable, flying in awful confusion through the expanse of heaven, fell before, behind and on either side of him; while in the distance he saw the ships of the rebels standing erect, lofty as mountains. The fierce daring of the rebels was inconceivable; officers and men fell at their posts, every effort to resist and stay the onset was in vain, and a retreat became inevitable."

The Chinese officer who showed the greatest bravery was Chin Chang-ming, a Fukienese. He had been 50 years at sea and at the time of the battle was 76 years of age. Even after the others had fled, he remained at his post undaunted, and assisted in serving the guns. His remains were afterwards buried in the City Temple of Shanghai and an image was erected in his memory.

Altogether about 200 Chinese lost their lives in the battle.

Advance on Shanghai After the fall of the forts, the British advanced on Shanghai by land and water. Lt.-Col. Montgomerie was in charge of a landing detachment of about 2,000 men which proceeded across the fields, encountering no difficulties except those connected with transporting the heavy guns across the innumerable creeks intersecting the country. The villagers came out in crowds to see the unwonted sight of well disciplined foreign troops with horses and artillery quietly making their way to Shanghai, but showed no unfriendliness.

After a time the detachment struck the Soochow Creek, then known as the Woosung River, and arrived at the stone bridge at Sinza, i.e., "the new lock" or "canal gate."

Crossing the bridge the troops passed through what is now part of the International Settlement towards the suburbs of the city. While so doing they heard the sound of firing on the left and saw a small native force in flight. When they came within sight of the walls a few shots were fired by the defenders but no real resistance was made. Some soldiers climbed over the wall at the North Gate, and opening it from the inside, admitted the troops. Inside the city they found a scene of great confusion, as some of the people were fleeing by the other gates and a rabble was engaged in looting.

The land force arrived first, but soon after its entry into the city the masts of the warships on their way up the river came in sight. The fleet, consisting of four fighting ships and four steamers to tow them, had left Woosung at eight o'clock in the morning, while a fifth steamer, the "Medusa," conveyed Admiral Parker, Sir Henry Gough and other officers.

There was no sign of opposition until the leading squadron came opposite the present site of the Hongkew wharves, when it was greeted by a salvo, fired from a battery stationed on what is now the lawn of the British Consulate. From this position, which commanded the approach to the city, much damage might have been done, but only a single volley was fired and that at such a distance that the missiles did not reach the British vessels. The reply of the British silenced the battery, and the Chinese garrison took to flight. This was the sound of firing that had been heard by the land force after crossing the Sinza Bridge.

The ships passed on, finding plenty of water and dropped their anchors in nine fathoms. A landing was effected close to the city, but a party under Captain Cunynghame went ashore some distance from the wall near a temple, which was afterwards converted into the Custom House and which stood on The Bund until it was torn down to give place to the building erected in 1893.

In the city all signs of authority had vanished. Looting was the order of the day and rich prizes were obtained from the pawn shops. At first some of the British troops also engaged in plunder, and carried on a brisk trade selling their ill-gotten gains to the Chinese on the water front and over the walls of the city. This lasted, however, only until strong patrols of British troops were sent to restore order. After that the people who remained in the city went about their usual business without disturbance, and there was no further fear of violence.

While the force occupied Shanghai, a survey of the upper Whangpoo River was made by a part of the fleet as far as the vicinity of Soochow, and Admiral Parker and some of his officers paid a visit to Sungkiang.

The occupation of Shanghai lasted for only a week. On June 23rd it was evacuated, and the forces left to take part in the expedition up the Yangtze. Some attempts were made by the Chinese to enter into negotiations, but the British postponed the final settlement until the conclusion of the expedition.

CHAPTER II.

THE BEGINNINGS
OF THE FOREIGN SETTLEMENT, 1843.

The British Expedition up the Yangtze The British expedition passed on up the Yangtze River, and bombarded Chinkiang, an important city at the junction of the Yangtze and the Grand Canal. Although the place was defended with courage by the Manchu garrison, after a severe struggle, in which many were killed, it was forced to yield.

From Chinkiang an advance was made on Nanking, at which place the expedition arrived on August 9th, 1842. This occupation of the Yangtze led the Chinese to sue for peace, inasmuch as the blockade of the river hindered vessels carrying the tribute rice from proceeding to the capital by way of the Grand Canal.

Ilipu and Ki-ying, both Manchus, were appointed Imperial Commissioners to treat with Sir Henry Pottinger, the British Plenipotentiary, who had come up from Hongkong.

The Treaty of Nanking The first treaty between China and Great Britain, known as the Treaty of Nanking, was signed on board the "Cornwallis" on August 29th, 1842.

Among other provisions of the Treaty, Canton, Amoy, Foochow, Ningpo and Shanghai were opened to foreign trade and were to be known as Treaty Ports. It was agreed that fair tariff rates should be imposed.

In the wording of the Treaty no direct mention was made of settlements, and the only safeguards provided for foreign merchants were that "they with their families and establishments shall be allowed to reside for the purpose of carrying on their mercantile pursuits, without molestation or restraint" in the five ports.

The Treaty was ratified at Peking, and was brought to Hongkong by Commissioner Ki-ying in June, 1843.

A careful study of the Treaty shows that in many ways it was unsatisfactory and that it did not take account of many of the problems which were sure to arise. At the same time, it reveals that the object of the British was not conquest, but solely to obtain a footing so that trade might be carried on more freely than had hitherto been possible.

American and French Treaties The fruits of England's victories were shared by other nations. The Hon. Caleb Cushing was appointed Commissioner and Envoy Extraordinary and Minister Plenipotentiary of the United States, for the purpose of negotiating a treaty with China. On July 3rd, 1844, the Treaty of Wang-hsia was signed, Ki-ying acting as representative of the Imperial Government. It was so called because the negotiations were carried on in a village of that name outside Macao.

The French Government despatched Monsieur Theodore M. M. J. de Lagrene to China to negotiate a treaty and one was signed at Whampoa on October 24th, 1844. Thus these two countries also obtained the right of trade for their merchants in the five Treaty Ports.

Appointment of First British Consul Captain George Balfour, formerly of the Indian Artillery, was selected by Sir Henry Pottinger to be the first Consul at Shanghai and held this office for three years. He came up from Canton and arrived in Shanghai on November 8th, 1843. On the following day he called by appointment on the Taotai, Kung Moo-yun, accompanied by his staff, Mr. W. H. Medhurst, interpreter, Dr. Hale, surgeon and assistant, and Mr. A. F. Strachan, clerk, and the Taotai duly returned the call on board the "Medusa," Consul Balfour's ship.

The first question to arise was that of a residence for the Consul, and for a time it seemed as if no one would venture to rent a house to the unwelcome foreigner, but eventually he secured the lease of a large dwelling house, containing 52 rooms, in the city, on a street between the East and West Gates at a rental of $400 per annum.

Shanghai was declared open to foreign trade on November 14th, 1843.

Sir Henry Pottinger having neglected to make any agreement about the site of a foreign settlement, the matter had to be arranged between Captain Balfour and the Taotai.

The Chinese authorities immediately raised the point that it was illegal to sell outright any land belonging to His Imperial Majesty, but this obstacle was surmounted by permission being given to rent in perpetuity, an annual land rent being paid by the renters.

Land was bought from the native proprietors at rates varying from 50,000 to 60,000 cash a *mow*,[1] the actual value being from 15,000 to 35,000 cash a *mow*, or $15 to $35 Mex. The annual rent or land tax was fixed at 1,500 cash a *mow*.[2]

First Settlement Boundaries. No very definite boundaries were made in the first delimitation of the Settlement. The Whangpoo River was to mark its eastern and the Yangkingpang its southern boundary. The west was left entirely undefined, while on the north, what is now Peking Road was the first boundary.

---

[1] A *mow* is almost one-sixth of an English acre. Roughly speaking a thousand cash equalled a dollar at that time.

[2] The present land tax is estimated at one tael per *mow*.

Later the western boundary was put at the Barrier Road (the present Honan Road). Altogether about 150 acres were contained within the first boundaries.

The main portions of the land were fairly well raised and were under cultivation; other portions were lower and marshy. There were numerous creeks, ditches and ponds, and the lower grounds in summer were covered with reeds. Innumerable grave mounds dotted the land and the purchasers were obliged to agree that the former owners could visit them at stated periods and perform the customary religious rites.

For several years after the establishment of the Settlement, all west of the present Szechuen Road was regarded as being in the country.

The Bund was a towing path with a wide foreshore, covered or uncovered according to the state of the tide.

There were other difficulties connected with the acquisition of land in this area, for the owners sometimes demanded exorbitant prices or were unwilling to sell. Even after they had sold the land, for one excuse or another, they refused to move or went only when forcibly ejected.

For a considerable period the foreign residents had to be content to live in native houses in Nantao, outside the city walls, on the shores of the Whangpoo. The conditions of life were not very pleasant. One of the early residents, Mr. Fortune, gives the following description of the state of affairs in 1843, "Often in the mornings we would find ourselves drenched with rain; and if snow fell, it was blown through the windows and formed wreaths on the floor." The foreign population was then something over a hundred, of whom seven were ladies. There were twenty-five mercantile firms engaged in business. It was not until 1849 that the residents generally moved into the Settlement.

Arrangements for Trade The Taotai appointed six "partners" in the shroff shop to grant receipts for export and import duties and tonnage dues, and there was considerable danger lest trade should fall into the hands of a few monopolists, as at Canton. Consul Balfour protested vigorously against such a development, as contrary to the Treaty. An early attempt was made to introduce a bonding system by which goods could remain in bond without paying custom duties until sold, but this was opposed by the Imperial Commissioners.

Although it was a day of small things, it is interesting to note that during the first six weeks after the port was opened, from November 14th to December 31st, seven vessels entered the harbour. Their imports totalled in value Tls. 433,729 and the exports Tls. 147,172. As import duty they paid Tls. 16,564.80, and for export fees Tls. 7,537.19. Their tonnage dues amounted to Tls. 985, a marked contrast to the large "squeezes" formerly enforced on vessels at Canton.

Legal Status of Foreign Residents Before the signing of the Treaty of Nanking, there was constant friction between foreigners who came to Canton and the local Chinese authorities. The Chinese refused to recognize the rights accorded by International Law (for example, in regard to the status of ships of war in foreign ports), and the foreigners refused to recognize the due authority of the local law courts.

The Treaty of Nanking marks the legalization of extraterritorial rights as well as the formal treaty relations in regard to commerce. Extraterritoriality was not expressly granted in the Treaty, but provision was made for the functioning of British consular officials, with the understanding that extraterritorial rights should be enjoyed by British traders.

Article XIII of the General Resolutions issued in connection with the Treaty reads as follows:

"Whenever a British subject has to complain of a Chinese he must first proceed to the Consulate and state his grievance. The Consul will thereupon enquire into the merits of the case and do his utmost to arrange it amicably. In like manner, if a Chinese have reason to complain of a British subject, he shall no less listen to his complaint, and endeavour to settle it in a friendly manner. . . . If unfortunately, any disputes take place of such a nature that the Consul cannot arrange them amicably, then he shall request the assistance of a Chinese Officer that they may together examine into the merits of the case, and decide it equitably. Regarding the punishment of English criminals, the English Government will enact the laws necessary to attain that end, and the Consul will be empowered to put them into force: and regarding the punishment of Chinese criminals, these will be tried and punished by their own laws, in the way provided for by correspondence which took place at Nanking, after the concluding of the peace."

The exercise of extraterritorial rights received a still more explicit statement in the Treaty made between the United States and China in 1844.

Article XXI of that Treaty reads as follows:

"Subjects of China who may be guilty of any criminal act towards citizens of the United States shall be arrested and punished by the Chinese authorities according to the laws of China, and citizens of the United States who may commit any crime in China shall be subject to be tried and punished only by the Consul or other public functionary of the United States thereto authorized according to the laws of the United States; and in order to secure the prevention of all controversy and disaffection, justice shall be equitably and impartially administered on both sides."

Another article of the same Treaty applies this arrangement to civil cases.

In Article XXV it was declared:

"All questions in regard to rights, whether of property or person, arising between citizens of the United States in China, shall be subject to the jurisdiction of, and regulated by the authorities of their own Government, and all controversies occurring in China between citizens of the United States and subjects of any other Government shall be regulated by the treaties existing between the United States and such Governments, respectively, without interference on the part of China."

According to what is known as the "most favoured nation" clause, these extraterritorial rights could be claimed by all nations entering into treaty relations with China. By the phrase "most favoured nation" is meant that China undertakes to extend to all the Treaty Powers those special rights which from time to time she has granted to particular Powers. In other words, it is agreed that no one Power shall enjoy privileges to the exclusion of other Powers.

The Chinese authorities appear to have entered into this arrangement in regard to extraterritoriality without protest. They were glad to be freed of the responsibility of controlling those who appeared to be turbulent foreigners, and to hand them over to their own authorities.

The Status of the Settlement   It was natural for the British authorities to regard the Settlement as exclusively under the jurisdiction of the British, and this was the attitude assumed by Consul Balfour, and no land in the Settlement could be acquired without his consent. After the signing of the American and French Treaties, the merchants of these two countries claimed that they had equal rights in the Settlement with the British. This led to many misunderstandings and controversies which might have been avoided if the Treaty of Nanking had been a little more explicit in its statements.

Mr. H. G. Wolcott, the first Acting American Consul in Shanghai, established his consulate in the Settlement, and raised the American flag. This was objected to by both the British Consul and the Taotai, as it was held that no national flag, except the British, could be raised in the Settlement. Mr. Wolcott persisted, and for a considerable time the American was the only national flag displayed in the Settlement, as the British Consulate was still situated in the native city.

The view held by Consul Balfour was not shared by the British authorities in Hongkong, who, in a despatch to the British Consul, made the following statement:

"It is doubtful whether a British authority can assume a ceremonial jurisdiction over foreigners, in which case the act of hoisting a national flag loses much of its importance."

First Land Regulations Land Regulations put forth in 1845 by the Taotai, Kung Moo-yun, by agreement with Consul Balfour, are important, as they form the basis of the subsequent enactments governing the cosmopolitan community of the Settlement.

The boundaries of the Settlement were again roughly defined, the western boundary being extended as far as the Defence Creek. Foreigners were not allowed to employ police, but could engage watchmen, subject to the approval of the Chinese officials. Native domiciles were forbidden in the then existing Settlement, or its further extension. Natives in the Settlement were prohibited

2

from "renting to each other, nor may they again build houses there for the purpose of renting to Chinese merchants."

The land-renters as a body were to be responsible for the upkeep of the Settlement and its revenue was to be derived from contributions from the residents. The assessments were to be made by a committee of the merchants, nominated by the Consul, to be known as the Committee on Roads and Jetties. The land-renters were vested with the control of the revenue and expenditure.

Foreigners, other than those of British nationality, were subject to the same regulations, the revision thereof being possible only by the consent of the British and Chinese authorities.

Four large roads were to be made in the Settlement —the present Hankow, Kiukiang, Nanking and Peking roads, running east and west. Kiukiang Road was to be 25 feet wide and the others 20 feet wide.

Establishment of the French Concession M. Montigny, first Consul for France at Shanghai, entered into an agreement with Ling Taotai on April 6th, 1849, for the establishment and government of a French Concession.

The tendency of the British to claim exclusive jurisdiction over the territory of the Settlement was also manifested by the French in regard to their Concession. The principle was adopted that no Chinese or foreign official would be allowed to exercise his power within the boundaries of the French Concession.

The boundaries of the Concession were clearly defined. On the south a part of the moat along the city wall, on the north the Yangkingpang, on the east the river side from the Canton Guild to the Yangkingpang, on the west from the creek named after the war god's temple, Kuan-ti Miao, up to the Bridge of the Chow family, subject to further extension if desired.

This settlement has always been known as the French Concession, and attempts were made from the beginning to place it on the same footing as the concessions that afterwards came into existence during the period of 1858-1863 (Newchwang, Tientsin, Hankow, Kiukiang, Chinkiang, and Canton).

The Establishment of the American Settlement   As Mr. H. B. Morse points out in *The International Relations of the Chinese Empire*, "the American Settlement was not created, but just 'growed.'" The merchants lived in the English Settlement, but some of the missionaries, seeking cheaper land for residences, purchased property in the outskirts. The American Episcopal Church Mission, under Bishop William J. Boone, established itself in Hongkew,[1] across the Soochow Creek. On the arrival of the first official Consul of the United States in February, 1854, he made his residence and raised his flag in this American Settlement. It was some time, however, before its boundaries were defined.

When Bishop Boone was asked what he considered the south boundary of his property, he replied, "the tow path in front of the Mission buildings." Had he said the edge of the river, legally all the property afterwards accreted would, upon payment of the *Sheng-ko*[2] fees, have belonged to his Mission.

At first neither the French Concession nor the American Settlement flourished.

The Jesuit missionaries alone showed any interest in the new site, and, in the neighbourhood of the Concession, at once started to build Tung-kia-tu Cathedral, the corner stone being laid on November 21st, 1849. This contains

---

[1] The Chinese characters for "Hongkew" mean "The Rainbow Mouth." This section was called by that name because of the bend in the shore making it resemble the shape of a rainbow.

[2] Land accretion caused by the movement of the tides and changes in the course of a stream.

an organ constructed by the French Fathers, which is unique, as the pipes are made of bamboo, and, as far as we know, is the only one of its kind in the world. It is pointed out as an object of curiosity to the traveller who visits the Cathedral.

The Americans found their situation so unfavourable that for a time even the Consul was obliged to establish his office in the British Settlement. Undoubtedly the exclusive privileges claimed by the British authorities for their Settlement was the chief reason for the French and American Governments wanting territory for the residence of their own nationals.

The dissension between the first residents in regard to jurisdiction was not, however, of so serious a nature as to cause real trouble. A healthy feeling grew up among the foreigners, and they recognized from the start that they had similar interests, which could only be attained through a spirit of unity.

As we shall see later, in 1863 the American Settlement was amalgamated with the British, and the present International Settlement came into existence.

Acquisition of the Present British Consular Site Consul Balfour, who at first was obliged to live in the native city, was anxious to acquire property in the Settlement for the British Consulate. At that time, according to the ruling of the Home Government, the Consuls to foreign countries were not allowed to purchase land or erect buildings, but were obliged to carry on their work in rented premises. In spite of this, Consul Balfour determined to secure a proper site for the erection of consular offices.

On April 28th, 1846, five months before ne resigned, he made arrangements for the purchase of the Li Chia Chang property, north of the boundary of the Settlement, consisting of over a hundred *mow* of land, for $17,000. Not having authority from the Government, he advanced

$4,000 of his own money.   His successor, Mr. (afterwards Sir) Rutherford Alcock, upon his arrival, proceeded with the matter and after much difficulty persuaded the Home Government to sanction the purchase. In this way the splendidly situated piece of land now occupied by the consulate buildings was obtained, and on July 21st, 1849, the consular offices were removed to this site.

The first Consulate, built in 1852, was destroyed by fire on December 23rd, 1870, and most of the records were lost. The present building was erected in 1872.

The Making of The Bund   From time immemorial, trackers had used the tow path along the shore of the Whangpoo River and the Chinese authorities in the first Land Regulations issued by them reserved this right. A space of 30 English feet was to be reserved between buildings erected on the foreshore and the edge of the river. Foreigners, therefore, when putting up their buildings on river lots, drove in piles to that distance in front of each lot, and filled it in. This was the origin of The Bund, now a beautiful promenade, but then a muddy road, not fit for walking. One of the features of Shanghai to-day is the wide open space between the river and the buildings on the water front. It was secured, in the first place, not from any aesthetic sense, but because of the necessity of leaving a path for the trackers.

Life in the Settlement during the First Few Years   The foreign population of the Settlement gradually increased. In 1844 it was 50, in the following year, 90, and after five years it had grown to 175. In addition there was a floating population, consisting of the men on shore from the ships in harbour.

Compared with the life in the factories of Canton where the merchants were confined in a small circumscribed area, the residents of Shanghai enjoyed considerable freedom, but they were not allowed to penetrate into the country around the Settlements so far that they could not return to Shanghai the same day. As the shooting was excellent, and the villagers friendly, these expeditions into the country were most enjoyable.

The Committee on Roads and Jetties experienced difficulties in carrying out their functions. As was perhaps natural, the early residents of Shanghai were not far-sighted, and did not plan much for the future. They were satisfied with a few jetties for the landing of goods from the ships and did not see much necessity for roads, as the native paths were sufficient for the coolies who carried the bales of silk and boxes of tea. Where roads had to be made, they decided that they must be at least 25 feet wide, and in those days that looked over-generous. Following the line of least resistance, the roads followed the banks of the creeks, and this accounts for their somewhat serpentine windings.

The buildings erected had little claim to architectural beauty and have been wittily described as of the "compradoric" order. Many of them were bungalows and all had deep verandahs. They were adapted to a tropical climate, and the builders seemed to have had only the four months of hot weather in mind, and to have overlooked the need of sunshine in their homes during the rest of the year.

Very little was done in regard to sanitation, and for a long time refuse was disposed of by depositing it on the shores of The Bund.

Attack on Three Missionaries, 1848 On March 8th, 1848, three missionaries, Drs. Medhurst and Lockhart, and the Rev. William Muirhead, made a visit to Tsingpu, a town about 25 miles from Shanghai. It so happened that at that time the town was crowded with some 13,000 men who had recently been discharged from the junks carrying tribute rice, because the Government was sending a large amount of it to Tientsin by the sea route. While the missionaries were preaching and distributing tracts, a dense crowd gathered around them and an attack was made by a party of junkmen armed with poles, bars, and an iron chain. They were rescued by some runners from the Magistrate's Yamen, who arrived just in time to save their lives.

When the matter was reported to Mr. Alcock, he decided to take strong measures to bring those who were guilty of the assault to justice, and take the affair up with the Shanghai Taotai. Failing to receive prompt redress, he informed the Taotai that until justice had been done, no British ship would pay duties, nor would any grain junks be allowed to leave the port. The Commander of the "Chiltern" detained 1,400 rice junks, while the "Espiegle", with the British Vice-Consul on board, was despatched to Nanking to bring the matter to the attention of the Viceroy and to lay before him a formal complaint. In this way the matter was speedily settled. The ten leaders in the assault were cangued[1] in front of the Custom House, S200 were paid as damages, and the junks were released. The Viceroy blamed the Shanghai Taotai for having erred and failed in the discharge of his duties.

The British Government was at first inclined to censure Mr. Alcock for exceeding his authority, but when his measures proved successful, its rebuke was considerably softened. The Taotai was removed from office, and another—Wu—known to foreigners as "Samqua," was appointed in his place.

---

[1] The cangue was a large square wooden collar placed around the neck of a criminal.

CHAPTER III.

THE "SMALL SWORDS" OCCUPY SHANGHAI, 1853.

The Taiping Rebellion broke out in Canton in 1851 and gradually spread northwards. At about the same time the "Small Swords," a branch of the Triad Society, began its operations and succeeded in capturing Amoy. This society was repudiated by the Taipings because it did not hold the same religious tenets and allowed the use of opium.

The Rebels Seize the City
In 1853 a small body of these rebels came up to Shanghai, and by the following ruse obtained possession of the Chinese city. Early in the morning of September 7th, which happened that year to be the day of the Autumnal Sacrifice to Confucius, when the gates were opened 600 men rushed in with the crowd going to witness the sacrifice, and attacked the Yamens. The city magistrate was put to death and the Taotai was kept under guard in his own residence. Sympathizers in the city threw bundles of red cloth into the streets which the rebels used for making turbans, and from this headgear they became known as the "Hung T'ou" or "Red Heads." The chief leader of the rebels was a man named Lew, a Cantonese who had been a sugar broker and who had established the Triad Society in Shanghai a few years before. He was an emaciated opium smoker, but was reputed to be a man of capacity and resolution. The most active spirit, if not the actual leader, was a man named Chin-a-lin.

General dissatisfaction with the Government is a sufficient explanation of the willingness of the people to support a movement having as its object the overthrow of the Manchus.

Before long, dissension broke out between two factions of the rebels, the Cantonese and the Fukienese, the former claiming that the latter had obtained the greater share of the plunder. This led to increased disorder, until the quarrel was settled by a compromise.

Two gentlemen from the Settlement, Dr. Hall and Mr. Caldecott Smith, succeeded in rescuing the Taotai. They entered the city and having gained access to the Taotai, disguised him and let him down by ropes from the city wall. He was first taken to the home of Dr. M. T. Yates, a missionary living close to the wall, and later was given refuge in Messrs. Russell and Company's Hong.

The Imperialists Attempt to Retake the City The Taotai, realizing what was in store for him from the Peking Government, attempted to regain favour by recapturing the city with the aid of an Imperialist force which had made its headquarters on the Soochow Creek, a little above the Sinza Bridge. The Imperialists might easily have reduced the city, had it not been that supplies of all sorts found their way inside of the city walls through the Settlement.

Wu Taotai purchased a small ship and fitted her out as a war vessel, and with that and some war junks that had come down from Sungkiang, bombarded the city in December, 1853, from the water front. Landing parties set fire to the Nantao suburb, but the attempt to breach the walls was unsuccessful.

Shortly before this, the Imperialists, hearing that the rebels were obtaining supplies of guns from a foreign firm, determined to invade the Settlement and secure possession of them. A party penetrated as far as the Custom House, and was in the act of carrying off the guns when some men from H.M.S. "Spartan" appeared on the scene and drove the invaders away.

The Taotai was desirous of obtaining the aid of the Settlement and the foreign Powers in driving the rebels out of the city, but the foreign authorities deemed it wiser to adopt the policy of neutrality. This neutrality, however, as far as business was concerned, was not strictly observed, and trade was carried on more or less openly with both sides.

The little community in the Settlement passed through an exciting period. Both Imperialists and rebels encroached upon the western boundary, and missiles often fell within the Settlement area.

The hospital, situated on Shantung Road under the management of Dr. Lockhart, was often in the line of fire but escaped from being attacked, and the wounded from both sides received treatment within its walls.

Assaults by soldiers on foreigners who went into the western district were frequent, and the New Park and Race Course, situated where Lloyd Road now is, became a dangerous locality.

Formation of a Volunteer Corps The peril arising from the proximity of the Imperialist camp on the Soochow Creek and from the rebels in Shanghai city made it necessary to provide some sort of a defence force for the Settlement.

On April 12th, 1853, a general meeting of the whole community was convened, at which were present the Consuls and Naval Officers of the three Treaty Powers, England, France and America; Mr. Alcock was in the chair. It was determined to adopt a policy of armed neutrality and for that purpose to organize a volunteer corps.

Captain Tronson of the Second Bengal Fusiliers was appointed in command, and immediately took in hand the drilling of the force.

Thus the Shanghai Volunteer Corps came into being, a force which was destined in succeeding years to play an important part in the defence of the International Settlement.

The Battle of Muddy Flat   The newly organized corps did not wait long for its baptism of fire, and soon saw active service in hostilities with the Imperialist forces.

The Provincial Judge and Governor of the Kiangsu Province, a Manchu official, named Keih-er-hangah (Koer-hangah) had been appointed commander-in-chief of the camp at Sinza, consisting of between twenty and thirty thousand men. Being a civil official, he found it difficult to control the soldiers and camp followers.

The nearness of the camp to the western boundary of the Settlement brought about a grave situation, as bands of soldiers were continually invading the Settlement and committing serious assaults on the foreign residents. Moreover, a target had been erected so close to the western boundary that stray shots frequently endangered the lives of foreigners using the Race Course, the western stretch of which was at that time on the present Thibet Road.

Owing to the danger thus arising from the location of the camps in the immediate vicinity of the Race Course, it was decided to request General Keih to remove his troops to the southern side of the native city, and on the morning of April 4th, 1854, Consul Alcock sent an ultimatum, stating that if the camps were not removed before four o'clock in the afternoon, they would be attacked by the foreign forces. General Keih replied to this asking for delay, and entreating Consul Alcock not to resort precipitately to arms. His answer was regarded as a refusal to evacuate, and at three o'clock in the afternoon the various units of the foreign force assembled in front of the English Church, standing on the site of the present Holy Trinity Cathedral. Captain Kelly of the U.S.S. "Plymouth" gives the following estimate of the numbers employed, "At 3.00 p.m. we landed, the English landing about 200 men, and our ships 75; the Volunteers, being all English, joined their countrymen, while the Americans with two field pieces placed themselves under my command, increasing my force to a hundred—the English to 250. About 30 sailors from the American merchant vessels were added to the American force." Altogether the attacking unit numbered 380 men.

Captain O'Callaghan of H.M.S. "Encounter," with Lieut. Roderick Dew as second in command, was in charge of the British contingent, the Volunteers being under Ex-Lieut. T. F. Wade, H.B.M.'s Vice-Consul; Captain Kelly was in charge of the American contingent.

At 3.30 p.m. with drums beating and flags flying, the advance was made up Park Lane (now Nanking Road) and the adventurous little army proceeded as far as the present junction of Nanking and Chekiang Roads (at that time the eastern stretch of the Race Course) and there the column halted. It was hoped that this display of force might be sufficient to cause General Keih to pay some attention to the ultimatum. When it was discovered that the situation was unchanged and that the small band would have to attack a force of some twenty thousand men, there was, according to an eyewitness, "a marked decline in the exuberance which had characterized the march out."

It was decided that the force should be split into two divisions, the Americans following the bend of the Race Course, and veering to the left so as to deliver a frontal attack on the camp, and the British proceeding straight ahead as far as possible, so as to take the enemy on the flank.

Mr. W. S. Wetmore, the eyewitness to whom we have referred, followed the movements of the Americans. They, with two guns, took up a position among the grave mounds, within two or three hundred yards of the camps in front of them.   Precisely at four o'clock the engagement began, Captain Kelly opened with his guns, and the British did the same from the point which they had reached.   No sooner had the guns begun to boom, when, according to Mr. Wetmore, one could see "the dreary waste of graves and mounds brighten up with scarlet spots moving rapidly in and out of the intricacies of the ground."   These were the rebels from the city who had come to join in the fray. and to assist in the attack on the Imperialists.   The red turbans became more and more numerous, with the result that the Imperialists were seized with consternation and were soon in full retreat.

Captain Kelly immediately gave the order to charge, but his men were unexpectedly halted by a creek of mud and water four feet deep and fifteen to twenty feet wide, which served as a moat to the camp parapets, six or seven feet high, on the far bank.   As the force reached the brink of this creek, they were exposed to a lively fire, and were compelled to take cover again behind the grave mounds.

In a short time the humming of the bullets ceased, and for the Americans the battle was practically over.   The creek which had checked the advance of the Americans was the Chow-king-pang which in after years formed a part of Defence Creek.

Turning to the British contingent, they had proceeded straight ahead and were able to cross the Chow-king-pang by a bridge.   Then changing direction to the left they took the first camp in flank and delivered an assault.   As it was defended by a cannon placed in the entrance, there were several casualties.   The camp was reached, however, and Lieut. Dew was the first to enter it.   After this there was little fighting as the Imperialists took to flight.   The deserted camps were destroyed by fire.

Gallant as was the conduct of the small force against overwhelming odds, the determining factor causing the flight of the Imperialists was probably the sudden appearance of the rebels on the battlefield.   There is some uncertainty as to whether the rebels took part in the operation of their own initiative, or whether the assistance of the rebel leaders had been invited by some of the foreigners.

Mr. Wetmore, while attributing the victory to the "unexpected co-operation of the rebels," thinks that General Keih, seeing the foreigners in earnest, may have given orders for his forces to retire.

The casualties of the British and American forces were two killed and fifteen wounded, of whom two died later.   The losses of the Imperialist troops were not more than fifty.

This skirmish has always been known as the "Battle of Muddy Flat," but as it was fought in clear weather on perfectly dry ground, it is difficult to account for the origin of the name.

The battle produced the desired result, as the main force of the Imperialist army withdrew to the south side of the native city, and the western boundary of the Settlement was no longer disturbed by bands of marauding troops.

The French Assist the Imperialists   The native city remained in the hands of the "Small Swords," and it became evident that if the city was to be recaptured by the Imperialists, supplies from the Settlement must be cut off.

The French Admiral Laguerre held that the obstinate resistance of the rebels was due to foreign encouragement, and to supplies from the English Settlement, and criticized the English for not observing stricter neutrality.

When the rebels raised a battery near where Rue Tourane now is, Admiral Laguerre ordered it to be demolished, and upon their refusal to comply with his request, joined forces with the Imperialists in an attempt to take the city.   An attack was made on the North Gate, close to the site of the present St. Joseph's Church, but although the French succeeded in making a breach in the walls and fought bravely, lack of support on the part of the Imperialists hindered them from accomplishing their object.   The French casualties were two officers killed and four wounded, seven men killed and thirty-two wounded.

The Rebels Evacuate the City   Later, a wall was built by the Imperialists from where the French Bund now is to where a bridge on Honan Road then crossed the Yangkingpang, to isolate the city from the Settlement.   Cut off from supplies, the beleaguered city was soon reduced to sore straits, and the rebels evacuated it on February 17th, 1854, as rapidly as they had entered, after having occupied the city for seventeen months.

When the Imperialists obtained possession of the city, it was given over to three days' looting, and the eastern half was almost entirely destroyed by fire.   The Imperialists showed no mercy to the rebels, and all who were captured were immediately executed.

Effects upon the Settlement   The Settlement was affected in many ways by the struggle between the Imperialists and the insurgents.

Trade was greatly disorganized.   The Taiping Rebellion, which is described in a later chapter, had closed the whole of the Yangtze basin from Chinkiang upwards, and the greater part of the Chekiang Province, so that there was no market for goods imported into Shanghai. Although the immediate vicinity of Shanghai had remained quiet, yet the feeling of uncertainty caused a decline in purchases. The result was that general imports, consisting mainly of cotton goods, remained unsold and accumulated in the merchants' godowns.

The amount of opium imported and sold, however, greatly increased at this time. The opium was delivered into receiving ships at Woosung and then smuggled into the country. Between 1847 and 1849 the average deliveries of opium amounted to 18,814 chests, the average value being $11,185,000 annually. In 1853 they had increased to 24,200 chests, valued at $14,400,000, and in the course of the next few years amounted to 33,069 chests.

Although conditions affected all imports except opium, the exports largely increased. Tea came to Shanghai, not by the Yangtze but over the mountains from Anhwei, Kiangsi, Fukien, and Chekiang. In 1853, 69,000,000 pounds were exported. This fell off in 1854 to 50,000,000 pounds, owing to the coming of the "Small Swords" to Shanghai, but increased again in 1855 to 80,000,000 pounds.

The same is true in regard to silk. In 1851, 20,360 bales were exported and in 1853, 58,319 bales. This was largely due to the fact that after Nanking fell into the hands of the Taipings the people were destitute and could no longer afford to purchase silk, and the output of the great silk producing district between Soochow and Hangchow was forced to seek a foreign market. Thus for a considerable time the exports exceeded the imports and this led to a large importation of silver dollars to balance the trade.

Origin of the Maritime Customs

While Shanghai was in the hands of the "Small Swords," all Imperial authority broke down. The Custom House was plundered and demolished and the Taotai was unsuccessful in his attempts to establish another place for the receipt of customs dues.

Many residents considered that as there was no longer any Imperial authority, it was not necessary to observe the Treaty. Neither the British nor the American officials concurred in this view, and held that the mere fact that the city had fallen into the hands of rebels was no just excuse for robbing the Chinese Government of its rights. It was arranged that both British and American Consuls should request their nationals to give guarantees for the payment of legal duties. This, of course, was not welcome to many of the merchants who were anxious to evade paying the regular charges. The French Consul, on the other hand, intimated that he would clear ships of his nationality without calling on them to pay duties, and the Consuls of other nations, who were all merchants, took the same line.

The Customs authorities themselves were largely responsible for the confusion that arose, for they allowed vessels to enter and leave the port after making partial or no payment at all.

Wu Taotai made an attempt to set up a floating Custom House in the Whangpoo opposite what is now the Public Gardens, but this did not work well. He had not been allowed to re-establish the former Custom House in the Settlement, as it would have been subject to attacks from the rebels, and would have had to be defended. Claiming neutrality, the foreign merchants were unwilling to guard it and at the same time were equally unwilling to permit the Imperialists to protect it.

In January, 1854, the U.S. Vice-Consul gave notice that he would allow American ships to sail without requir-

3

ing the payment of duties, so long as ships of other nations were allowed to do so.   Mr. Alcock, however, held out until the Taotai, being pressed for money, allowed a Bremen ship to clear on payment of only part of the duties.

On February 14th, 1854, it was agreed that a Custom House should be placed on the Hongkew side of the Soochow Creek.   As, however, it was discovered that certain ships managed to get in or to clear without paying dues, there was a determination on the part of many to regard Shanghai as a free port and to evade entirely the payment of duties.

Consul Alcock conceived the idea of bringing order out of chaos by placing the Chinese Customs under foreign supervision, so as to ensure integrity in administration. After consultation with the Taotai, the Consuls of the three Treaty Powers nominated delegates for the proposed foreign Inspectorate.   The nominees were: Mr. T. F. Wade of the British consular staff, Mr. L. Carr of the American diplomatic service, and Monsieur A. Smith of the French consular service.

The Custom House was re-established on July 12th, 1854, in a godown at the corner of Nanking and Kiangsi Roads.   The new plan was successful beyond expectation and was a great improvement on the past corrupt native administration.

Mr. (afterwards Sir) Thomas Wade was later succeeded by Mr. H. A. Lay, who received from the Chinese Government the appointment of Inspector-General.   The Imperial Maritime Customs, beginning thus at Shanghai, was, after the Taiping Rebellion, extended throughout China.

The promissory notes and securities for duties given by British and American merchants during the period when the Chinese Government was unable to make regular collections were eventually returned in 1855.

CHAPTER IV.

THE LAND REGULATIONS OF 1854.

It had become evident that, whatever may have been the original purpose, the Chinese Government was unable at that time to provide adequate protection for the Settlements; and that some more efficient form of government must be devised.

The Consuls for the three Treaty Powers, Rutherford Alcock for Great Britain, R. C. Murphy for the U.S.A., and B. Edan for France, conferred together and drew up a new set of Land Regulations which afterwards received the approval of the Taotai.

Meeting of Land Renters, July 11th, 1854
These Regulations were placed before a public meeting of the Land Renters on July 11th, 1854, at the British Consulate, held under the auspices of the three Consuls, and were adopted.

The Committee on Roads and Jetties appointed by the Consul was dissolved and a Municipal Council for the Settlements was *elected*. Thus for a time the three separate Settlements were united and placed under one municipal administration, exercising control over all foreign residents.

Of the Land Regulations some merely re-enacted the provisions of the Regulations of 1845. It was, however, clearly stated that for the acquisition and registration of land, the land renter "must first apply to the Consul of his nation, or, if none be appointed, to the Consul of any friendly Power," and this implied that the original claim of the British authorities for complete jurisdiction had been waïved and would no longer be asserted.

Article X of Land Regulations
Article X was of great importance. It reads in part as follows: "It being expedient and necessary that some provision should be made for the making of roads, building public jetties and keeping them in repair; cleaning, lighting, and draining the Settlement generally, and establishing a watch or police force; the foreign consuls aforesaid shall at the beginning of each year convene a meeting of the renters of land within the said limits, to devise means of raising the requisite funds for these purposes: and at such meeting it shall be competent to the said renters to declare an assessment in the form of a rate to be made on land and buildings, and in the form of wharfage dues on all goods landed at any place within the said limits: and to appoint a committee of three or more persons to levy the said rates and dues and apply the funds so realised to the purposes aforesaid. . . . The committee shall be empowered to sue all defaulters in the consular courts under whose jurisdiction they may be. . . . "

Thus was delegated to the governing body of the Settlement the highest powers in all government, those of taxing and policing the community. The authority of the Municipal Council and its legal status was not acknowledged by the legal authorities of Hongkong until twenty years later, on the ground that the Diplomatic Body had not been consulted when the Land Regulations were amended in 1854.

One significant feature of the Regulations was the definite acknowledgment of Chinese sovereign rights to the land. The Chinese Government was to receive an annual land tax, and land deeds were to be sealed by the Chinese authorities.

Taxation
of
Chinese

Nothing was said in the Regulations about the legality of letting houses or selling land in the Settlement to Chinese.

There was already a large number of Chinese living within the Settlement, most of whom had come in as refugees, and it was decided that they were to pay a house tax of 8 per cent. in return for the protection afforded them. The foreign population numbered about 300 residents with their families. The Chinese, barely 500 before the taking of the Shanghai city by the "Small Sword" rebels, now exceeded 20,000, including many wealthy families.

The First
Council

The first Council consisted of Messrs. W. Kay, E. Cunningham, D. O. King, C. A. Fearon, and the Rev. Dr. Medhurst.

The early experiences of the Council are full of interest. The first Municipal Budget amounted to a total of $25,000,[1] of which $14,000 was to be expended upon the Police, leaving but little for the construction of roads and municipal improvements.

The services of Mr. S. Clifton, an ex-army man who had served as Inspector of Police in Hongkong, were secured, at a salary of $150 a month, as Superintendent of Police.

The estimate for lighting the streets with oil lamps was $12 a month and a similar amount was appropriated for sanitation.

In October a special Land Renters' meeting was held to obtain permission for borrowing $12,500 for the erection of police barracks. The Land Renters were generally

---

[1] Small as the amount appears to us now, it is interesting to remember, as Mr. Lang pointed out in a lecture in 1871, that the budget of the original committee of three appointed by the Consul was $2,000 and that after paying all necessary expenses a reasonable balance was left in hand.

opposed to the raising of loans or to increase in taxation but this proposal was sanctioned by a small majority, 18–15.

In November of the same year at a meeting of the Land Renters a resolution was passed "That the Municipal Council be not empowered to assess the Foreign Residents and Foreign Trade of the Port to a greater amount than $6,000.00 in all without express sanction."

All through these early days there is no indication that the Land Renters were able to take a large view of the future possibilities of the Settlement.

Another serious difficulty arose in regard to police matters. When the rebels departed in 1855, the Consuls, who did not approve of the Police being entirely under the control of the Council, called attention to the fact that they were not "sworn constables," and that therefore no fire-arms could be placed in their hands, and that they could not interfere with the Imperial authorities or their officers in the Settlement. When any Chinese was arrested, it should be reported to the Senior Consul, and as "None but magistrates can without illegality have parties apprehended and brought before them for hearing" which the Councillors were doing, the Consuls thought that the sooner the Police were disbanded the better it would be.

A test case arose when a member of the police force stopped and detained for a considerable time at the Barrier Gate, the Imperial Commissioner, H. E. Keih. The policeman was punished by the British Consul, and the Municipal Council was informed that it should take care not to issue orders to its servants of an illegal nature, the carrying out of which subjected them to legal penalties.

Finally the police force was reorganized in such a way that the men became duly "sworn constables," deriving their authority from the Consuls and the Chinese Government as well as from the Municipal Council.

Residence
of the Chinese
in the Settle-
ment

As we have pointed out, there had been a great influx of Chinese into the Settlements owing to the troublous conditions in the vicinity of Shanghai caused by the fighting between the Imperialist troops and the "Small Sword" Rebels. From the beginning a great difference of opinion was manifested between different sections of the foreign residents. Those who profited by building houses and renting them to Chinese naturally were in favour of allowing them to reside in the Settlements, but some saw the difficulties and dangers that might arise by departing from the terms of the Treaty.

When the Consuls brought the matter to the attention of the Taotai, he stated that the influx of Chinese refugees into the Settlements was due to the foreigners themselves, who built tenements for their accommodation, and housed them regardless of the risk incurred by harbouring people of doubtful character, and the difficulties that might arise if criminal offences were committed within the bounds of the Settlements.

One of the reasons for the Taotai and the Chinese authorities being generally opposed to the residence of Chinese in the Settlements was the fear that the latter might claim exemption from taxation by the Chinese Government.

The Taotai accordingly issued a proclamation prohibiting native residence in the Settlements without special permission of the respective Consuls.

The consular authorities instructed the Municipal Council to take measures for the disposal of the native tenements, pointing out the importance of abiding by the original regulations of the Treaty.

The Council, however, considered such a step as beyond its control, but undertook to clear up some brothels and gambling dens. Evidently it did not dare to try and carry out a measure so unpopular with the majority of the Land Renters.

The refugees tnemselves showed no disposition to move, and foreigners continued to build tenements for them, so that their residences became more widely scattered than ever.

Consul Alcock then took upon himself the responsibility, and made the necessary arrangements for the removal of objectionable Chinese, and the demolition of certain tenements. Provision was made for legalizing the residence of such Chinese as the Consuls and the Taotai might consider entitled to remain, either from their original occupation of lands and houses or on account of other circumstances connected with their legitimate interests and occupations.

As the squatters on the Yangkingpang refused to move, they were, by order of the district magistrate, forcibly ejected and their tenements destroyed. Unfortunately this occurred during cold winter weather and was the means of stirring up considerable anti-foreign feeling.

In his despatch of February 24th, 1855, the Taotai made some proposals to the Consuls to which they assented. As a result, the following regulation was drawn up and issued in the form of a proclamation.

> "Any native, before being admitted to the Settlement, must secure a licence from the consular and local authorities and enter into securities, in his own name, if wealthy and of sufficient standing, or otherwise in the person of two well-known residents, for keeping the Land Regulations and contributing his share to any general assessment. Any native guilty of a breach of registration rules will be subject to a penalty of fifty dollars for the first offence and cancellation of his licence in the case of a repetition thereof."

These regulations were never very strictly enforced, and the right of the Chinese to reside in the Settlement gradually became established by usage.

There now arose the question as to how these Chinese residents were to be regarded—as rightful members of the community, or as persons admitted on sufferance. The Chinese residents were taxed equally with the foreign members of the community, but had no voice in the expenditure of collected revenues, and could not participate in the municipal government. From a theoretical point of view this seems to have been an unjust arrangement. When we take into consideration, however, that the Chinese residents at that time had different political, social, and intellectual backgrounds from the foreign residents, one can see that admitting them to full privileges as citizens of the community was fraught with many difficulties. It would have resulted in the elimination of the Settlement as a place under foreign control, as, numerically, the Chinese far outnumbered the foreigners. In other words, the Settlement as we know it to-day would never have been developed. Shanghai would have reverted to the status of a Chinese city in which foreigners had the right to reside and carry on trade.

It probably never occurred to early Chinese residents that there was any injustice in the arrangement. They were quite accustomed to being taxed without representation and were not familiar with democratic ideas of government. They were ready to pay the taxes for the sake of the protection afforded and for the benefits of being able to carry on their trade in peace and safety.

CHAPTER V.

For a few years after the evacuation of the "Small Swords" from the city of Shanghai, the Settlements enjoyed peace and prosperity, but they were soon threatened with a more serious danger, that of invasion by the Taiping Rebels.

Mr. Laurence Oliphant, who visited Shanghai at that time, in his narrative of Lord Elgin's Mission, gives the following picture of life in those days. He describes people "riding or gyrating daily on the race course, as though they were being lounged. Those who prefer gossip to exercise frequent The Bund, a broad quay which extends the whole length of the Settlement, and which is crowded with Chinese porters all the morning and sprinkled with European ladies and gentlemen in the afternoon. The harmony and hospitality of Shanghai make it infinitely the most agreeable place of residence in China to the Mission."

Origin of the Taiping Rebellion The Taiping Rebellion began in the Province of Kwangsi in 1850. Its leader, Hung Hsiu-ch'uan, had been influenced by Christian teaching, and his original purpose was a crusade against idolatry, and the establishment of a society called the "Shangti Hui," "Association for the Worship of God."

He believed in using force for the promotion of his object, and soon came into conflict with the authorities. This led to open rebellion on his part, and the heading of a movement for the overthrow of the Manchu Dynasty and the inauguration of a new dynasty to be known as the "Tai-ping-tien-kuo," that is, "Great, Peaceful, Heavenly Kingdom."

He became more and more fanatical in his religious views, claiming for himself the Third Place in the Divine Trinity—consisting of God (the Heavenly Father), Jesus Christ (the Heavenly Elder Brother), and himself (the Heavenly Younger Brother).

Spread of the Rebellion The rebellion spread northwards through Hunan to the Yangtze River and established its capital at Nanking on March 19th, 1853. The expedition sent to the North to attack Peking was repulsed at Tientsin and the rebels were obliged to fall back on Nanking. Here they were closely invested by the Imperialist forces, but one of the four princes, Chung Wang (Loyal Prince), who had been appointed by Hung Hsiu-ch'uan as his principal assistant, cut his way out from Nanking and began the invasion of Chekiang and Southern Kiangsu. Through the activity and strategy of this leader the rebellion, when about to collapse, entered on a new lease of life.

Taking of Soochow After the taking of Soochow by the Taipings in June, 1860, there was consternation in Shanghai, as it was felt that before long an attack would be made on the rich Settlements.

Policy of Neutrality The original policy adopted by the foreign Powers towards the Taiping Rebellion was that of neutrality. Among the foreign officials and missionaries some were inclined to sympathize with the rebellion, and to regard it as the dawn of a new era for China, when a better government than that of the Manchus would be established. Their hopes, however, were soon dispelled, when it was discovered that the whole movement was destructive, and had nothing constructive about it.

Another reason for following a neutral policy was that England and France were at war with China.

This second war between Great Britain and China began in 1856, and may be divided into three stages.

In the first, hostilities were confined to the South, and an attack on Canton; in the second, Lord Elgin, who had been sent out from England to be Commander-in-chief, carried the war to the North, and forced the Chinese Government to agree to the Treaty of Tientsin, which was signed on June 26th, 1858; in the third, the British and French armies advanced on Peking because of the refusal of the Chinese authorities to permit the exchange of the ratification of the Treaty in the capital. This led to the taking of that city by the Allied forces (British and French) and to the signing of the Treaty of Peking, October 22nd, 1860.

Among the public monuments in Shanghai there is one erected to some members of the British force who took part in the advance on Peking in 1860. Lord Elgin had sent forward a small party under Mr. (afterwards Sir) Harry Parkes to carry a letter to the High Commissioners at Tungchow, who had been appointed by the Chinese Government to treat with the English and French commanders. On their way back they were seized and sent to Peking, where they were imprisoned and suffered great indignities. Of the twenty-six British seized on September 18th, thirteen, including Mr. Parkes and Mr. Lock and one English dragoon, were returned alive, the other thirteen, according to Lord Elgin's account, " were barbarously murdered." Some of the bodies were sent back, but some were never recovered.

Of the thirteen French seized, five were released alive, the bodies of six were returned, and two were not accounted for.

A large granite cross was sent out from England in memory of those who lost their lives. As there were difficulties connected with its being put up in Peking, it was erected in Shanghai, and stands on the lawn in front of the British Consulate. On the sides of the steps forming the base of the cross are inscribed the names of William de Norman, Robert B. Anderson, John Phipps, Luke Brabrazon, and Thomas William Bowlby, with the dates of their birth and death.

The cross bears the following quaint inscription:

> Born in its light,
> Passing through the dark valley,
> In its power,
> Resting in its shadow.
> In its great glory,
> Behold it, O Heathen,
> Enquire, believe, and live.

The Treaty of Tientsin and Opium

It is unnecessary here to give the full terms of the Treaty of Tientsin, but one of the provisions of the Treaty, that of legalizing the opium trade, calls for some remarks as it had much to do with the commercial life of Shanghai.

After the first war with Great Britain, the trade in opium had been declared illegal. In the American Treaty of Wanghsia, 1844, as Mr. Cushing pointed out, it was expressly stipulated that " In regard to opium, which is not directly mentioned in the English treaties, it is provided by the Treaty of Wanghsia, that citizens of the United States engaged in this or any other contraband trade shall receive no protection from the American Government, nor shall the flag of the United States be abusively employed by other nations as a cover for the violation of the laws of China."

The attempt to keep out opium resulted in a disastrous failure, and led to smuggling on an extensive scale, in which American ships played no small part.

At Shanghai, but moored at Woosung, were a large number of receiving ships.   Up to 1854 there were ten; four for opium consigned to British firms, four to Jewish or Parsee firms, and two to American firms.   In 1854 the two American ships were withdrawn from service.

Swift and well-armed clipper schooners carried the opium from point to point along the coast.   The arming of these ships and of the receiving ships was not for the purpose of forcing the noxious drug on the people, as some hostile critics have stated, but for the purpose of guarding against pirates.   The drug was in great demand and found ready purchasers, who obtained it from the receiving ships. The officials connived at the illegal traffic, inasmuch as they could obtain a large revenue by taxing the smugglers.

The following figures show the rapid increase in this illegal traffic in Shanghai.   In 1847, 16,500 chests were disposed of and in 1857, 31,907 chests.

The Chinese Government, having become convinced that it was impossible to prohibit the importation of opium, and that the attempt resulted in lawless smuggling, adopted a change of policy.

In the negotiations carried on for drawing up the Treaty of Tientsin, Lord Elgin proposed the legalization of the opium trade to the Chinese deputies.   To this they agreed on the following terms:

"Opium was to pay Tls. 30 per picul import duty.   The importer was to sell it only at the port.   It was to be carried into the interior by Chinese only, and only on Chinese property; the foreign trader would not be allowed to accompany it.   The passport and transit dues were not to be extended to it, and the transit dues were to be arranged as the Chinese Government saw fit; and tariff revision was not to apply to opium."[1]

---

[1] Morse: *International Relations of the Chinese Empire*, Vol. I, p. 535.

The opium traffic, whether carried on legally or illegally, resulted in great harm to China, and we have arrived now at a time when specious arguments are no longer used to defend it. Condemned, both on moral and physical grounds, the great problem confronts the nations as to the best way of limiting the drug to its legitimate uses in all countries. China has never been able to deal with the problem effectively. Prohibition led to smuggling. Legalization of the trade led to the more rapid spread of the habit throughout the country, and to the planting of the poppy in China itself.

The agreement on the part of the British Government in 1908 to restriction of the importation of Indian opium into China, and to ultimate prohibition led for a time to a crusade for the suppression of the planting of the poppy. Recent years, however, have brought a recrudescence of its cultivation, and although for many years Great Britain has prohibited the export of Indian opium to China, opium still remains one of the great curses of the country.

For Shanghai the legalization of the trade meant the appearance of the opium hulks moored along The Bund. Old sailing ships were converted into receiving stations for opium, which was stored on them until it could obtain a market. These unsightly monsters disfigured The Bund for many years, and the last of them did not disappear until after the cessation of the importation of opium from India in 1917.

The Defence of Shanghai Returning to the Taiping Rebellion, the question uppermost in everyone's mind was how Shanghai could be defended in the case of an attack by the Taipings.

The Chinese officials were anxious to get foreign assistance to keep the rebels out of Shanghai and the Taotai actually proposed that the foreign forces gathered at Shanghai for the expedition against the Government in the North, should be employed to fight against the Taipings. The inconsistency of warfare between China and the foreign forces in the North, and an alliance between China and the foreign forces in the South was not appreciated. This is indicative of the lack of the spirit of nationalism at that period.

Measures of Defence As a first step in taking measures for defence, the Volunteer Corps, which had practically ceased to exist, was in 1860 reorganized.

Both the French Minister, M. de Bourboulon, and the British Minister, the Hon. Mr. (afterwards Sir) Frederick Bruce, acceded to Wu Taotai's appeal to join in the defence of Shanghai, but the British policy at first was confined to defensive measures and was opposed to aggressive action against the rebels.

Chung Wang announced in a letter to the foreign ministers that he was about to attack the city of Shanghai, but that if the foreigners observed neutrality the Settlements had nothing to fear.

The Attack on the City, August 18th, 1860 On August 17th, 1860, the approach of the rebels was heralded by a dense cloud of smoke in the west, due to the burning of villages. Chung Wang seized the Mission premises at Siccawei for his headquarters, and on the next day launched an attack on the city of Shanghai. The Taipings found to their surprise British and French flags flying on the walls of the native city, which were manned by the Allied troops; the British under Captain Budd of the Royal Marines, and the French under Captain Faure.

The rebels advanced under cover of thickets, grave mounds and buildings towards the South Gate, held by Captain Budd. When the attacking force came out into the open they were met with a brisk fire of rifles and of large guns which had been brought from the ships.

Driven from the South Gate, the Taipings moved toward the south-west corner of the wall, but there encountered a telling fire from the Marines and Sikhs, and the attacking force, numbering about 3,000, was obliged to retire.

During the night, parties were sent out from the city to fire the western and southern suburbs, which afforded shelter for an attacking force.

Under cover of darkness the Taipings managed to get into Nantao, inhabited by leading Chinese merchants and containing a large supply of merchandise. Here they seized the Custom House, and proceeded to pillage and massacre. The French force, as a defensive measure, set fire to the whole of this rich suburb.

Settlement Threatened On the morning of the 20th, the Taipings advanced to the West Gate, and then turned toward the Settlements, whose defence was in the hands of Colonel March. No sooner had they planted their standards close to the Race Course than they were attacked by shells and rockets. The river despatch boat "Nimrod" sent shell after shell over the Settlements far out into the fields beyond, and the "Pioneer," which had taken up her position on the Soochow Creek, attacked the rebel force with 13-inch shells. After submitting to a two-hour bombardment the rebels retreated towards Siccawei.

Within the Settlements, the Volunteers under Colonel Neale guarded the barricades which had been erected at the entrance to every street on the western boundary. Mr. Forrest, the Interpreter to the British Consulate, rode out to the camp at Siccawei, accompanied by an orderly

4

named Phillips with a letter to the rebel chiefs in which they were told that the city of Shanghai was under the protection of the British and French, and that they could not be permitted to enter it. He was civilly received and invited into the camp. This invitation he did not think it wise to accept, and departed after leaving his despatches.

Withdrawal of the Rebels In consequence of the severe check suffered by his troops Chung Wang decided to withdraw from Siccawei. Before doing so, however, he sent a letter to the foreign Consuls, threatening to stop the silk and tea trade if any further aid was given to the Imperialists, and stating that he had come at the invitation of certain foreigners who sympathized with the Taipings, and that his object had been to negotiate a treaty. On the next day, when Mr. Forrest returned to Siccawei for his answer, he found only a few ill-clad soldiers at the rebel camp. The army had evacuated, leaving some stuffed straw figures to represent soldiers.

With the departure of Chung Wang, Shanghai enjoyed a brief respite. Had it not been for the presence of the foreign forces gathered in Shanghai at that time in connection with the expedition of the Allies to the North, its fate might have been sealed.

Influx of Chinese into the Settlements Just as when the "Small Swords" seized Shanghai there had been a great influx of Chinese into the Settlements, so it was at the approach of the Taipings, only on a much larger scale. Officials and merchants, rich and poor, all alike rushed in, seeking a place of safety. Every available space was soon occupied, even the creeks and the river being crowded with boats of all descriptions. The population of the native city fled into the Settlements or across to Pootung. Twenty dollars became the regular price for conveying people across the river in a sampan.

Soon the Chinese population had increased to 300,000 and the cost of living advanced rapidly. Real estate values also began to soar, and land purchased originally for £46 to £74 per acre was sold for £8,000 to £12,000 per acre.

After the war in the North came to an end, Vice-Admiral Sir James Hope, in February, 1861, proceeded to Nanking and had an interview with Tien Wang (Heavenly Emperor) i.e., Hung Hsiu-ch'uan, who was persuaded to agree that his forces should not approach Shanghai nearer than a hundred *li*, or thirty miles. This promise, however, was given for a year only, and nothing was said of what might happen after thai time had expired.

Visit of Vice-Admiral Sir James Hope to Nanking, February, 1861

Shanghai consequently enjoyed a year of peace and steamers began to ply on the Yangtze, which was opened to trade as far as Hankow.

Shortly after the fall of Soochow the Chinese residents at Shanghai, under the direction of Wu Taotai and a wealthy banker named Ta Chi (Yang Fang), formed a Patriotic Association for the purpose of resisting the Taipings.

Chinese Employ the Service of Foreigners

In the meantime Tseng Kuo-fan, who had become titular Viceroy of Nanking and High Commissioner, with jurisdiction over the provinces of Kiangsu, Kiangsi, Chekiang and Anhwei, called to his assistance Li Hung-chang. The latter came into prominence by his vigorous actions against the rebels in Anhwei, and in consequence in July, 1862, had been appointed titular Governor of Kiangsu. These two officials adopted a bold and aggressive policy against the Taipings and saw the advantage of employing foreigners to assist the Imperialist forces in resisting the rebels.

Frederick Townsend Ward, born in 1831 in
Engagement of F. T. Ward Salem, of an old Massachusetts family, took
to the sea at the early age of fifteen. He
found his way to Shanghai as master of a barque in 1851,
and spent several years in the seafaring world on the coast
and the Yangtze River. He was a born adventurer and
entered into an agreement with Ta Chi, Chairman of the
Patriotic Association, to recapture Sungkiang, which had
fallen into the hands of the rebels, for a sum of Tls. 30,000,
the payment of the money to be conditional on his success.

He proceeded to enlist a hundred men, chiefly foreign
sailors attracted by the prospect of plunder, and with these
he attempted to take the city of Sungkiang, but failed.
Undiscouraged, he then enlisted the same number of
Manila-men (Filipinos) with two foreign lieutenants, E.
Forrester and Henry Andrea Burgevine. With this force
he delivered a second assault, this time successfully, and
drove out the Taiping garrison. Next he undertook to
retake Tsingpu (Chingpoo) with a force of 200 men,
accompanied by 10,000 Chinese troops, but here he found
foreigners were assisting the rebels, and was repulsed,
being himself severely wounded. He was obliged to retire
to Sungkiang, and for over a year made it his headquarters,
while he drilled his troops.

Foreigners generally regarded Ward as a filibuster,
and the Americans objected to his actions, as up to this
time the policy of neutrality had been adopted by their
government. The British authorities were incensed because the temptation to join Ward's force and to enrich
themselves by plunder led to many desertions from the
Navy. In May 1861, Admiral Hope arrested Ward on the
charge of enticing sailors to leave their ships and he was
brought before the American Consul for trial. He secured
his acquittal by declaring he had renounced his nationality
and had become a Chinese subject.

Being obliged to abandon his policy of enlisting foreigners, he undertook to raise and drill a body of Chinese troops to serve under foreign officers, retaining his own body-guard of Manila-men. In this new venture he showed marked powers of organization, and developed a force which proved capable of winning many victories.

Owing to the fact that their uniforms were semi-foreign and because they wore foreign hats, at first his men were nicknamed "the imitation foreign devils."

The Second Attack on Shanghai On January 11th, 1862, some 30,000 Taipings, with 200 foreigners enlisted in their service, began an advance on Shanghai from the direction of Woosung. They reached a point a mile and a half north of the British Consulate, but withdrew when they found they were opposed by the Volunteers and a battalion of Indian troops. At the same time another force threatened Sungkiang, and a third army advanced from Hangchow. The force attacking Sungkiang was defeated at Kwangfuling (a town half-way between Sungkiang and Tsingpu) by Ward's well disciplined troops, and retreated to Pootung. The rebels advancing on Shanghai were prevented from taking the field by a heavy fall of snow, early in January, which lasted 58 hours and covered the Settlements and country to a depth of 3 feet in many places. This gave the forces in the Settlements time to organize their defence.

On February 24th, a combined force of English and French sailors led by Admiral Hope, and 700 of Ward's men attacked the Taipings at Kaokiao (Kajow) on the Pootung side between Shanghai and Woosung—and defeated them, and a short time afterwards another body of about 6,000 Taipings were put to rout by this same force at Nankiao (Najow). For these victories Ward was promoted by Imperial decree to the rank of Brigadier-

General in the Chinese army, and the title of the "Ever Victorious Army" was bestowed on his force.

CHAPTER VI.

SHANGHAI
DURING THE TAIPING REBELLION—(*Continued*).

Foreigners Adopt an Aggressive Policy More and more it became apparent that the policy of defensive neutrality was futile, and that the safety of Shanghai could only be secured by aggressive measures in co-operation with the Imperialist forces. Admiral Hope permitted the transport in British steamers of 9,000 troops of Tseng Kuo-fan's army, from Anking to Shanghai, and after consultation with his French colleague, Admiral A. L. Protet, it was agreed to clear the country of the Taiping marauders within a thirty-mile radius of Shanghai. This was approved by the British and French authorities, and it was decided to transfer the British troops in garrison at Tientsin to Shanghai. For the carrying out of the new policy, the assistance of Ward's unit was sought. Admiral Hope in writing to Mr. Bruce said, "in the force organized and led by Mr. Ward I see the nucleus and beginning of a military organization, which may prove most valuable in the distracted state of China."

The Thirty Mile Radius By the arrival of the garrison from the North, the Allied force was increased to 2,824 men, and these with the 1,000 troops under Ward were thought sufficient for the carrying out of an aggressive campaign.

The command was exercised jointly by Admiral Hope, Admiral Protet, General Staveley, who had come with the troops from Tientsin, and General Ward, but the general direction of operations was entrusted to Admiral Hope.

Victories were gained over the rebels at Waykiatze, Tsipao, Nanziang, Kiating, Tsingpu, Nankiao and Tselin (Cholin).

Admiral Protet, a man of remarkable bravery, was killed in the assault on Nankiao. His remains were taken to Shanghai[1] and his funeral was attended by many influential Chinese. An Imperial decree was issued, extolling the Admiral and commanding that a sacrifice be offered to his spirit.

The Summer of 1862 The gains made by the allied troops were not retained for any length of time, as the Imperialist garrisons proved unable to hold them. Owing to the oppressive heat of the summer weather, and to the prevalence of cholera, the troops retired to Shanghai and for a time there was a cessation of hostilities.

During this period, the Volunteer Mounted Rangers, a force consisting of about twenty young men of the Settlements, were of great service, reconnoitring the country and bringing back reports of the movements of the enemy.

Chung Wang, the rebel leader, exasperated by frequent defeats, was stirred to greater activity, and with a large force penetrated as far as the Bubbling Well, within two miles of the Settlement boundary, which at that time was at Defence Creek. Refugees, in great numbers, flocked into the Settlements, increasing the Chinese population to 500,000.

Only Sungkiang and Nankiao remained in the hands of the allied troops, and the outlook was serious.

---

[1] In the grounds of the French Town Hall in Rue du Consulat stands a bronze statue on a granite pedestal erected in honour of Admiral Protet, and the French troops who lost their lives in China during the Taiping Rebellion.

Although the foreign Powers had now espoused the cause of the Imperialists, the rebels continued to obtain large supplies of guns and ammunition from foreign firms in Shanghai and undoubtedly they were thus enabled to prolong the rebellion.

Death of General Ward Ningpo fell into the hands of the Taipings on December 9th, 1861, and from that centre a campaign was directed against the surrounding towns. General Ward's help was solicited to resist the advance of the rebels. In an attack on Tzeki, a town about ten miles north-west of Ningpo, on September 21st, 1862, he was killed by a stray bullet.

Thus ended the adventurous career of one who had proved himself a loyal servant of the Imperialist cause. General Gordon paid the following tribute to his memory, "He was a brave, clear-headed man, much liked by the Chinese Mandarins, and a very fit man for the command of the force he had raised."

Later, on March 10th, 1877, a Memorial Hall was erected by Imperial order at Sungkiang, containing a spirit tablet before which incense was burnt. In recent years an annual pilgrimage has been made to this shrine by members of the American Legion of Shanghai, and measures have been taken to keep the place in repair.

Appointment of Burgevine After the death of General Ward the " Ever Victorious Army " came directly under the control of Li Hung-chang. The question arose as to who should be put in command, and it was finally decided to appoint Burgevine, one of Ward's faithful lieutenants.

At about this time the Russian Government proposed to come to the help of the Imperialists with a force of

10,000 troops, but this offer was refused by Li Hung-chang. The Russian fleet, however, was allowed to co-operate with the British and French against the rebel forces.

After the summer, there was renewed activity on the part of the allied forces. The city of Kiating was retaken and victories were gained at Huangtu and Paohokiang (Paokong), and in January, 1863, General Staveley was able to announce that the country within the thirty-mile radius had been entirely cleared of the Taipings.

Dismissal of Burgevine Burgevine did not have Ward's faculty of getting on with the officials, and was never popular with Li Hung-chang. The payment of his troops fell into arrears, and he refused to carry out the orders to assist in an attack on Nanking until his army had been paid. He quarrelled with the banker Ta Chi in an attempt to extract money from him and in consequence was dismissed from the Imperial service. His later career darkened his reputation. He went over to the side of the rebels, and was finally taken prisoner by the Imperialist forces in Fukien, and was drowned (whether accidentally or not was never determined) while being conveyed as a prisoner to Soochow.

Appointment of Captain Holland On January 15th, 1863, Captain J. Y. Holland of the British Marines was appointed in command of the "Ever Victorious Army." He started out from Sungkiang on February 10th, on an expedition against Tai-ch'ang (Tai-tsang), but met with a disastrous repulse, 190 men being killed and 174 wounded. Having lost the confidence of his own men and of the British authorities, he felt obliged to resign.

Appointment of Major Gordon
Although there was a desire on the part of the officers and men for the reappointment of Burgevine, the Chinese authorities would not give their consent, and on March 24th, Charles George Gordon, afterwards known as "Chinese Gordon," received the appointment. He had come out to the East as Major in the Royal Artillery in connection with the second war between Great Britain and China. His appointment was made possible, as a British Order in Council had been issued on January 9th, permitting British officers to take service under the Chinese Government.

He soon gave proof of military genius. Like Ward, he dominated his men by his strong will. He went into action with utter fearlessness, carrying only a short rattan cane, and soon became a hero in the eyes of his men. Unlike Ward he had no personal ambition and refused to receive any emoluments apart from his salary.

Gordon's Victories in Kiangsu
Gordon secured a succession of brilliant victories. Changshu, which had been invested by the rebels, was relieved, Taich'ang was retaken, and Kunshan (Quinsan) was captured. The latter city with its hill, 200 feet high, was of great strategical importance, as it was connected by waterways with Soochow, Shanghai, and the Yangtze River, and was protected by shallow lakes on the north and west.

Mutiny in the Army
When he decided to remove his headquarters from Sungkiang to Kunshan and gave orders to that effect, a mutiny broke out among his soldiers. It was dealt with promptly and severely but resulted in his force being reduced from 3.900 to 1,700 men. To fill the vacancies he enlisted bodily 2,000 Taipings, taken prisoners at Kunshan. In his diary he writes, "Recruit rebel prisoners, who are much better men."

Surrender of Soochow

Next he advanced with his force on Soochow, the headquarters of Chung Wang. Before making a direct assault on the city he captured the neighbouring towns. His movements were facilitated by the use of two small steamers, a part of the Lay-Osborne fleet[1] which had been purchased by the Chinese authorities from England. Gradually his force worked its way closer and closer to the city of Soochow, causing great consternation within the walls and resulting in its surrender on December 4th.

Gordon had agreed that if the city surrendered, the lives of the eight rebel "Wangs" or princes would be spared. When he discovered that Li Hung-chang and General Chen of the Imperialist army had summarily executed these men, he felt his honour was involved, and threatened to resign.

He was persuaded, however, by the British authorities to retain his command a little longer, by the argument that only so could the safety of Shanghai be secured.

Resignation of General Gordon

After further victories and the taking of Changchow on May 11th, 1864, the Taiping Rebellion in Kiangsu rapidly collapsed. General Gordon resigned his command and the "Ever Victorious Army" was disbanded at Kunshan. Gordon was offered Tls. 10,000 reward upon the fall of Soochow, and the offer was renewed when he resigned his command. On both occasions it was refused.

Memorial to the "Ever Victorious Army"

Li Hung-chang made a grant of $1,500 for erecting memorials to those who died in the service of China. The Shanghai memorial now stands just within the southern entrance to the Public Gardens on The Bund. It is a stone monument and bears the following inscription:

---

[1] See page 61.

"In memory of the officers of the ' Ever Victorious Army ' who were killed in action while serving against the Taiping Rebels in the Province of Kiangsu, A.D. 1862-64."

On it are 48 names of foreigners, headed by that of General Ward.

Strangely enough, with the exception of a street named after him, no memorial has been erected in Shanghai to General Gordon himself, a man who did so much for keeping the Settlements from utter destruction.

The Lay-Osborne Fleet and the Appointment of Robert Hart as Inspector-General of Customs During the course of the rebellion, in 1882, the Imperial Government resolved to create a properly organized navy to be manned by Europeans, and instructions were sent to Mr. H. N. Lay to purchase and equip a steam fleet in England. When the matter was discussed with the British Government, the question arose as to what flag the vessels should fly, for at that time China had no national flag. The question was referred to Peking, and Prince Kung gave orders that a triangular flag with the dragon design should be adopted and flown on all Chinese warships.

A small squadron of seven steamers and one store ship were bought and equipped and sent out to China.

Mr. Lay appointed Captain Sherard Osborne to be in command of the fleet for four years.

As soon as the fleet arrived a bitter controversy broke out between the Chinese Government on the one side and Mr. Lay and Captain Osborne on the other. The Chinese Government wished to appoint a Chinese Commander-in-chief, and to make Captain Osborne assistant Commander-in-chief, having authority over the foreign naval officers. He was to receive his orders from the Viceroys and Governors within whose jurisdiction he might happen to be.

Mr. Lay insisted that Captain Osborne should be Commander-in-chief, and furthermore held that all orders to Captain Osborne were to be transmitted through himself.

The two points of view differed so radically that it was impossible to effect a compromise. Finally the Chinese Government refused to take over the ships and they were purchased by the British Government. Mr. Lay was dismissed from his post as Inspector-General of Customs, and Mr. (afterwards Sir) Robert Hart was appointed in his place, and began to build up what became a very remarkable service.

Kiangnan Arsenal   As one of the results of the Taiping Rebellion, the Kiangnan Arsenal was established by Tseng Kuo-fan and Li Hung-chang in 1865. It was located at first in Hongkew, and moved to its present site near Lunghua in 1867.

It manufactured rifles and large guns, and constructed naval ships. A school and a translation department were attached to it. The former at one time was under the direction of Dr. Young J. Allen, and the latter was for many years conducted by Dr. John Fryer, and did useful work in supplying China with books on Science in the Chinese language.

CHAPTER VII.

MUNICIPAL DEVELOPMENT, 1860–1870.

During the Taiping Rebellion and the years immediately following there was considerable development in municipal affairs.

Establishment of the French Municipality, 1862

In the beginning there had been a fair prospect of municipal affairs being carried on under one administration. The French, however, fearing lest their interests might be overlooked, determined to set up a separate municipal government. They held they were free to do this, for although the Land Regulations of 1854 had been signed by the French Consul, they had never been ratified by the French Government. Accordingly on May 13th, the Municipal Council of the Concession Francaise was formed. It differed from the English Municipal Council in that all its decisions were subject to the approval or veto of the French Consul.

Inasmuch as for some time after this the foreign trade of Shanghai was largely carried on in the English Settlement, the French Municipality found it difficult to raise a revenue, and depended largely on income derived from licenses to opium divans, brothels and gambling houses.

Amalgamation of the American Settlement with the English

In the American Settlement which had been founded in Hongkew, across the Soochow Creek, were the premises of the American Episcopal Church Mission, the Shanghai Dock, some wharves, and some establishments for the entertainment of sailors. It was justly called "the Cinderella among the settlements." It had the disadvantage of becoming a refuge for the criminal class, driven out of the English Settlement by its more efficient police force, and the authorities found it difficult to control the large Chinese population which flowed into it during the Taiping Rebellion. The Hongkew Municipal Committee was obliged to come to an arrangement by which the Hongkew police (consisting of a body of six men) were amalgamated with the police of the English Settlement, so as to gain the co-operation of the latter.

A movement for one municipal government for both Settlements was put forward by Mr. Edward Cunningham of Russell and Company and Mr. George F. Seward, the American Consul. On September 21st, 1863, a union was effected, and the International Settlement, north of the Yangkingpang, came into existence.

At the same time, Consul Seward and Huang Taotai agreed to the following boundary line of the American Settlement. Starting from a point opposite the Defence Creek it extended down the Soochow Creek and the Whangpoo to three miles up the Yangtszepoo Creek and then in a straight line back to the point facing the Defence Creek.

Proposal to Make Shanghai a Free City The Shanghai Municipal Council (the Municipal Council of the International Settlement) realizing the burden of providing a government for hundreds of thousands of Chinese, as well as for the foreign residents, seriously contemplated the practicability of converting the International Settlement into a free city—or, in other words, into an independent republic.

The British Consul, Mr. W. H. Medhurst, son of Dr. W. H. Medhurst, pointed out that such a step would be a violation of the Treaties, as "the territory belongs to the Emperor of China, who merely accords to the Foreign Powers, that have entered into treaties with himself, an extraterritorial jurisdiction over their own citizens

The Custom House in the Fifties.

SIGNING OF THE TREATY OF NANKING, 1842.

resident at this port, but retains for himself all authority over his own territory and subjects."

The British Envoy, Sir Frederick Bruce, was even more emphatic in his opposition to the proposal and declared that the "English Concession at Shanghai was neither a transfer nor a lease of the land in question to the British Crown, the land so acquired remaining Chinese territory."

It can readily be seen that the scheme proposed was impracticable. It would not have been possible to obtain the consent of the Chinese Government, and if the plan had been attempted, in face of Chinese opposition, it would have been easy to wreck the new republic by placing round it a cordon of Custom barriers preventing trade with the interior.

Proposal of the Envoys The Envoys, especially Sir Frederick Bruce, made counter proposals in regard to the administration of the Settlements.

"It was proposed that a municipality should be created, to include if possible the English, French, and American settlements; that each resident should be subject, in both criminal and civil suits, to the jurisdiction of his own authorities but that arrests for the Chinese authorities should be made only by the Municipal police; that a Chinese element should be introduced into the Municipal Council, and that no measure affecting the Chinese residents should be taken without its consent, but this proposal was contingent on the extension of the scheme to all three settlements; that territorial jurisdiction should rest solely on grants from the Emperor or his representatives; and that if necessary to obtain such grants, certain revenues, or a percentage of revenues, should be paid to the Imperial authority." [1]

---

[1] H. B. Morse: *International Relations of the Chinese Empire*, Vol. II, p. 126.

An important part of the proposal was not carried out. The three Settlements did not come under one administration, the French preferring to have a separate Municipality and as a consequence, the admission of a Chinese element into the Council was not effected, and the Chinese ratepayers were left without representation.

Taxation of the Chinese within the Settlement In July, 1862, the Taotai called attention to the expense to which his government was put in protecting Shanghai, and asked permission to impose a poll tax on the Chinese residents of the Settlements similar to that which had been paid in the native city.

The British Envoy was in favour of granting this permission and maintained that there was nothing in the Treaties exempting the Chinese population of the Settlements from paying taxes to their own government. The merchants in Shanghai saw more clearly than the Envoy the difficulties that might arise, as it would bring about dual and rival jurisdiction within the same area. They were obliged, however, to bow to the will of the Envoy and to admit the right of the Chinese Government to tax her own subjects for national purposes. As a compromise it was arranged that the tax should be collected by the Municipality and handed over to the Chinese authorities. Accordingly on June 12th, 1863, it was agreed that the Shanghai Municipal Council should collect from Chinese residents 20 per cent. rental tax and that half the proceeds of this tax should be paid to the Taotai and half to the Council, and that no further tax should be imposed by the Chinese Government.

Although theoretically it would appear that the Chinese authorities had the right to impose taxes on the Chinese residing in the Settlements, yet practically, if this right had not been restricted, it might have resulted in a great hardship on the Chinese themselves and would have subjected them to increasing exactions on their commerce and personal property. One of the chief reasons for their seeking a home in the Settlements was to be free from government interference with their trade. As a matter of fact the Chinese Government had done little or nothing for the protection of the Settlements and the expense had fallen almost entirely on the foreign governments having extraterritorial jurisdiction therein.

The Establishment of the Mixed Court The exercise of jurisdiction over the Chinese residents raised many questions. How were Chinese offenders to be dealt with? Should the Chinese set up a court in the Settlements? The solution was found by the establishment in 1864 of what is known as the "Mixed Court," presided over by a deputy of the Shanghai Magistrate. Police cases were to be heard by the deputy alone. In criminal cases against Chinese, in which a foreigner was interested, a delegate from a consulate was to sit as assessor with the deputy. In civil cases, where it was between Chinese, the deputy was to sit alone; where it was a suit of foreigners against Chinese, a consular assessor was to sit with the deputy. Appeals were to be heard by the Taotai sitting with a Consul as assessor.

At first the court was held in one of the outbuildings of the British Consulate, and did not command much respect, partly because of the low rank of the Chinese deputy appointed.

The procedure was amended in 1869, when it was agreed that the court was to be presided over by a deputy who had the rank of sub-Magistrate. All cases affecting the interests of foreigners were to be heard with an assessor, but the deputy sat alone where both parties were Chinese; servants of foreigners could be summoned only with the consent of the Consul concerned; criminal charges punishable by death were to be tried by the Shanghai Magistrate.

In later years there was further modification. The consular assessor became a party to the judgment in every case—in police cases because of the interest of the foreign community, and in suits between Chinese, on the ground that "the Chinese official, with his traditional methods of enforcing judgments, must not be admitted to an unfettered jurisdiction within the area reserved for foreign trade and residence." These changes, as we shall see later, came to be regarded by the Chinese as an infringement of their sovereign rights.

Land Regulations of 1869   In 1866 the Land Regulations of 1854 were revised by the land renters in concert with the Consuls, without previous consultation with the foreign Ministers in Peking.

The new rules recognized the establishment of the French Concession. The Council was increased to nine members, vested with amplified powers, and *personally* exempt from any claim arising out of their administration. The Municipal Council, *as a body*, however, was liable to the jurisdiction of the Court of Consuls, established for this special purpose. Upon requisition of twenty-five land renters the Consuls might jointly or singly convene a public meeting and adopt measures which, if passed, should have the force of laws. The land renters should have the right to vote by proxy. Chinese were to have the right to participate in the Municipal Government.

These new rules and bye-laws were not sanctioned by the foreign Ministers at Peking until 1869, and in sanctioning them, the Diplomatic Body eliminated the clause in regard to Chinese participation in the Municipal Government.

The new Land Regulations were drawn up without consultation with the local Chinese authorities, but the latter made no objection to their being put into operation as the changes did not affect Chinese interests.

Shanghai is probably the only municipality in the world where proxy voting is permissible, and naturally this has given rise to much criticism, inasmuch as it lodges a dangerous power of blocking progressive legislation, in the hands of absentee landlords.

Detailed rules for the Court of Consuls were not promulgated until thirteen years later on July 10th, 1882.

Although attempts, as we shall see, were made in later years to amend the Land Regulations still further, yet no change was endorsed by the Diplomatic Body until 1898, and the revision made at that time did not materially alter the Regulations of 1869.

In 1860 Mr. Pickwood was employed as Secretary of the Council. He was succeeded in 1862 by Mr. R. F. Gould and reforms were made in the internal working of the Municipality. A small staff of assistants, including a qualified engineer, a European interpreter, and an officer to supervise the Municipal revenues from wharfage dues were appointed. The police force was increased, and in 1864 consisted of 164 foreigners. On account of expenses this number was cut down, and Chinese were drafted into the force. In 1870 the foreign police numbered 112[1].

Fire Brigade   The crowding of the Settlements with cheaply constructed Chinese houses during the period of the rebellion added to the danger of fire.

---

[1] During the first ten years, the Consular Constables and the native watchmen sufficed for the policing of the Settlement.   In 1853 eight foreign constables were employed with Mr. S. Clifton as Superintendent. In 1855 the foreign police force was increased to 30.

In order to cope with this menace fire wells were sunk in the main thoroughfares to serve as reservoirs for water. Before the introduction of a system of waterworks, these fire wells, the creeks, and the river were the only available sources upon which the one fire engine could draw. This engine was imported from the United States in 1863 by the Council, and formed the nucleus of a voluntary fire brigade service organized in 1866. Captain J. P. Roberts was elected first Chief Engineer, and Mr. C. J. Ashley, foreman of the Mih-ho-loong (destroy fire dragon) Hook and Ladder Company. The French joined heartily in the enterprise and the three Settlements worked in complete harmony.

The Brigade was not at first under the control of the Municipal Council, and, as it was largely supported by the Insurance Companies, was not a great drain on municipal resources.

Fire alarms were in the beginning given by the ringing of the church bell and the firing of three guns from the senior man-of-war in port, and the ringing of the bells of the steamers in harbour. Owing to the fact that the church bell could not be heard distinctly, a tower was erected at the Hongkew Police Station, and one of the church bells not in use was lent by the trustees as a fire alarm.

In 1880 a large bell weighing 5,150 pounds was purchased from the Meneely Founders of West Troy, N.Y. The bell had been cast in 1865 and was obtained at the low cost of $1,500 gold. It was hung in the one hundred feet high tower erected at the Central Fire Station on Shantung Road and the one in use there was transferred to the tower at the Hongkew Police Station. Some time after bells ceased to be used for fire alarms, the large bell purchased in 1880 was moved to Jessfield Park and mounted on a stone pedestal in front of a small Chinese pavilion where it may now be seen.

The second and third articles of the constitution of the voluntary Shanghai Fire Department read as follows:

" Article II.—The Shanghai Fire Department is instituted for the better preservation of all property exposed to conflagration and its motto shall be ' We Fight the Flames.'

" Article III.—That the American, English and French Settlements be known respectively as Fire Districts Nos. 1, 2, and 3, and the operations of the S. F. D. shall be within the foreign settlements of Shanghai, and these limits shall not be passed except in cases of urgent necessity, and by order of the Chief Engineer."

The Fire Brigade played an important part in the life of the Settlements. The young men took up the service with considerable eagerness and enjoyed the excitement and the social life connected with it. Some of them lived at the fire stations, so as to be on hand when alarms were given, and no matter what social functions they might be attending, at the sound of the fire bell, they rushed off so as to be at their stations as quickly as possible. There was keen competition among the different units as to which would reach the scene of the fire first.

As we shall see later, owing to the extension of the Settlement area and to great increase in the number of fires, it became necessary to abandon the voluntary system, and to introduce in its place a paid fire brigade, with a trained Chief Officer at its head, appointed by the Municipal Council.

Cemeteries A Cemetery Company was formed in 1844 which by the sale of shares, raised S500 with which was bought the first burial ground behind the Custom House. Before it could be laid out as a cemetery.

Messrs. Lindsay and Company acquired this plot of ten and a half *mow*, by giving in exchange for it a piece of fourteen *mow* on Shantung Road, with a well built wall, a gateway and a mortuary chapel. It is known as the Shantung Road Cemetery. Here will be found many of the graves of the early residents of Shanghai including those of Dr. E. C. Bridgman, the first American Missionary to China and the Rt. Rev. William J. Boone, the first Anglican Bishop in China.

During the years 1844-1851, 54 seamen died in Shanghai and were buried in the foreign cemetery. Later on a special cemetery was set apart for seamen, in Pootung.

An interesting cemetery is situated at the corner of Rue Hué and the Boulevard des Deux Républiques. Here are the graves of the British soldiers and sailors who lost their lives during the time of the fighting around Shanghai, in 1861-1864. They were buried at first just under the city wall, but when this was demolished, after the Revolution of 1911, the graves were removed to the present site.

In September, 1863, it was decided that a new cemetery was necessary and that it should be located outside of the Settlements. This led to the purchase by the Municipalities of the Pahsienjao Cemetery, at that time situated beyond the French Concession. In 1866 the Councils undertook the charge of all cemeteries.

In later times other cemeteries were acquired, first that on Bubbling Well Road and then the one on Hungjao Road.

Bridges   The fact that one of the Settlements, the American, which became a part of the International Settlement in 1863, lay to the north of the Soochow Creek, made better communication between the two sections necessary. At first the only way of crossing the Soochow Creek was by ferry, and this of course was inconvenient, especially in inclement weather. The need of a bridge was apparent, and in the first instance it was supplied by a man named Wills who organized the Soochow Creek Bridge Company. A bridge known as Wills Bridge, not a very sightly structure, was erected in 1856 at a cost of $12,000. It had a span of 450 feet, and a drawbridge in the centre that could be opened for the passage of boats. The company made a great profit from the tolls collected from those using the bridge, and claimed it had received a charter from the Taotai giving it a right to this monopoly for twenty-five years. The public, however, protested, and denied the authority of the Taotai to grant any such charter. When the company attempted the erection of a new iron bridge in 1871, two poles gave way and the part of the bridge that had been completed sank into the river. Some years later the Council obtained control, first, by erecting a free bridge by the side of the company's, and later by buying out the company, and erecting what was known as the Garden Bridge. This first wooden bridge was replaced by the present structure in 1906.

When the first Garden Bridge was built the authorities of the Settlement were of the opinion that the Taotai might be willing to help pay for public improvements of benefit to the whole community—Chinese and foreign alike—and he was asked to contribute one-half the cost. This he very positively declined to do, and the Municipality learnt that it must be self-supporting, and could not expect the Chinese authorities to pay for the expense of protecting the Settlements or to contribute for their upkeep.

Street Lighting
At first, the streets were lit at night with oil lamps, and were nearly as dark as those within the city walls. In 1864, the Shanghai Gas Company was formed and obtained permission to lay mains, and thus after 1865 gas was used for street lighting. There was considerable objection to this improvement on the part of the land renters as it increased their rates, and did not add much in the way of illumination, the lamps being placed a hundred yards apart.

Hospitals
During the early days of the International Settlement, the revenue of the Municipal Council was not sufficient to allow it to spend much on public works or to establish institutions for the benefit of the community, and a good deal was left to private enterprise. We see this especially in connection with the development of hospitals. Health conditions were poor, due to stagnant pools, to lack of proper drainage and to the unsanitary habits of the Chinese population. At times the death rate was exceedingly high, and there were frequent epidemics of cholera, smallpox and typhoid. The need of better hospital accommodation became urgent. In 1862 Shanghai had two hospitals for foreigners, the Shanghai Hospital and Dispensary, and the Marine Hospital. These proving to be insufficient, shares were sold for the establishment of a General Hospital. A sum of Tls. 31,000 was subscribed and trustees were appointed. The new hospital was first situated between the West Gate and the Ningpo Guild (popularly known as the Ningpo Joss House). The patients were cared for by the Sisters of Charity of St. Vincent de Paul, many of whom rendered devoted service.

As years went by it became necessary for the Municipal Council to assist in the support of this enterprise, and to make an annual donation towards its maintenance. In this way the large General Hospital, now standing on the north side of the Soochow Creek, between Chapoo and North Szechuen Roads, came into existence.

Gaols   The need of a gaol was soon realized, for Shanghai from the start had to cope with a criminal class. Sailors on shore often gave serious trouble, and the influx of Chinese into the Settlements brought many of the undesirable class.

The first gaol to be erected was on the grounds of the British Consulate, in 1856. Being the only foreign prison in existence it had to serve for all criminals, and we find that "by courtesy American criminals were confined there as well as the English," the American Government having made no provision for a gaol. In 1868 a new British gaol was erected on Amoy Road near the junction of the Defence and Soochow Creeks, where it still stands.[1]

Chinese criminals were handed over to the Chinese authorities, and it was not until later that a Municipal Gaol was built.

H.B.M. Supreme Court   In 1865 the British Government appointed Sir Edmund Hornby as Chief Justice of a British Court for Shanghai, and the jurisdiction in legal matters was transferred from the Consulate to the Supreme Court. The buildings for the new court were erected on land adjoining the Consulate lot.

Building of Roads   There was little money for the construction of roads, and as sedan chairs and wheelbarrows were the usual means of transportation, the importance of roads was not keenly felt by the early residents.

The original Land Regulations provided for four roads, those now named Hankow, Kiukiang, Nanking, and Peking, and for the preservation of the river frontage, formerly used for a towing path.

---

[1] Recently it has been purchased by the Municipal Council, and is now used as a Municipal Gaol.

Gradually the roads system underwent an extension. The land renters were obliged to make roads for their own convenience, and these were afterwards handed over to the Council. With the coming of the Chinese into the Settlements and the erection of houses for their occupation, more roads had to be opened.

For a long time these roads were in a poor condition and were quite impassable during the rainy season. The soil of Shanghai, being alluvial, can only be converted into good roads at considerable expense. At first broken brick was used as a foundation. Later on shingle was introduced, and then cinders and clinkers, obtained from the steamers. Granite chips were first used in 1856 on Mission Road (now Foochow Road). The present unmettled suburban roads will give a fair idea of what the roads must have been like in wet weather.

In road building we can trace the following evolution: first, the land renter made his own road and handed it over to the Municipal Council to keep up; second, the land owner bought the land for the road and the Council made it up; and thirdly, the Council bought the land and made the road. Before the Council had power to acquire land for public purposes, it was often obliged to pay large sums for the property it wished to purchase.

Originally in various parts of the Settlements, for greater security, wooden gates were erected on some of the streets to prevent a sudden inrush of mobs or rioters. These were closed at night and guarded by watchmen. The last was not removed from Nanking Road until 1866.

The haphazard way in which the roads were constructed accounts for the utter lack of system with which they were laid out, and makes it difficult for strangers to find their way about.

During the Taiping Rebellion, when Shanghai was occupied by military forces, some roads were made for transporting supplies and ammunition, and in this way Jessfield Road came into existence connecting with the Fan-wang-tu (Van-waung-doo) Ferry.   Afterwards this road was kept up for a time by Mr. James Hogg, and later was taken over by the Council

Jessfield   The origin of the name Jessfield recalls a romantic story of the early days.   A Portuguese gentleman, while passing a circus tent erected in Hongkew, heard the cries of a small girl who was being ill-treated.   He purchased her freedom from the circus company, and sent her, in care of a missionary, to the United States for education.   Upon her return, he married her, and as her name was Jessie, he called his country place, now the site of St. John's University, Jessfield. The road connecting it with Bubbling Well Road thus became known as Jessfield Road.

The Public Gardens   The way in which Shanghai secured the Public Gardens on the foreshore is interesting.   Originally the land it now occupies was known as the Consular Mud-flat, being formed by the silt deposited by the meeting of the waters of the Whangpoo and Soochow Creek.   The foundering of an old brig close to The Bund, led to the further accumulation of silt.

The land belonged to the British Consulate, but permission was obtained from the British Government to make it over to the Municipal Council on condition that it should be used as a public garden.   At considerable expense the land was filled in and thus gradually out of what had been an unsightly mud flat a beautiful park was developed.

Shanghai Volunteer Corps   In 1870 the control of the Shanghai Volunteer Corps was handed over to the Council "who shall, through their Chairman, decide upon all questions of organization, and shall generally control the actions of the Corps."   This, of course,

led eventually to its becoming a more efficient force.   A
Rifle Range, where Range Road is now situated, was constructed for target practice.   In 1897, owing to the rapid
growth of the Settlement, it became necessary to move the
Range to its present site on the road to Kiangwan.

CHAPTER VIII.

DEVELOPMENT IN THE SETTLEMENT, 1860–1870.

The last chapter gave an account of the changes which took place in the decade under consideration, in municipal administration. In this chapter, other developments in the Settlement affecting the trade and the life of the foreign residents will be considered.

Slump in Real Estate After the suppression of the Taiping Rebellion in 1864, contrary to general expectation, there was a great exodus of Chinese refugees, returning to their former homes.

Whole streets of newly built houses became empty, buildings were stopped half way in their construction, long lines of godowns along the river front, representing nearly Tls. 1,500,000 became disused, and recently constructed wharves stood deserted.

Many private capitalists were threatened with bankruptcy, and with the departure of the Chinese taxpayers, the revenue of the Council suddenly declined.

Land values had been greatly inflated, and the cost of building materials had become exceptionally high. It had been a time of wild speculation, and was followed by a brief period of panic.

It is almost impossible to say to what extent the population grew during the time when the Settlements were occupied by the refugees. Some estimate that in the three Settlements and the walled city the population may have been as high as 1,500,000. We know, however, that in 1865 the Chinese population shrank to 70,000 in the English Settlement, 47,500 in the French Concession, and 200,000 in Hongkew.   The foreign population was 2,750 residents in the Settlements and 2,832 in the Naval and Military forces.

Trade   During the Taiping Rebellion the Customs receipts fell to one half the usual amount. The privilege given to foreigners to visit Hangchow, Soochow and the silk districts was cut off, and for a time foreign trade suffered from the Imperialists and the rebels alike, both seizing the cargo in transit on the canals.

It is estimated that the export of silk decreased by 41,000 bales.

The over speculation in land and buildings and the financial collapse, had a disastrous effect on the banks and six out of eleven suspended payment.   The world-wide monetary crisis of 1866 made its effect felt in Shanghai also, and added further to the financial depression.

The Building of the Cathedral   It is sometimes said that wherever an Englishman goes he takes with him his Church and his Race Course.   This was true in regard to Shanghai, and we find the early residents making provision both for religious worship and for their favourite sport.

The first public worship was held at the British Consulate in 1843 when it was still within the native city, and was conducted by Dr. W. H. Medhurst and other missionaries, according to the ritual of the Church of England.

The first Episcopal Church to be erected was Trinity Church, in 1847, on the present site of the English Cathedral.   The land was given at a nominal price by Mr. Beale, of Messrs. Dent and Company.   The building cost only $6,000 and called for constant repairs.   In 1850 the roof fell in, involving an expenditure of $5,000 for repair, and in 1862 the original church became so dilapidated that it

First Day of Races—Spring 1881.

MUNICIPAL COUNCIL, 1857.

ANDREW A. RANKIN.   GEORGE G. GRAY.   JAMES L. MAN.

was abandoned and a temporary one erected.   In 1866 the
old church was pulled down and the building of the present
structure begun.

Plans were made in England by Sir Gilbert Scott for
an imposing church, but owing to the lack of money the
drawings were considerably modified by a local architect
named William Kidner.   The building was not completed
until 1869.   The style is Gothic of the early thirteenth
century.   For a long time it stood without a tower, but
this was added in 1893 and greatly enhanced its beauty.

In 1875 Trinity Church was offered to the newly
appointed Bishop of North China, the Rt. Rev. W. A.
Russell, as his Cathedral, and the Bishop "selected and
assigned" the Church as the Cathedral for his Diocese of
North China.   The successor of Bishop Russell, the Rt.
Rev. G. E. Moule, D.D., would not take the Cathedral on the
same terms, that is, that he should have the building as his
Cathedral during his term of office in life.   He required
that it should be "vested in him" and his successors.   To
this the trustees would not agree.

**Church of
Our Saviour**
One of the first churches in the Settlement
was the Church of Our Saviour in Hongkew,
built by Bishop William J. Boone of the
American Episcopal Church Mission in 1854.   It stood
then close by the northern bank of the Whangpoo, and its
tower was a landmark for many years to the captains of
ships coming up the river from Woosung to Shanghai.
Later, as the land accreted in front, this commanding
position was lost and it was hidden by the buildings
erected between Broadway and the river bank.   In 1916
the old church was pulled down and a new one was built,
off Dixwell Road, by the Chinese congregation.

**Church for
Seamen**
The large amount of shipping in the early
days gave occasion to work being undertaken
by the Seaman's Mission.   This was first

6

carried on by a floating "Bethel" on the Whangpoo and then by a barque called the "Euphrates," bought in 1860. Later it was decided to build a church on land, and a chapel was erected in 1867 near Pootung Point.   It was designed by Mr. E. H. Oliver, and built by Mr. Henry Lester at a cost of Tls. 3,500, the Council giving the site.

The cemetery adjoining the Church was used for the burial of sailors who died in port.

As time went on, it became necessary to transfer the work among seamen to the Hongkew side of the river, and finally it was arranged for the old site to be sold and the proceeds used for the building of another church.   In this way St. Andrew's Church for Seamen on Broadway was erected.

The care of the cemetery at Pootung was taken over by the Shanghai Municipal Council, and in 1927 the site came into the possession of the Council.

Union Church   The Union Church traces its origin back to the earliest days of the Settlement.   We find that the Rev. Dr. W. H. Medhurst of the London Missionary Society conducted services for foreigners in 1845 in the Shantung Road Compound, various members of the same Mission continuing these services for many years, among whom was the Rev. William Muirhead; but in 1864 the non-conformists organized themselves into a separate and independent church.   In the same year the first Union Church was built on a part of the London Mission Compound in Shantung Road.   After twenty-one years, the congregation purchased the present site on the corner of Soochow and Yuen-ming-yuen Roads, and in 1886 a new Church was opened which ever since has been known as the Union Church.   A Sunday School Hall and a Manse were added in 1899 and the church was altered and enlarged in 1901.

The Race
Course and
Recreation
Ground

Shanghai was not long without a Race Course. Before there was a Municipal Council, as far back as 1850, eighty *mow* of land had been secured for a park. This was on the northern side of Nanking Road, and its eastern boundary was the present Honan Road. Here were held the earliest race meetings. Next what was called the New Park and Race Course, situated east of the Defence Creek, was purchased in 1854. One can retrace this Race Course in imagination by starting from Nanking Road (which did not then exist as a road) following the straight Thibet Road around the curve of Pakhoi and Hoihow Roads and back by Hoopeh Road across Nanking Road along the present Chekiang Road and Chefoo Road as far as Yunnan Road, curving back to the point of departure on Nanking Road. It was used as a riding course as well as for racing. Four residents, whose names are worthy of remembrance —R. C. Antrobus, James Whittal, Albert Heard, and Henry Dent, in 1860 purchased 40 *mow* of land in the interior of the second Race Course, so as to provide a place for cricket and other sports.

The second Race Course was succeeded in 1862 by a third, the present one on Bubbling Well Road. When it was laid out, the gentlemen whose names have been mentioned above decided to sell the original piece of property which had greatly increased in value, and to purchase a new piece inside the third Race Course.

Shareholders in the first recreation ground consented to sell their shares to the committee at the original price. The land was sold for Tls. 49,425, and a Recreation Fund founded. Tls. 12,500 was used for the purchase of 430 *mow*, within the present Race Course in 1863, and a cricket ground was laid out.

As years passed this large piece of land was gradually converted into the splendid playing fields we have to-day, for all manner of sports. Situated as it is in a densely crowded part of the Settlement, it serves the purpose of an indispensable lung.

The Recreation Fund has been useful in many ways besides its original purpose. Loans were made out of it to aid other enterprises, not always advantageously, and involved it at one time in serious financial difficulties.

The Shanghai Club The Shanghai Club was built in 1862, and was planned on an extravagant scale, far beyond the means of those called upon to support it.

In order to finish the building a loan was obtained from the Recreation Fund, and as the Club was unable to pay off its indebtedness, a long altercation ensued. For many years the Club was run in such a way that there was an annual deficit, and it was not until 1870 that it was put on a sound financial basis. The present commodious Club erected in 1909 occupies the same site as the original building.

Social Life and Sports In the beginning, as we can well understand, means of recreation were somewhat limited.

Indeed an old resident has described wheelbarrow races up and down The Bund as an after dinner amusement on summer evenings! In a short time, however, many clubs and societies came into existence. Amateur theatricals began as early as 1850, the theatre in which they were performed being a transformed godown or warehouse. Later, in 1866, the Amateur Dramatic Club was formed, and steps were taken for the erection of a permanent theatre at the cost of Tls. 6,000. The first building of the Lyceum Theatre was a wooden one and was destroyed by fire in March, 1871. The one still in use was planned and built in 1874.

Royal Asiatic Society A Literary and Scientific Society was started as early as 1857 which in the following year became the North-China Branch of the Royal

Asiatic Society.   After a few years of vitality it passed through a period of suspended animation.   Then in 1864 it was revived and since then has steadily continued its existence, issuing its valuable *Journals,* which for many years have appeared annually.

For a long time it had no regular home.   In 1868, a letter was written by Sir Rutherford Alcock recommending to the Foreign Office a grant to the Society of a site for a building.   The grant of a piece of property, situated in Museum Road, near Peking Road, was made at once at a nominal rent on condition that if the Society should be dissolved or if buildings were not put up within three years the ground would revert to the government.

The offer came near being voided, but towards the close of the three years a great effort was made to collect funds for a building.   The Debating Society gave its balance on the understanding that it could meet in the Society's rooms.   Mr. Thomas Hanbury gave Tls. 500, Mr. Thomas Kingsmill prepared the plans free of charge, and the building was put up in 1871 at a cost of about Tls. 3,000.   Subscriptions were raised amounting to Tls. 2,700 by M. Henri Cordier, the Honorary Librarian, and by Mr. F. B. Forbes.

Of course a large part of the community was not deeply interested in the Society and regarded it as a dry-as-dust institution, but it has had a long and honourable history and has carried on valuable research in the language, customs, ethics, history, etc., of China.

It has a creditable museum and a very valuable library of books on the Orient, the nucleus of which was obtained by the purchase of the splendid collection of books belonging to Mr. Alexander Wylie.

In 1927 the Society celebrated its seventieth anniversary.

Shanghai Library
The Shanghai Library dates back to 1849. In 1854 we find that it contained 1,276 distinct works, and subscribed to 30 periodicals and newspapers, and met a great need of the young Settlement.

It was housed at different times in various locations, at the Shanghai Club, in rooms adjoining the premises of the Royal Asiatic Society, on Nanking Road and finally in the Town Hall.

When the Shanghai Club built its own library, the Shanghai Library lost about half its subscribers and for a time was crippled financially.

On condition that its Reading Room should be made free to the public, an annual grant was made to it by the Shanghai Municipal Council.

Masonry
Masonry has always played an important part in Shanghai life. We find that the first Lodge—the Northern Lodge—was established in 1849. This was followed by the Sussex Lodge in 1863. Its first home was in Park Lane, now Nanking Road. The foundation stone of the new Hall on The Bund was laid in July, 1865, and was one of the first buildings of pleasing character to appear on the water front. The present site and building have recently been sold and it is now planned to erect a large and handsome building in some other part of the International Settlement.

Sport
Turning to sport, we find, of course, that shooting was a favourite pastime. After the devastation wrought by the Taiping Rebellion in the vicinity of Shanghai, game became more plenteous than ever.

The first mention of a house-boat is in the year 1859. From that time on one of the most delightful ways of spending a holiday was an excursion up country in a house-boat for the purpose of shooting

Cricket, as already noted, was one of the chief forms of sport. The first recorded cricket match was played somewhere in Hongkew, and on this ground a match between a team of officers from H.M.S. "Highflyer" and a Shanghai eleven was played on April 22nd, 1858. The first interport match with Hongkong took place in 1866.

Rowing made its appearance in 1863, and a football club was formed in 1867.

The early history of the Fives Court, the Bowling Alley and Racquets Court is somewhat wrapped in mystery. The Fives Court was situated at the corner of Nanking and Honan Roads. Until recently an insignificant doorway in a Chinese wall at 49 Nanking Road, gave entrance to what is said to have been the somewhat exclusive Bowling Club, and to the Bowling Alley which was made in 1857. Although this old historic site has recently been sold and the building torn down, it is interesting to note that the Chinese still call that part of Nanking Road by the Chinese words *pau-jeu-dzang*[1] meaning "Bowling Alley."

By 1864 Paper Hunting as an outdoor sport became fairly established, but the club goes back to an earlier date. Its introduction was due to the military officers who were familiar with it in other parts of the world.

The first paper hunt was won in December, 1863, by Mr. Augustus Broom on a pony called "Mud." About a year later a pack of beagles was followed across country, the dogs having been brought out in 1864. Enthusiasts in regard to paper hunts refer with pride to a Royal Hunt. In 1881, Shanghai was visited by the late Prince Albert Victor, Duke of Clarence, Prince George (now the King of England), and Prince Louis of Battenberg. On December 3rd Prince Albert Victor and Prince George

---

[1] Shanghai pronunciation.

rode with the "foxes," and Prince Louis rode in the Hunt and was sixth on the card.[1]

Rowing became very popular, and an international cup was keenly competed for. In 1866 it was won by the American eight and in 1867 by the English. The races were rowed on the Soochow Creek. In later years as Shanghai developed, the congested traffic on the waterways near Shanghai made it necessary to hold the annual regatta out in the country at Henli.

The Missionary Community   As soon as Shanghai was opened as a Treaty Port, it became a centre of Protestant Missionary work as well as of trade.

The Roman Catholic Church had carried on important work in China since the seventeenth century, and a church had been built in the Chinese city, largely by the help of the well-known convert already referred to, Paul Zi, or Hsü. During a period of persecution this had been seized and converted into a temple of the god of war. In 1860, through the influence of General de Montauban, it was returned to the Fathers, and restored to its former use. It still stands, and is known as the "Lau Tong," or "Old Church."

In 1848 the foundation was laid of the important centre at Siccawei. The Orphanage, Industrial School, Library, Meteorological Observatory, T'usewei Printing Press, and Church form an interesting group at the present day.

As to the advent of the Protestant Missionaries, the Rev. W. H. Medhurst, D.D., and Dr. Wm. Lockhart, of the London Mission, who had formerly been stationed at Canton, arrived in Shanghai a little before Captain Balfour.

---

[1] The author is indebted for these facts to Dr. C. Noel Davis, the present Master of the Shanghai Paper Hunt Club.

At the beginning of things the services of Dr. Medhurst were much in demand as interpreter in the negotiations carried on with the Chinese authorities, "and thus the British Service at Shanghai benefited from the wide experience and fluency of men from the Mission field." These two were followed by the Revs. William Muirhead and Joseph Edkins.

Mrs. Lockhart, a sister of Mr. (afterwards Sir) Harry Parkes, was the first Western lady to set foot in Shanghai. She survived her husband for many years, and died in England on January 2nd, 1918, at the ripe age of ninety-five. She may be said to have been canonized by the public, inasmuch as St. Catherine's Bridge derives its name from her.

Among the first American Missionaries were Dr. E. C. Bridgman of the Congregational Church, who was transferred from Canton to Shanghai in 1847, and the Rt. Rev. Dr. William J. Boone, the first representative of the American Episcopal Church. He was first stationed at Batavia, then at Amoy, and came to Shanghai in 1845. He was the first missionary Bishop of the Anglican Communion to be sent to China.

The best known of the Southern Baptist Missionaries in Shanghai at an early date was Dr. M. T. Yates, who arrived in 1847. As he lived close to the walls of the native city he saw much of the fighting which took place when Shanghai was in the hands of the rebels.

Other distinguished missionaries connected with Shanghai, are Dr. W. A. P. Martin, who became a great Chinese scholar, Dr. Young J. Allen who both as translator and educator did a remarkable work, and Mr. Alexander Wylie (1847), Agent of the British and Foreign Bible Society, who was acquainted with many languages and became a leading Sinologue.

The number of residents being small, there was not the same clear line of demarcation between the missionary and business communities as exists to-day. Both alike had the interests of the new Settlement at heart and helped in its development. Of course there were times when they did not see eye to eye, and we find some of the missionaries objecting to being taxed for the erection of jetties, on the ground that as they were not engaged in commerce, they ought not to be asked to pay for what was of use only to the mercantile portion of the community. The majority, however, were public spirited, and were ready to support anything of benefit to the community. The name of Dr. W. H. Medhurst appears on the Council in the year 1854-1855 and that of Dr. M. T. Yates in the years 1868-1870.

Early Missionary Work   Missionary work was at first largely confined to Shanghai, but attempts were made to do evangelistic work in the neighbouring towns and villages. In one case this led, as we have seen, to serious friction between the British Consul and the Chinese authorities, when Medhurst, Lockhart, and Muirhead were attacked by a mob at Tsingpu.[1]

The efforts of the missionaries were exerted in founding churches, schools and hospitals.

Among the first churches to be built were Christ Church in the native city in 1850, and the Church of Our Saviour, which has already been mentioned. Another old church was that of the London Mission, on Shantung Road, erected in 1864. It has since given place to a new and more modern edifice. A Baptist Church outside the North Gate was also built at an early period.

---

[1] See Chapter II.

Among the first schools were those of the American Episcopal Church Mission in Hongkew, the schools founded by Dr. Bridgman at the West Gate, and the Anglo-Chinese School under the auspices of the Church Missionary Society.

The first hospital for Chinese was opened by Dr. Wm. Lockhart of the London Missionary Society in 1843, near the South Gate. The premises were found inconvenient, and a local committee was formed for the purpose of making an appeal to the foreign residents for funds to build a hospital on a piece of land outside the North Gate.

When the sum of $2,881.47 had been raised, the subscribers were called together on December 3rd, 1846, for the purpose of electing trustees. At this meeting seven trustees were elected, who were to hold the property of the hospital in trust, on condition that it should always be used as a Hospital for Chinese, and be temporarily rented to the resident medical officer of the Medical Missionary Society of the London Mission in China.

In 1861 this site was sold and a new building was put up on Shantung Road, and the hospital became known as the Shantung Road Hospital.

In 1873 the Hospital Trustees leased from the London Missionary Society for 25 years at $300 per annum, the land on which the present men's hospital stands. In 1901 the site was bought outright from the Society by the Hospital Trustees. In 1873 the hospital was entirely rebuilt.

After many years of useful service, it obtained means for building a modern well equipped hospital from the legacy of Tls. 2,000,000 from the Lester Estate,[1] and in 1927 adopted its new name, the Lester Chinese Hospital. Although strictly speaking not a mission hospital, it has

---

[1] See Chapter XXVIII.

always had close connection with the London Missionary Society and has permitted that Society to carry on religious work among the patients.

Another mission hospital, St. Luke's, was founded in 1866 under the auspices of the American Episcopal Church Mission. It was inaugurated by a gift of $150 gold sent to the Rev. (afterwards, Archdeacon) E. H. Thomson, by Mrs. Elizabeth Shields of Philadelphia. Mr. Thomson and Dr. McGowan opened a small dispensary at a rent of $5 per month. Several of the community doctors rendered their services free, among whom was Dr. R. A. Jamieson. On account of its location it was at first known as the "Hongkew Hospital." The name "St. Luke's" was adopted when it was moved to the present site in 1880. A wealthy Chinese, Li Chiu-ping, gave the land, and a little later helped to raise money to build two wards, with an office and operating room. In 1882 the Gutzlaff Hospital was amalgamated with St. Luke's. Recently this hospital also received a legacy of Tls. 200,000 from the Lester Estate.

Naturally as Shanghai developed into the largest and most important treaty port, it became the headquarters of most of the Missions carrying on work in China.

Visit of the
Duke of
Edinburgh
Shanghai was visited in 1869 by the Duke of Edinburgh, and as he was the first royal guest to be entertained by the community, he received a most enthusiastic welcome. Inasmuch as the Duke of Somerset in a speech in the House of Lords a few months previous had referred to Shanghai as a "sink of iniquity," much to the indignation of the residents of Shanghai, an effort was made to give the Duke of Edinburgh a better impression of the community that prided itself on being a "model settlement."

CHAPTER IX.

THE FIRST RIOT IN SHANGHAI, 1874.

The opportunities for friction between the small body of foreign residents and the large Chinese population in whose midst they lived were innumerable, and it is truly remarkable that serious disturbances were so infrequent. The avoidance of trouble was undoubtedly due in large measure to the fair-mindedness of the first British officials who had been sent out to represent their country.

Causes of Friction between Chinese and Foreigners

There were many causes leading to possible misunderstandings. The foreign community and the Chinese population had little in common, except the desire to trade. Their religious, moral, social, and political ideas were different, and had few points of contact. The foreign residents, with the exception of the missionaries, were content to live their own lives in their own way among a people whom they made little effort to understand. Outside of the missionaries and official interpreters few endeavoured to study the Chinese language, and communication between foreigners and Chinese was largely carried on in "pidgin" [1] English.

Merchants conducted their trade through compradores who acted as middlemen and thus the principals in a business transaction seldom came into touch with each other.

---

[1] Pidgin English is a form of English spoken according to Chinese idiom, with words altered in such a way as to make it easy for the Chinese to pronounce them. Some Portuguese and French words have been incorporated into it.

The foreign resident was too apt to regard himself as one of the elect and to look down upon the Chinese with a contemptuous and patronizing attitude.

Many of the Chinese disliked the foreigners who had forced an entrance into their country and regarded them as greatly inferior to themselves in culture. They did not welcome their coming, and resented the necessity of granting them a settlement.

They did not welcome the missionary. Prince Kung declared to Sir Rutherford Alcock on his departure from Peking in 1869, "Take away your opium and your missionaries, and you will be welcome!" At the same time Wen-siang, another high official, said to him, "Do away with your extraterritorial clause and merchant and missionary may settle anywhere and everywhere; but retain it and we must do our best to confine you and our troubles to the treaty ports."

The unpopularity of the missionary was due not so much to his teaching or to his good works as it was to the fact that his religion was foreign, and considered unnecessary for China. Furthermore, as missionaries were not content to remain in the treaty ports but wanted to carry on propaganda throughout the whole country, it was feared they would introduce a disturbing element into Chinese social and political life. The fact that mission work was protected by the treaties gave rise to the criticism that the Christian Church relied on force for its extension. A great deal of the opposition to mission work was caused by the ignorance and superstition of the masses, who were stirred up to believe that missionaries carried on nefarious practices, such as taking out children's eyes and making them into medicine.

But enough perhaps has been said to show how easily good relations between the foreign residents and the Chinese could be upset.

Attacks on Missionaries We find that in the years 1868 and 1869 attacks were made on missionaries in different parts of the Empire, first at Yangchow and then in Szechuen, where two French priests were murdered.

The Rev. J. Williamson was beaten to death in his boat at Tientsin. These attacks culminated in the Tientsin Massacre in 1870, when the French Consul and his Secretary, a number of Sisters of Mercy in the Roman Catholic Orphanage, a Russian merchant and his wife, and several others—numbering nineteen in all—were cruelly done to death by the Imperialist troops.

Further, a party of five foreigners had met with rough handling in the vicinity of Shanghai, when they were returning to the Settlement along the shores of Pootung. One of them, Mr. Grant, was found lying bleeding and senseless in a creek, with bound hands and feet.

Shanghai is sensitive to all that goes on in China, and fears began to be felt for its own safety. One immediate effect was to revive the Volunteer Corps which has ever since been maintained on an effective footing.

Riot in the French Concession The first riot in Shanghai occurred in 1874 in the French Concession, and originated in the following way. A portion of the Chinese population who had their homes in Ningpo had erected a Guild House toward the back of the French Concession, with a mortuary hall for the deposit of coffins, to be sent later to their ancestral homes, and with a cemetery for the burial of those whose families were too poor to send the coffins back. In 1863 this area had been included in the extension of the French Concession. The French Municipal Council drew up plans for the making of new roads, one of which was to run through the cemetery, and in 1874 it was decided to begin the construction. The Ningpo Guild on January 27th, 1874, made representations, objecting to the opening of the road through the cemetery, pointing out that the ground should be regarded as sacred, and that it would offend the Chinese people to have the bodies removed and the spirits of the departed disturbed. The Council, perhaps not realizing how much Chinese susceptibilities would be injured, was determined to carry out its purpose. A lengthy discussion was held between the Taotai and the French Consul, but both parties remained obdurate. Consequently the populace became more and more excited and on May 3rd, a riot broke out.

An attempt was made to destroy the residence of M. Percebois, the French Council's Road Inspector, and he, with his wife and family of young children, narrowly escaped being murdered. Houses were set on fire and the lives of foreigners were imperilled. Many were wounded, some severely and some slightly, but none were killed. Although the riot was directed against the French, it was difficult for the rioters to distinguish between French and English and both alike were in danger.

The spread of the riot was prevented by the active measures taken by M. Voisin, the Chairman of the French Council, and M. Barbe, the Captain of the French Police, who called in the aid of the volunteers, police and firemen of the International Settlement. In addition, twenty men were landed from the French gunboat "Couleuvre," and seventy-eight men, with a Gatling gun, from the U.S. despatch boats " Ashuelot " and " Yantic." The Taotai later sent one hundred and fifty Chinese troops.

In fighting the fire on that occasion, the firemen of the International Settlement under the District Engineer,

Mr. Brodie A. Clarke, had to be escorted by armed police and soldiers through a wildly excited mob.

On the night of the same day, rioting was renewed and some seven Chinese were shot and twelve severely wounded by the men from the "Couleuvre," who broke loose from discipline, and used their weapons as often as not against innocent people, allowing the ringleaders to escape.

Attitude of the French Consul During the crisis, the French Consul, M. Godeaux, acted with indecision. He hesitated about getting men from the ships, and the Council had been obliged to take matters into its own hands.

On the day following the riot, when the Consuls and Taotai met to consider what should be done to restore peace, the French Consul put out " an Urgent Proclamation " in which he abandoned the proposed road and enjoined the Guild to enclose its land with a wall.

The residents in the International Settlement felt that the French had shown little tact at the beginning of the affair, and that Godeaux's hasty concessions appeared to be placing a premium on mob-violence. Many of the French, and the Swiss, who were under the care of the French Government, criticized their Consul severely and in retaliation he withdrew for a time his protection from his Swiss protégés.

Attitude of the British Authorities Mr. Medhurst, the British Consul, refused to send British bluejackets to assist in putting down the riot, on the grounds that the English should not be mixed up in a quarrel between the French and a Chinese clan, that the native authorities should be called upon to restore order, and that no intervention should take place unless the native authorities failed.

7

The British Minister, Sir Thomas Wade, was of a different opinion.   He approved of the actions taken and pointed out that if there had been no ships in harbour, the whole French Concession might have gone up in a blaze before order could have been restored.

Terms of Settlement   In the settlement of claims for damages, it was arranged that the Chinese authorities should pay for the cost of damage to foreign property, a sum of Tls. 37,000, while the French should pay Tls. 7,000 to the families of the Chinese who were killed.

One unscrupulous foreigner attempted to get rich by claiming that Tls. 10,000 was due him on account of a bruise received on the head and the loss of two teeth!

It was agreed that the Ningpo Joss House and cemetery should remain the property of the Guild forever and that no roads or drains should be made through the burial ground.   As we shall see, the agreement was broken in 1898, at a time when the Chinese were less able to resist than in 1874, and the road was then constructed.

We have dwelt at length upon this first riot, as it is a good example of difficulty arising between two peoples on account of their different points of view.   To the Westerner, with his desire for that which is useful, it seemed absurd that the construction of a road should be held up by the unwillingness of the Chinese to remove some graves.   To the Chinese it seemed that the Westerner was wanting in respect for the dead, the strongest cult in China.

CHAPTER X.

SOME FRUSTRATED ATTEMPTS AT DEVELOPMENT.

Trade in Shanghai After the failure of the wild speculation in property and buildings connected with the increase of Chinese population during the Taiping Rebellion, the business of Shanghai developed on a sounder basis, and we find from statistics that commerce made satisfactory progress.

In 1874 the gross imports were valued at Tls. 52,902,102, and the gross exports at Tls. 43,764,978, whereas in 1864 the imports had been Tls. 30,522,183.

The absence at that time of deep water ports in the North made Shanghai the distributing centre for North China as well as for the Yangtze basin.

The foreign residents began to realize Shanghai's possibilities and to plan for its further development, and the Shanghai Municipal Council became more active in regard to public works. Many new roads were made and The Bund, Bubbling Well Road and some others were planted with trees. Broadway was extended and a road was built as far as the Yangtszepoo Creek, only stopping there for want of a bridge.

Founding of China Merchants S. N. Co. An American company, known as the Shanghai Steam Navigation Company, for traffic on the Yangtze, had been formed in 1867 by Russell and Company. The Chinese merchants saw the importance of Shanghai as a port and in order to secure a large share in its shipping, the China Merchants Steam Navigation Company was founded in 1872 by the initiative of Li

Hung-chang. The old P. and O. steamer "Aden" was bought, and for the first time the Chinese flag was flown over a merchant steamer. In 1877 the fleet and property of the Shanghai Steam Navigation Company was purchased by the "China Merchants," for the sum of Tls. 2,000,000, but the fact that many officials were connected with the company prevented it from becoming a prosperous enterprise, and from realizing its great opportunity.

Need of Harbour Improvement
Trade was the life of Shanghai, and anything interfering with a good harbourage for ships was fatal to its further development.

The accessibility of the harbour in Shanghai was rendered difficult by the shallow water over the outer and inner Woosung Bars. These are formed by the tidal Whangpoo River emptying itself into the tidal estuary of the Yangtze River. The low water depth of the river bar varied in different months of the year from 6 feet to 13 feet 6 inches and was in the midst of a crossing that cut diagonally from one bank to the other of the Whangpoo River.

Conference with Mr. Robert Hart
In 1863 when Mr. Robert Hart, Inspector-General of Customs, was in Shanghai, a deputation, representing the leading shipping firms, put before him the importance of conserving the Whangpoo and of dredging the Woosung Bar, so as to allow the entrance of the larger ships then being despatched to China. He agreed to lay the matter before the Chinese Government. To all requests the answer of the Chinese Government was "No," and the Chinese Ministers maintained an attitude "even more obstructive than the obstruction of the Bar." It is well to remember that in the early days, the Chinese sometimes referred to

the bar as a heaven-sent barrier intended to prevent war vessels of heavy draught and ironclads from entering the harbour.

After the lapse of a year, Mr. F. B. Johnson, the Chairman of the Chamber of Commerce, reopened the subject by a memorable despatch to Sir Thomas F. Wade, the British Minister, in which he asked that in case the Chinese Government would do nothing about the matter, it should grant such additional powers as would enable the Ratepayers of Shanghai, by means of special taxes upon native and foreign shipping entering the port, and by taxes upon land and property, to provide for the conserving of the river and the dredging of the bar. Sir Thomas Wade seems never to have replied to this communication, and we may infer that his attitude was also unfavourable.

Appeal to Sir Thomas Wade

Mr. Robert Hart, in 1875, published in a memorandum the result of his deliberations in regard to the advisability of dredging the Woosung Bar. His opinion is worth quoting at length, for it is an excellent example of the fallibility of human reasoning and the difficulty of prophesying the future.

Opinion of Mr. Robert Hart

"The trade consequent on opening the Yangtze River has so far been diverted into a false channel by the vested rights or money spent in Shanghai. This agency is in turn counteracted by the opening of the Suez Canal, through which steamers have begun to pass, making London and Hankow their termini . . . Teas will be shipped at Hankow and Kiukiang, and Shanghai silks and Ningpo teas at Chinkiang. They will be the return cargoes of the steamers which carry what China may continue to demand from Europe. In twenty years time Chinkiang will have taken the place of Shanghai as a semi-terminus and trans-shipment

port . . . Thus looked at, as it affects and is
affected by natural and artificial agencies now at
work at the mouth of the Yangtze, the question
of the Woosung Bar is seen to mean that dredging
there may possibly be nothing more than a means
of making the last days of Shanghai a little more
comfortable than they would otherwise be; it will
not prolong or avert the commercial death of the
place, but it will make a show of vitality during
its declining years more possible. Given the
natural and commercial agencies at work, it may
be taken for granted that—certainly for ten, or
perhaps twenty or thirty years to come, the commercial status and foreign community of Shanghai
will be such as to make it worth while to prevent
the river from being blocked up at any one point
—for instance by the Woosung Bar. Dredging
can do this and then only for a time; it cannot
secure for Shanghai either a navigable channel or
a continuance of commercial prosperity . . . .
The circumstances of Shanghai, its present position as a commercial centre, the interests of the
community are in themselves sufficient reasons
why the demand for dredging ought to be assented
to, but it must be borne in mind that no one can
say how soon commerce may cease to ask for access
to Shanghai, or natural forces acting elsewhere
make dredging operations at Woosung useless."

Thus were the efforts at developing the harbour frustrated
for a time.

In 1881 the Chinese authorities, at their own cost,
ordered a steam dredger to be used in removing the
"heaven-sent barrier," but dredging alone was found
to be of slight value, and the results were small. It
was not, as we shall narrate later, until after the Boxer

Outbreak that the matter was taken in hand seriously. **Woosung Railway** At about the same time as the foreign merchants were agitating for the conservancy of the Whangpoo and the dredging of the Woosung Bar, an attempt was made to build the first railway in China. As far back as 1863, when General Gordon was on the point of taking Soochow, a group of English and American firms petitioned Li Hung-chang for a concession to build a railway from Shanghai to Soochow. The petition was refused and Li Hung-chang stated that "railways would only be beneficial to China, when undertaken by the Chinese themselves and conducted under their own management; that China's objection existed to the employment of numerous foreigners in the interior; and that the people would evince great opposition to being deprived of their land for that purpose."

In 1865 the foreign merchants of Shanghai formed a company to build a railway from Shanghai to Woosung, but met with extreme opposition. They secured permission, however, to reconstruct the military road from Shanghai to Woosung, and to acquire by purchase the land necessary to widen and straighten it. They bought the land, made the embankments and culverts needed for a raised road in a flat country, intersected by creeks liable to be flooded. Later on the promoters of the Woosung line announced that they intended to lay rails for a tramway along the new road, and obtained permission for this from the British Envoy. The rails for the "tramway" were landed in Shanghai in December, 1875, and, to the surprise of every one, work was begun on a *railway* line of 30-inch gauge. When the Chinese discovered the subterfuge, the Taotai enjoined the promoters to stop the construction until he could refer the matter to Peking.

The line, notwithstanding the Taotai's objection, was completed over a distance of five miles to Kiangwan by June 30th of the following year, and from that time six trains a day, for passengers only, were run each way. The trains were crowded and the new method of travel proved popular, but on August 3rd a man walking on the line was killed "under circumstances which suggested, either extremely dense stupidity or a malicious intention to commit suicide, and thereby create a prejudice against railways." [1]   The people became excited and hostile, and Sir Thomas Wade, who happened to be in Shanghai at that time, gave instructions that the trains should cease running. The Chinese authorities then began negotiations for the purchase of the line, but while negotiations were in progress the train service was resumed.

On October 21st, 1877, a sum of Tls. 285,000 was paid for the land, rolling stock, and rails, being the actual cost to the promoters. The last train which ran was pulled by the engine "Victory" followed by the "Celestial Empire." A crowd of Chinese was present to take a last look at the unfamiliar sight—the like of which was not to be witnessed again until twenty years had elapsed.

After the purchase, the rails were torn up and shipped with the rolling stock to Formosa, where for many years they were left rusting on the beach. Thus a second important development was frustrated.

Telegraphs   The first attempts to introduce the telegraph into Shanghai also resulted in a failure. In 1865 Mr. E. A. Reynolds undertook to establish telegraphic connection between Shanghai and Woosung, so that the people in the Settlements could be informed of the movements of the shipping at the mouth of the river.

---

[1] H. B. Morse: *International Relations of the Chinese Empire*, Vol. III, p. 76.

The country people, with the connivance of the Chinese authorities, destroyed the poles, which they said had a bad effect on the "fengshui" (the influences of wind and water). In proof of this they produced the body of a man, who had died in the shade of one of the poles! As a result the Chinese authorities forbad the use of the line.

A year later Russell and Company, with the permission of the Councils, put up a line from Kin-le-chong godowns (French Bund) to Ke-chong in the American Settlement. This was the first line worked in China, but it was entirely within the settlement limits.

Owing to the number of accidents to shipping at the entrance to the Whangpoo, the necessity of telegraphic communication between Shanghai and Woosung became pressing. The Taotai, however, remained unconvinced and in his reply to the joint despatch from the Consuls pointed out that there was no provision whatever in the treaties in regard to the introduction of telegraphs. He said it was "entirely without precedent," and that the wooden poles undoubtedly affected the "fengshui" and would thus do harm to the agricultural interests. He could see no reason for a telegraph line in China.

In 1870 when a cable was laid between Shanghai and Hongkong, according to agreement, the cable at the Shanghai end was not to be landed on shore but on vessels anchored outside the limits. No part of the line went overland; and at each port where the company had an office, the telegraph service was conducted on hulks.

The line to Shanghai at first had its end moored at sea 25 miles south of Videa Island in the Chusan group, and was thence carried via Gutzlaff Island to Woosung. From Woosung a small cable came up river and was brought ashore in Hongkew. The cable at Woosung was brought ashore secretly. Afterwards, when this was discovered by the Chinese authorities, there was a protest, and it was insisted that the cable must end on a vessel anchored outside.

The opposition to telegraphs yielded sooner than that to railways, and in 1878 the Chinese authorities permitted the construction of an overland line along Woosung Road, the poles being erected on foreign owned land.

The Chinese were thoroughly converted to the use of the telegraph during the trouble with Russia over the territory in Central Asia, and in 1880 and 1881 the Chinese authorities employed the Great Northern Telegraph Company (Danish) to construct a line connecting Shanghai and Peking at a cost of Tls. 140,000.

The Jinricsha A new form of conveyance came into Shanghai in 1874, which proved in some ways to be a nuisance and in others, a great convenience. This was the Jinricsha—"the man power carriage." It was imported from Japan. At first the ricshas were not very popular, but they soon proved their usefulness and became more and more numerous.

The Burlingame Mission Mr. Anson Burlingame, the American Minister in Peking, was commissioned by the Chinese Emperor in 1867 as Ambassador Extraordinary to all the Courts of the world. The purpose of his appointment, as expressed in the words of Mr. Robert Hart, was "to cultivate and conserve friendly relations by explaining to each of the Treaty Powers the many difficulties that China cannot fail to experience in attempting to change existing conditions and to introduce novelties; to bespeak forbearance and prevent, in as far as possible, any resort to hostile pressure to wring from China concessions for which the government did not as yet feel itself ready."

Mr. Burlingame had the oratorical temperament, and in his addresses in the United States and other countries gave an exaggerated statement of Chinese readiness to enter upon the path of progress. For instance, he asserted that China was prepared to invite the missionaries to "plant the shining cross on every hill and in every valley," and to engage Western engineers to open mines and build railways and to modernize her ancient civilization.

The Burlingame Mission did not arouse as much enthusiasm in England as in the United States. Lord Clarendon, head of the Foreign Office, declared that "the policy to be adopted by his government and its agents was that an unfriendly pressure shall not be applied, inconsistent with the independence and safety of China, and that the British Government desires to deal directly with the central government rather than with the local authorities. China was expected to observe the treaties she had entered into, and the British Government reserved the right to use force to protect life and property immediately exposed."

From London, the Mission proceeded to Paris, Berlin and St. Petersburg. In the last named city, Mr. Burlingame, unable to withstand the severity of a Russian winter, succumbed to an attack of pneumonia and died on February 11th, 1870.

The residents of Shanghai were somewhat sceptical in regard to the promises made by this Ambassador in his tour around the world, owing to the opposition they encountered in the attempts to introduce the railway and telegraphs, and the unwillingness of the Chinese authorities to dredge the Woosung Bar, and improve the harbour of Shanghai.

The Margary Memorial   The Indian Government in 1874, acting under instructions from the British Home Government, despatched an expedition under Colonel Browne to proceed into Yunnan by way of Bhamo, in order to open up a trade route between Burmah and China. It was arranged that at the same time Mr. A. R. Margary, of H.B.M.'s Consular Service, should travel overland through China, to meet the expedition at Bhamo, and, acting as interpreter, should conduct it through Yunnan and then overland to Hankow.

At Manwyne, on the border between China and Burmah, Margary was assassinated under circumstances which were never cleared up. Out of this incident came the Chefoo Convention between Great Britain and China.

A memorial monument to Mr. Margary was erected by subscription in Shanghai in 1880, and placed at the division of The Bund into Soochow Road and the Garden Bridge approach. In 1907 the monument was removed to the north end of the Public Gardens, where it now stands.

CHAPTER XI.

DEVELOPMENT IN THE EIGHTIES.

Early in the "eighties," progress was made in regard to the introduction of two great public utilities, water and electricity.

Waterworks, 1883. For many years the principal source of water supply had been the Whangpoo River or the Soochow Creek. The water from wells was brackish and unfit for drinking purposes, and the water carried from river or creek in buckets to the various houses was muddy and subject to contamination from sewers or refuse. It was poured into large *kongs* or jars and settled by the use of alum. Then it was boiled, but even so there was considerable danger connected with using it for drinking purposes. Probably it was the cause, in many cases, of typhoid fever and cholera.

The first proposal for the introduction of a system of waterworks was brought forward at an early date by Dr. M. T. Yates, but largely owing to financial reasons it received no support.

The subject was repeatedly discussed but nothing definite was done about it until 1880. The Shanghai Municipal Council then entered into terms with a company, known as Drysdale, Ringer and Company, and the work of laying pipes was begun. A water tower was erected in Kiangse Road and the pumping of water began in April, 1883. The Viceroy, Li Hung-chang, who happened to be on a visit to Shanghai, accepted an invitation to take part in the ceremony of turning on the water.

A year later the system was extended so as to meet the needs of the Chinese. The object was not philanthropic but based on the ground that disease among the Chinese might spread to the foreign community, and that better native health meant greater safety for the whole population.

At first there was no great eagerness on the part of the Chinese to avail themselves of this new source of supply. Their reluctance was due not only to there being a small tax on those who used the water, but to prejudice founded on ignorance. There were rumours that the water was poisonous, or spoiled by lightning, or that people had been drowned in the water tower, and the Mixed Court Magistrate was obliged to issue a reassuring proclamation.

In the beginning there were complaints that the company overcharged for its supply, and this caused dissatisfaction. Although in 1888 it was proposed that the Council should buy out the company, and take the matter of water supply into its own hands, as is generally the case in other cities of the size of Shanghai, it was found to be too expensive a project. The waterworks have remained a private company known as the Shanghai Waterworks Company up to the present day, although negotiations have recently been completed for bringing the company under the control of the Municipality.

The waterworks were of great value not only for the health of the community but also in increasing the facilities for extinguishing fires, the firemen previously being dependent entirely on the fire wells sunk in various localities.

Street
Lighting
The lighting of the streets by gas had never given complete satisfaction, and in 1882 proposals were made for the introduction of electricity. Mr. R. W. Little secured permission to use the Council's poles, and to erect others for a trial of the Brush system, promising that it would prove cheaper

than gas. In June a sample light was exhibited on the Band Stand in the Public Gardens, and was greatly admired.

The company formed by Mr. Little was allowed to put up wires for some Chinese houses, and the Shanghai Club, and for some residences in the French Concession.

Electric lighting, like all other modern improvements, met with serious obstacles.

In the first place, the Taotai objected on the ground that it was not safe, inasmuch as the current could kill a man, burn up a house or destroy a whole city.   In his letter to the Council he stated, "This electric disaster will happen, if you do not put an end to electricity."

In the second place, the Gas Company opposed its introduction, fearing it would supplant the use of gas for street and residential lighting.   The struggle between the two companies began in 1882 and was long drawn out. In the end Electricity triumphed, but the Gas Company was able to survive by providing gas for other purposes than lighting.

At first electric light did not prove as satisfactory as anticipated. It was more expensive than gas and less dependable, and the machinery frequently broke down.

The company entered into a contract with the Council in 1883 for the lighting of The Bund, Nanking Road, and Broadway.

In 1884 the company asked the Council to buy up its plant, but to this proposal the Ratepayers would not listen. Matters began to improve in 1888 when a new company was formed and important changes were introduced.

A new era began in 1893 when the company's entire plant and business was taken over by the Council at a cost of Tls. 66,100, and the present efficient service began to be developed.   At the present day Shanghai has one of the largest electric plants in the world, supplying power and

heat as well as light.   A very large amount of capital has
been invested in the enterprise, and it has proved a source
of revenue to the Municipality.

**Revision
of Land
Regulations**   Towards the close of 1879 a committee
was appointed by the Shanghai Municipal
Council to revise the existing Land Regula-
tions, and at the Ratepayers' meeting held in 1880 a report
was presented.   One of the objects in view was to enlarge
the body of voters, and to increase the number of those
eligible to serve as Councillors.   At that time only 112
residents were eligible as Councillors under the existing
qualifications.   Another object was to extend the power of
the Council so as to give it the right to impose new taxation,
and to compel the surrender of property for roads.

The authority of the police was to be arbitrary, including the right to enter a private domicile without a warrant.

"In the event of a riot or a grave disturbance,
the Council having notified the Senior Consul at
once, was at liberty to adopt such measures as
it might deem necessary for public safety.   A
volunteer corps was to be organized under the
command of the Council's Chairman; and in case
of serious danger to the Settlement, the Council
was empowered to place all residents under such
laws as circumstances might require, subject to the
consent of the Consuls or a majority among them."

Such a constitution would have gone a long way
towards making the Municipality a free city, a proposal
which had been rejected by the Diplomatic Body in 1862.

The new Land Regulations were approved by the Ratepayers in March, 1881, and forwarded in 1883 for ratification to the Foreign Ministers in Peking.   For a long time
they were pigeon-holed, and sanction was not given until
15 years later, in 1898, and then in a much modified form.
Some of the objects desired were secured, especially the

extension of the franchise, and the increase in the number of those eligible as Councillors, but the Council's status was limited to being an executive body, all measures adopted at the Ratepayers' meeting being subject to the approval of the Consular Body in Shanghai and the Diplomatic Corps at Peking.

This was the last revision of the constitution of the International Settlement, a constitution which, with all its limitations, has proved fairly workable.

Clause XXVIII restricted the Council to the policy advocated by Sir Frederick Bruce and Mr. Anson Burlingame in 1864, and provided that "Hereafter should any corrections be requisite in these Regulations, or should it be necessary to determine on further rules, or should doubts arise as to the construction thereof, or powers conferred thereby, the same must be consulted upon and settled by the Foreign Consuls and local Chinese authorities, subject to confirmation by Foreign representatives and the Supreme Chinese Government at Peking."

The Government of the International Settlement — Having followed the development of the Land Regulations, we may now give a brief summary[1] of the way the Shanghai Municipality has been governed.[2]

A Council of not more than nine or less than five is elected annually by foreign land-renters and ratepayers.

The electorate is limited to foreigners who own land of not less than five hundred taels in value and who are householders paying an assessed rental of not less than five hundred taels per annum and upwards.

---

[1] This summary is largely derived from an address given by Sir Edward Pearce to the Shanghai Civic League, October 26th, 1920.

[2] The Government of the Shanghai Municipality underwent an important change in 1928, when Chinese representatives were admitted on the Council, see Chapter XXVIII.

8

The ratepayers have their annual parliament or meeting once a year, when a report of the work of the Council for the past year and the estimates for the next year are presented for consideration.

Special meetings may be called when it is desired to deal with any matter which cannot or should not be left over for decision by the annual parliament.

The powers of the Council are restricted, and the approval of all the Consuls and of the Chinese authorities and of the Diplomatic Body is required for the amendment of the Land Regulations.

The channel of communication between the Council and the Chinese authorities is the Consular Body.

Judicial powers over foreigners are, under the grant of extraterritoriality, vested in the Consular Courts of the foreigners concerned, or, in the case of unrepresented foreigners or Chinese, in the Mixed Court.

The Council has a right to sue in these courts, and may in turn be sued in a court elected from the Consuls of the Treaty Powers, known as the Court of Consuls. The Municipal police force provides the executive for all these courts. No arrests, as a general rule, can be made except on a warrant of the proper court, and in the case of the Mixed Court, it must be countersigned by the Senior Consul.

From 1911 until the rendition of the Mixed Court in 1927 the execution of Mixed Court summons and warrants was entrusted to the Municipal police.

The election of the Council takes place during the month of February, and the ratepayers' annual meeting is held in April.

At its first meeting the new Council elects its Chairman and Vice-Chairman and then divides itself into three

Committees, the Finance, Works and Watch Committees, which have oversight of the various departments and sub-committees.

The Secretariat acts as the Chief Executive of the Council, and as a clearing house for all departments.

Although in some ways the government is cumbersome, and many difficulties arise from the limited powers of the Council, yet on the whole it has proved satisfactory. Its success has been due in no small measure to the time and labour given by the members of the Council, who render their services freely.

Critics have called the Council a Taipan[1] oligarchy, but it would be more fitting to refer to it as a good example of the efficiency of Commission government.

Political events in recent years have made it exceedingly difficult to get all the Treaty Powers to agree with any unanimity to any proposals put before them in regard to the amendment of the Land Regulations.

Development of The Bund

For a long time it looked as though utilitarian considerations would gain the day, and the foreshore would be used for mooring ships. If that had happened, its appearance would have been similar to that of the present French Bund, and it would not have become, as it is now, a beautiful esplanade.

It was made unsightly by the erection of sheds, used as work shops for builders, with annexes for kitchens and latrines. The sewers, which did not reach to low water mark, deposited considerable garbage and refuse on the mud banks.

At last the work of filling in and bunding was taken in hand, but it was not until May, 1886, that the grass plots, extending from the Public Gardens to the Customs shed, were thrown open to the public. All respectable and

---

[1] A Taipan is the head of a business firm.

decently clad Chinese were admitted to them, but when it was found that coolies used the benches for siestas, notices were posted on the benches restricting their use to foreigners.

It was not until some years later that the whole foreshore was filled in up to the line approved by the authorities.

War between France and China   During this period China engaged in another foreign war. The French were desirous of opening up a trade route from Cochin-China into Yunnan by way of the Red River which flows through Tongking, one of the provinces of Annam. China claimed that Annam was a vassal state, and supported her in resisting this demand. This led to a state of hostility between the two countries from 1881 to 1885.

Shanghai being far from the actual seat of warfare, was not directly concerned. There was, however, great trepidation among the Chinese in the Settlements, and attempts were made on the part of the Canton merchants in Hongkew to raise a volunteer corps to help in the defence of Shanghai.

In order to secure the safety of the China Merchants fleet, the steamers were temporarily sold for a nominal sum to Russell and Company and were put under the American flag.

The Chinese authorities threatened to close up the channel at Woosung by sinking junks laden with stones across the bar. If this had taken place, it would have resulted in a serious injury to trade, but fortunately, although preparations were made, the project was never actually carried out.

In August, 1884, the day the French fleet bombarded Foochow, the French Consul-General issued a proclamation declaring the neutrality of the French Concession, and later the French Envoy, M. Patenotre, gave assurances that as long as Shanghai and Woosung maintained the *status quo*, they would not be attacked.

The dangerous position of the Settlements, in case of a war between China and a foreign Power, became apparent, and led to endeavours on the part of the Diplomatic Body to have the Settlements regarded as a neutral zone during war periods.

Statue to Sir Harry Parkes Shanghai has not been very generous in the way of erecting statues in memory of those who have played an important part in its development. There is, however, one outstanding exception. Sir Harry Parkes, G.C.M.G., who as a diplomat did so much for opening up of commercial relations between Great Britain and China, has been remembered, and a monument has been erected to his memory on The Bund, at the entrance to Nanking Road. It bears the inscription "erected in 1890 by the foreign merchants in China in memory of his great services." It was unveiled by H.R.H. the Duke of Connaught who paid a visit to Shanghai in that year.

CHAPTER XII.

EDUCATION.

Need of Educational Facilities It is somewhat surprising to find how long it took the residents of the Settlements to make plans for the education of their children.

The Missions had developed schools for Chinese boys and girls and laid the foundation of what afterwards became important and influential institutions, long before anything was done for the education of foreign children. This was largely due to the fact that the early residents had no intention of remaining permanently. They regarded themselves as " exiles " and looked forward to the day when they would have accumulated sufficient wealth to enable them to return to their homelands. Furthermore, both for climatic and social reasons, Shanghai was not considered a good place for bringing up children, and they were sent home at a very early age for their schooling.

When, however, the period of residence of the foreign community, owing to economic reasons, became more prolonged, the providing of education for the children became increasingly urgent.

The need at first was supplied to a certain extent by Roman Catholic institutions which opened departments for the education of foreign children, St. Francis Xavier's for boys, and St. Joseph's for girls.

St. Francis Xavier's College, which had been founded in Hongkew in 1864, reported in 1893 that 875 scholars had been received up to that date, one-fourth being British or American, and that out of 309 charity boys,

80 British and Americans paid little or nothing, and that in some instances clothing was provided as well as instruction. On this ground it asked and received from the Shanghai Municipal Council a yearly grant of Tls. 1,500. This amount has since been gradually increased.

The attention of the Settlements seems at first to have been directed towards the needs of children of mixed parentage, Eurasians, who were left without means of securing an education.

As far back as 1869, the *North-China Herald* pointed out the necessity of providing boarding schools for this class, so that the fact of their mixed parentage might not be a handicap to them in competition with pure whites.

School for Eurasian Children A school for Eurasian children was opened the following year by a Mrs. Bonney in Hongkew, and a year later Mr. (afterwards Sir) Thomas Hanbury provided a ten-roomed house for this purpose. A committee was formed and money was raised for the support of this enterprise.

In 1882 Mr. Hanbury offered to transfer the school to the Municipality on condition that it should be exclusively for Eurasians and be called " The Hanbury School for Eurasians." The Council found it impossible to undertake this responsibility at once, but began to make annual grants.

In 1889 the Eurasian School and a newly founded " Children's Home " were amalgamated as the " Thomas Hanbury School and Children's Home," and the trust deed of the school property was handed over to the Council.

A new building was erected on Boone Road in 1891. In the new scheme the school was to be for Eurasians and other children, and hence it became increasingly cosmopolitan, the pupils being the poor children of many nationalities.

The boys' and girls' departments were carried on in the same building for many years, but as the work grew it became necessary to separate them, and a new building for boys was put up on Haskell Road.

Plans are now on foot for a new building on a more convenient site for the girls' department, which reached a high state of efficiency under Miss E. H. Mayhew before her retirement in 1926.

When this is accomplished the Municipality will have made excellent provision for this class of children.

Schools for Foreign Children The Freemasons in 1886 took the initiative in providing a school for foreign children, but in a short time encountered financial difficulties. As the school was being run at a loss, it was proposed to hand it over as a private school to Mr. and Mrs. Barnes Dallas, the committee representing the Freemasons retaining some control.

Next the school became the "Shanghai Public School" under the headmastership of Mr. G. Lanning. In 1890 the Ratepayers were called upon to make a grant of Tls. 1,000 to put it on a sounder basis and inasmuch as the number of pupils had grown from 54 to 94, acceded to the request. A few years later Mr. Lanning proposed that the school should be taken over by the Council and become a Public Municipal School.

At the Ratepayers' meeting of 1892, a grant of Tls. 3,000 was made, and later in that same year the Council appointed a school committee.

In 1893 an agreement was signed by the trustees of the Masonic School Fund and the Council, by which the Masonic property was handed over to the Municipality, and the Council agreed in return to give free education to four Masonic children.

The school premises originally were at the corner of Peking and Honan Roads. Later a new building was erected on the corner of Boone and Chapoo Roads, and was ready for occupation in 1895.

From that time the Council's growing interest in education is evidenced by the increased appropriations for schools, in the successive annual budgets.

At first the school on Boone Road served for both boys and girls, but it soon outgrew its quarters and a well-equipped new school for boys was erected on North Szechuen Road Extension.

With the growth of the Settlement and the removal of residents to the western district, the need of a school for that part of the city became apparent, and hence in 1922 a very fine school for girls and small boys was erected on Yuyuen Road.

The French Municipal Council established two schools, one for Chinese boys on Boulevard de Montigny in 1910, and one for French and other foreign children on Avenue Joffre in 1911.

In addition to the efforts put forth by the Municipalities for the education of foreign children, many private schools have been founded for the same purpose. There are two Cathedral schools founded by the Very Rev. A. J. Walker, former Dean of the English Cathedral, one for boys and one for girls. That for boys has been carried on in the school building on the Cathedral grounds. Recently it received a large bequest from the will of the late Mr. Henry Lester, which will make possible the erection of a large and up-to-date building, and in this way Dean Walker's dream of a British National School will be realized.

The Americans have established a large school for American children on the outskirts of the French Concession on Avenue Petain.

School for Chinese Children It was not until 1899 that the Shanghai Municipal Council began to do anything for the education of Chinese children living in the International Settlement. In that year a proposal for a public school for Chinese, drawn up by Doctors Timothy Richard, J. C. Ferguson, and F. L. Hawks Pott, was presented to the Council. It was approved and adopted at a meeting of the Ratepayers. According to the plan, the Chinese gentry furnished the land, and the Municipality erected the building. The Chinese community subscribed Tls. 37,000 for this purpose, and the first Public School for Chinese was built in 1904 on Elgin Road. It proved so popular that in succeeding years other schools of a similar character were established by the Municipality.

In 1912 the Council took over complete control of the Ellis Kadoorie School on Carter Road.

In 1916 Mr. C. C. Nieh gave a site on Baikal Road, and the Nieh Chih Kuei School for Chinese was opened.

In 1917 the Council assumed responsibility for carrying on the Polytechnic Institute on Kwangse Road. The history of the Institute is as follows: in 1876, by the initiative of Consul Medhurst, a Polytechnic Institute had been founded in Shanghai largely by Chinese subscriptions. Its main object was to extend a knowledge of the natural sciences. One of the chief movers in the enterprise was Dr. John Fryer. It did not have, however, a very prosperous career and in 1917 the trustees decided to turn over their property and buildings to the Shanghai Municipal Council on condition that steps would be taken for the establishment of a new school on the same site, in which science subjects were to be taught.

By the building of these schools the Municipality did much to remove the reproach sometimes made, that foreigners were entirely indifferent to the welfare of the

Chinese population in whose midst they made their homes.
Mission It would be impossible in the brief compass
Schools of this book to give any detailed account of
the many schools and colleges founded in Shanghai under
missionary auspices for the benefit of the Chinese.

Among others there are the schools at Siccawei; St.
Francis Xavier's College on Nanzing Road, founded in
1864, first under the auspices of the Jesuits and later of
the Marist Brothers; St. John's University at Jessfield,
founded in 1879 by the American Episcopal Church
Mission, the outgrowth of schools begun in Shanghai in
1865-1866; the Aurora University on Avenue Dubail,
founded in 1903 by the Roman Catholic Church; Shanghai
College at Yangtszepoo, founded in 1906 by the Northern
and Southern American Baptist Missions; the Lowrie
Institute at South Gate, founded in 1850 by the American
Presbyterian Mission; Anglo-Chinese School on Range
Road, founded by the Church Missionary Society in 1850;
Medhurst College on Chaoufoong Road, founded by the
London Missionary Society in 1908; Mary Farnham Girls'
School at the South Gate, founded by the American Presby-
terian Mission in 1861; St. Mary's Hall for girls on Brenan
Road, founded by the American Episcopal Church Mission
in 1881; McTyeire School for girls on Edinburgh Road,
founded by the Southern Methodist Mission in 1890; and
the Eliza Yates Memorial School for girls on Paoshing
Road, founded by the Southern American Baptist Mission
in 1897.

The establishments at Siccawei, St. John's University, Shanghai College, St. Mary's Hall, and McTyeire
School are among the places of interest pointed out to
tourists visiting Shanghai.

CHAPTER XIII.

A TROUBLOUS PERIOD, 1891–1897.

In 1891 serious riots occurred along the
Yangtze River and dispelled the vision of
China's immediate entrance on the path of
progress. The prime instigator was a
scholar in Hunan, named Chou Han, who employed the
members of a secret society, known as the *Kolaohwei*
(venerable brothers) for carrying on anti-foreign propaganda. This society is said to have been founded by
disbanded troops at the close of the Taiping Rebellion. A
series of vile posters accusing missionaries of barbarous
crimes, such as the kidnapping and vivisection of Chinese
children, were spread broadcast, and the people were
incited to rioting and murder.

**The Yangtze
Riots, 1891**

Disturbances broke out in many places along the
Yangtze, churches were demolished, missionary residences
wrecked and looted, and missionaries themselves were
obliged to abandon their stations and to seek refuge in
Shanghai. At Wusueh two British subjects were murdered, one, an officer of the Maritime Customs, and the
other, a missionary.

Posters were put up calling on the people to rise and
attack the important mission establishments at Siccawei
and Jessfield. Naturally there was considerable apprehension in the Settlements and the volunteers were ordered
to stand by.

The Legations in Peking felt that the riots must be
checked, and made strong representations to the Tsung-li
Yamen (Foreign Office), and brought pressure to bear on

the Chinese Government by the assembling of foreign warships, British, French, and American.

Ultimately, the riots were suppressed, reparations were made and the danger passed away.

In connection with the *Kolaohwei* riots an attempt was made by an Englishman named Mason to start a rebellion.   He was a fourth class assistant in the Maritime Customs at Chinkiang where he became connected with the *Kolaohwei*.   Having entered its service, he undertook to procure arms and ammunition, and to smuggle them into Chinkiang for the purpose of starting a revolt against the Manchus.

Proceeding to Hongkong, he secured 35 cases of arms and ammunition and shipped them in piano cases as freight on board the S.S. "Chi-yuan."   He and his associates took passage on the same ship, intending to start a mutiny, gain control of the vessel, and proceed directly up the Yangtze to Chinkiang, without calling at Shanghai.   At the last moment his nerve failed, and instead of assisting in the mutiny, he helped to suppress it. On arrival at Chinkiang, his share in the plot having been discovered, he was arrested and sent to Shanghai.   At his trial he pleaded guilty and was given nine months' sentence.   While in gaol he tried to escape, but was recaptured and finally deported.

The trial caused a good deal of discussion in Shanghai and it was followed with considerable interest.   It is generally supposed that Mason was obsessed by the idea that he might, through a successful rebellion, make himself Emperor of China.

He was the type of adventurer found occasionally in China, ready to take part in any nefarious traffic, and causing the reputation of his fellow countrymen to suffer accordingly.

The Shanghai Jubilee   Shanghai celebrated its semi-centennial on November 17th and 18th, 1893, and the International Settlement was *en fête*.

There was considerable discussion in regard to the establishment of some permanent memorial of the occasion and various proposals were made, such as the opening of a new park, the founding of a hospital for infectious diseases, the building of a school for foreign children, the starting of schools for Chinese, and the erection of a Town Hall, but it was finally decided to collect a sum of Tls. 15,000, the capital and interest to be placed at the disposal of the Shanghai Municipal Council to be used at its discretion to benefit public institutions.

An elaborate programme was carried out. On Friday, November 17th, there was a parade of the Shanghai Volunteer Corps and men from the men-of-war in harbour. An address by the Rev. Dr. William Muirhead was delivered from a raised platform on The Bund, at half past eleven in the morning, in which the orator reviewed the history of the past fifty years and the progress made during that period. A salute of 50 guns was fired by the artillery at noon, a banquet was held at one o'clock, and at two o'clock there was a children's *fête* on the Race Course. The fountain in the Public Gardens was illuminated at night and made a very beautiful spectacle. The Bund, Nanking Road, the Garden Bridge and a part of Hongkew were bright with illuminations after dark. At night there was also a procession of the Shanghai Volunteer Fire Brigade, followed at ten o'clock by a display of fireworks.

On Saturday, November 18th, in the morning there was a parade of the native guilds and in the afternoon there was a performance for the children by the Amateur Dramatic Club at the Lyceum Theatre.

Among the distinguished guests were the Governor of Hongkong and Admiral Sir Edmund Fremantle, R.N.

In connection with the Jubilee Mr. Thomas Hanbury, who was visiting Shanghai, presented a gift of Tls. 5,000 to be used for some permanent memorial.

Sino-Japanese War The next stirring event in the history of China, which had an important influence upon the future of the Settlements, was the war between China and Japan, which began in 1894.

It is not necessary to enter into the causes of the conflict, more than to state that the control of Corea was the matter in dispute. The Japanese, fearing encroachment by Russia from the north, were anxious to dominate the government of Corea, so that it could be used as a buffer state between Russia and Japan.

There was considerable excitement in Shanghai when the British steamer "Kowshing," commanded by British officers, was sunk by the Japanese man-of-war, the "Naniwa," while transporting Chinese soldiers to Corea. Inasmuch as the British Foreign Office was of the opinion that war had already broken out, it was held that the Japanese were within their rights in sinking a transport on which enemy troops refused to surrender when summoned to do so.

On account of the war, the status of Shanghai caused anxiety to the commercial nations interested in the Settlements. The Taotai informed the Consuls of his intention to block the Woosung Bar, but as this would seriously cripple trade, it met with a general protest.

The British representative in Tokyo obtained from the Japanese Government an undertaking to "regard Shanghai as outside the sphere of its warlike operations." Notwithstanding this assurance, the Woosung Bar was for a time partially blockaded.

The Japanese authorities soon found they had been too generous in regard to Shanghai, as the Kiangnan Arsenal was located on its outskirts, and the port was used to ship ammunition, supplies, and troops. The American Government, however, joined with England and France to bring pressure upon Japan to carry out the neutrality agreement.

The result of the war was in some ways disastrous for China. Her weakness was still further revealed, and Western nations, realizing her inability to resist, became more insistent in their demands. China, yielding under pressure, became resentful, and the seeds of future trouble were sown.

In the Treaty of Shimonoseki made at the conclusion of the war, there was one article in the subsidiary treaty of commerce signed at Peking on July 21st, 1896, which was calculated to introduce a new element into the industrial situation in China. The right was conceded to carry on trade, *industries*, and *manufactures* at any of the treaty ports. Hitherto China had opposed the introduction of factories, but from this time it became permissible. The privilege gained by Japan could be shared by other nations, under "the most favoured nation clause," and this prepared the way for an Industrial Revolution in China.

The Second Riot in Shanghai
At a Ratepayers' meeting held in 1897, the Shanghai Municipal Council was authorized to raise the price of wheelbarrow licences. When, on April 1st, an attempt was made to carry out this regulation, the wheelbarrow coolies went on strike, and for two or three days there were minor disturbances.

On April 5th a mob from the French Concession crossed a bridge over the Yangkingpang, and, streaming into the International Settlement, started a riot. The alarm bell was rung, the volunteers called out and shore parties landed from H.M.S. "Linnet," H.M.S. "Plover" and U.S.S. "Monocacy." The rioters were dispersed, but for several days there was a state of tension. Much to the indignation of the foreign community, it was announced on April 6th that the Council had backed down and agreed to a compromise. At a meeting of the community which was very largely attended, a strong protest was made against the Council's action, and the opinion was expressed that owing to it, the prestige of fifty years had been lost.

As no satisfaction could be gained from the Council, a special Ratepayers' meeting was called on April 21st, at which the Council was subjected to the severest criticism. The Chairman, Mr. E. A. Probst, not only justified what the Council had done, but claimed that a victory had been won. It appeared that the Consular Body had deputed the Senior Consul to confer with the Taotai on the situation, and that the latter had promised to see that the increased licence fee would be paid by the wheelbarrow coolies, if the date for imposing the new tax was postponed for a short time.

Mr. Probst claimed that by this arrangement the Taotai acknowledged the right of the Council to increase taxes, and that it prevented the occurrence of similar trouble in the future.

This explanation not being satisfactory to the Ratepayers, a resolution was passed expressing "the most profound regret that the Council should have so far disregarded the interests and dignity of the community as to agree to the compromise which had been effected." The mover and seconder of the resolution declared that the Council should resign, as they had no right to make an agreement in opposition to a vote of the Ratepayers. This scathing vote of censure was passed unanimously, with the result that the whole Council retired.   The Chinese are past masters at compromise but it is difficult to persuade the Westerner to adopt that method, and unwillingness to compromise has been a constant source of friction between the Oriental and European.

Queen Victoria's Diamond Jubilee

The Queen's Jubilee of 1887 was observed in Shanghai without any great display of enthusiasm, but it was quite otherwise with the Diamond Jubilee of 1897.   The fountain in the Public Gardens was built as a memorial of the first Jubilee, and the Victoria Nursing Home was presented to the Municipality as a gift at the Diamond Jubilee.[1]

Shanghai being a cosmopolitan Settlement, it was impossible for the Council to take an official part in the Diamond Jubilee, and therefore the celebration was carried out under the auspices of the British Consular authorities and the British residents.   The people of all nations, however, co-operated in making the day memorable, and the rejoicings were truly international.   The Settlement was decorated, there was a great service in the English Cathedral, there was speech making and a reception, and at night there were illuminations and a torchlight procession.   It was a recognition not only of a great and good Queen, but a tribute to the prestige of the British nation throughout the world, as a pioneer in international commerce and the upholder of law and order.

Anti-Footbinding Movement

A great deal has been written about the evils of footbinding.   The credit for starting a movement against the practice belongs to the late Mrs. Archibald Little, who, in the year 1895,

---

[1] Recently there has been considerable discussion in regard to the future of the Victoria Nursing Home.   On the ground that since the erection of the Country Hospital, it is not needed as much as before, it is proposed to dispose of it, and to erect a Nurses' Training Home in connection with the Country Hospital.

started the *Tien Tsu Hui* or Natural Foot Society.   Much was done in the way of rousing public opinion and the reform was eventually taken up by the Chinese themselves. Nothing is more convincing of the advent of the new China than the discontinuance of the barbarous practice of foot-binding.   In a city like Shanghai, the modern young Chinese lady has complete freedom of movement.   She now takes part in athletics and is as fond of dancing as the Western girl.

CHAPTER XIV.

THE BEGINNINGS OF AN INDUSTRIAL REVOLUTION.

Cotton Mills Cotton manufacturing in China, according to modern methods, did not begin until comparatively recently.

China is a great cotton producing country, and this can be easily understood when we consider that the clothes worn by the people are for the most part made of cotton cloth. As a rule, only the rich wear ·silk, and China has rightly been called "the land of the blue (cotton) gown." It has been estimated that the annual consumption of cotton cloth is worth about $1,000,000,000, and that four-fifths of the amount used is produced by the Chinese themselves and manufactured by the hand loom.

It was in 1889 tnat Li Hung-chang undertook the erection of a modern cotton mill, under the name of "Foreign Cloth Factory." Unfortunately after three years of careful planning and construction, the mill was destroyed by fire.

The Modern Spinning and Weaving Factory, started at the same time, was completed in 1890.

Sheng Hsuan-hwai (Sheng Kung Pao) realized the importance of introducing machinery for the manufacture of cotton, and undertook to organize a joint stock company with a capital of Tls. 800,000. Only one-third of the amount was ever paid up, but the balance was arranged for by other means, and a mill was erected in 1894 with 65,000 spindles and 600 looms, and was called the Hwa Shen Cotton Mill.

After the Sino-Japanese War, by the Treaty of Shimonoseki, as already stated, foreigners obtained the right to engage in manufactures in the Treaty Ports, and this led to increased activity in the erection of mills. Firms like Jardine, Matheson and Company, Ilbert and Company, and Arnhold, Karberg and Company, which were originally dealers in piece goods and cotton yarn, immediately took up cotton manufacturing enterprises, and cotton mills under the names of Ewo, Laou Kung Mow, and Shui Kee were built along the northern bank of the Whangpoo.

In a short time the Japanese followed suit and before long surpassed the British in the number of mills erected.

Shanghai at the present time has 58 cotton spinning and weaving mills, with 1,865,344 spindles.

Some of the factors that have led to the establishment and development of the cotton manufacturing industry in Shanghai are as follows: (1) It is surrounded by a prosperous cotton growing section of the country, and the cotton can be easily transported to Shanghai. (2) There is a great demand for cotton goods throughout China, and Shanghai is the principal distributing centre for Central and North China. (3) Shanghai has an abundant supply of both Chinese and Japanese coal. (4) Shanghai has better financial facilities than any other city in China. (5) Shanghai has a good supply of labour and has trained up a number of hands who have become experts. (6) It has a cheap supply of electricity.

Importation of Machinery Of course the erection of mills resulted in increased demand for machinery, and the Customs statistics show a gradual ascent for this import. Inasmuch as the modern cotton spinning and weaving industry started in the British

Empire, where cotton machinery was first invented, it was natural that British machinery should be used in the beginning.

Recently, however, with the return of American-trained students, there is a growing demand for American machinery.

Flour Mills[1] Some time during the early "nineties" the first roller process flour mills were brought to China by Fobes and Company. The modern flour milling industry dates from 1897, when the late Mr. Sun Tao-sung became especially interested in the matter, being convinced that flour made by machinery could be sold at better prices than native ground flour. Hearing that American machinery was cheaper than British, he sent his brother, Mr. Sun Tao-shing, with Mr. Yen Ts-ching as interpreter, to America. With G.S22,000 a fully equipped American plant was procured, and in 1899 the Fou Foong Flour Mill was organized. There were many difficulties at the beginning, but these were overcome and at the end of the first year the success of the new mill was assured.

The Fou Foong Mill had one rival in 1899, the China Flour Mill Company, established by some German merchants with German machines. Owing to lack of support this enterprise resulted in a failure.

The success of the Fou Foong Mill encouraged others, and to-day in Shanghai and vicinity there are 16 modern flour mills, with an aggregate daily producing capacity of 10,500 bags.

Silk Filatures One of the most valuable of silk products exported from China is raw white, steam filature silk. China's steam filature silk realizes a better price than any other in the market, and that produced in Shanghai is considered better than that from Canton.

---

[1] This information was courteously supplied by Mr. R. Y. F. Sun and Mr. A. F. Ollerdessen.

Among the oldest of the silk filatures in Shanghai is Jardine, Matheson and Company's Ewo Silk Filature, situated in Chengtu Road. It was established in 1882 and has now about 500 bassines.

One of the principal silk filatures founded by Chinese capital is the Sin Chong in Wuchow Road. At present there are in Shanghai over 15 large steam filatures and several smaller ones.

The Kiangsu Chemical Works Among the first industrial establishments founded in Shanghai was the Kiangsu Chemical Works, started by the Major Brothers in the early "sixties," near the old stone bridge which crossed the Soochow Creek. In 1875 it was converted into a limited company, and new buildings were erected some distance above the old premises. Great care was expended on the purchase of the most up-to-date plant, and the whole equipment cost Tls. 230,000. There is a department for the refining of gold and silver, and sulphuric and nitric acids are manufactured.

Shipbuilding The shipbuilding industry in Shanghai began at an early date. We find Boyd and Company in 1862 and then S. C. Farnham in 1865. These two companies united to form a new company known as the Shanghai Engineering, Shipbuilding and Dock Company, Limited. The present name of the company, The Shanghai Dock and Engineering Company, Limited, was adopted in May, 1906. The company owns the Pootung Engine Works, the Old Dock, the Cosmopolitan Dock, the International Dock, and the Tungkadoo Dock.

Other forms of industry followed in successive years and Shanghai gradually developed into a great manufacturing centre. Starting as a treaty port for trade, it became a city of factories, and the general appearance of the place greatly changed in consequence.

The mills and factories were first built in the Yang-tszepoo region on the Whangpoo, and then, on the Soochow Creek. On the latter waterway they now reach to several miles beyond Jessfield.

As the traveller enters the harbour of Woosung, his attention is attracted to the numerous high chimneys belching out their smoke, and he becomes conscious that he is nearing the great industrial port of the East.

Effects
It is impossible here to do more than refer briefly to the social and economic consequences of the beginnings of an industrial revolution. Industry has attracted a large number of labourers to Shanghai from different parts of the country. It has led to the gathering together of men, women, and children in the mills and factories, breaking down the old strict family life and customs, especially bringing women out of their former seclusion. It has made the young girls wage-earners, adding to the family income, instead of being an economic burden.

The standard of living has tended to rise, as a result of the larger earning capacity of the families. It has brought about the formation of labour unions, and to the conflict between capital and labour with which we are familiar in the West, resulting often in disastrous strikes. Owing to the absence of factory laws at that time, many evils developed in connection with a cheap labour market, such as the employment of young children, and the injury to life and health, but we must postpone the consideration of these until a later chapter.

CHAPTER XV.

Many things combined to make the year 1898 an important one for the International Settlement. Among others, there was the establishment of an efficient Health Department under Dr. Arthur Stanley, who did much for the improvement of health conditions in the International Settlement, and introduced the Pasteur treatment. A railway line, built by the Chinese between Shanghai and Woosung, was opened to traffic, and thus an enterprise which had ended so disastrously in 1877 was now successfully achieved.

The most important event, however, was the extension of the Settlement.

There was real need for enlarging its boundaries. The Chinese population, attracted by the advantages of living within this area, was steadily growing, and the number of mills, filatures, and other industrial enterprises was rapidly multiplying. It became evident that if Shanghai was to become the great city which it was capable of becoming, further room for expansion must be secured.

The Council, according to the Land Regulations, could not approach the Chinese authorities directly on the matter, but must act through the Consular Body. A letter therefore was addressed to this Body on January 3rd, 1896, requesting its assistance in securing such an extension of the settlement area as would provide ample room for future development. While official negotiations were in progress the Council sounded the local Chinese officials and gentry and sought their co-operation. Much to its satisfaction, it was able to clear the atmosphere of distrust. The local officials and gentry ceased to oppose the scheme, and the native landowners as a class became favourably disposed towards it.

Encouraged by the attitude of the local Chinese authorities, the Council revised the original proposal of 1896, and asked for a larger extension, taking in a considerable portion of land adjoining Jessfield Road in the western district, the Paoshan *hsien,* and Pootung, sections where foreigners had already purchased large tracts of land and where mills had been erected.

It so happened that at the same time, the French were seeking for the extension of their Concession towards Siccawei.

In connection with the enlargement of the Concession, the question of putting a road through the Ningpo cemetery was revived. In 1898, in spite of the agreement arrived at in 1874, the compulsory surrender of this cemetery was decided upon by the Taotai and the French Consul-General, who offered to pay the owners of the land its duly assessed value. Before proceeding to carry out their plan the French took strong precautionary measures and landed some men from one of the men-of-war in harbour. On July 16th, the walls of the cemetery were demolished. This resulted on the following day in a riot, which was sternly quelled, with twelve fatal casualties among the rioters.

Although great indignation was aroused among the Chinese residents by this high-handed action, the French authorities continued to press for the extension of their Concession. They demanded not only an extension in the direction of Siccawei, but also land on the right bank of the Whangpoo, and the Pootung frontage opposite the French Bund, where large tracts of land were owned by

British and American shipping firms. The owners vigorously protested and objected to being deprived of the jurisdiction of their own courts by being included in the French Concession. The British and American Ministers upheld these protests in Peking, and the matter was referred to the Home Governments.

On the other hand, the French Minister protested against the extension of the International Settlement on the ground that it included land already earmarked for the French Concession. This friction between the International Settlement and the French Concession brought about a deadlock.

As far as the Chinese Government was concerned, since it was opposed to the extension of both the French Concession and the International Settlement, any excuse for procrastination was welcome. The Chinese authorities were unwilling to have any land in the Paoshan *hsien* included in the International Settlement, as it was very thickly populated, and was a separate administrative district from the Shanghai *hsien*. Furthermore the inclusion of land in the Paoshan *hsien* was objectionable as it would put the Shanghai railway station of the Shanghai-Woosung line within the limits of the foreign Municipality.

A special General Meeting of the Chamber of Commerce of the International Settlement was held on July 17th, 1898, at which it was unanimously decided to bring the matter to the attention of the foreign Ministers at Peking, individually. Mr. J. S. Fearon, Chairman of the Shanghai Municipal Council, paid a visit to the Capital for this purpose. His representations were favourably received, but the conflict between British and French interests still prevented any active measures being taken.

After some time, the dispute between these two countries was settled by their respective governments, and then their representatives, with the American and

German Ministers, joined in addressing identical notes to the Tsung-li Yamen, pressing the Chinese Government to instruct the Viceroy at Nanking to grant the extensions.

On April 13th, 1899, the Ministers of the Tsung-li Yamen informed the foreign Legations verbally that the Viceroy of Nanking had been instructed to act in accordance with the request of the Ministers.

The yielding of the Chinese Government was due in no small measure to the fact that after the disastrous war with Japan, it was too weak to risk giving offence to the foreign Powers.

To expedite matters the Council asked Mr. (now Dr.) J. C. Ferguson, former President of Nanyang College, to interview the Viceroy at Nanking. This visit resulted in the Viceroy's appointing Mr. Ferguson as one of the two deputies to negotiate in regard to settlement extension. At the same time the deputies were instructed not to include any land in the Paoshan *hsien* in the new area. The actual delimitation of the boundaries was carried out by the Public Works Department of the Municipal Council, in conjunction with the Shanghai Magistrate and Messrs. J. C. Ferguson and Yü, and was accomplished in an amicable manner.

A special meeting of the Ratepayers was held June 29th, 1899, at which a motion adopting the new boundaries was carried unanimously and forwarded to the Senior Consul, who in turn transmitted it for ratification to the Diplomatic Body and the Chinese Government.   In July, 1899, the Council was informed that the extension had been sanctioned.

In the meantime the Taotai issued a proclamation, which was posted in the new territory, giving the Council authority to collect taxes and to exercise municipal control.

The boundaries of the International Settlement after the extension were as follows:

1.—*Upon the North*:—The Soochow Creek from the Hsiao Sha Ferry to a point about seventy yards west of the entrance thereinto of the Defence Creek, thence in a northerly direction to the Shanghai-Paoshan boundary, thence following this boundary to the point where it meets the Hongkew Creek and thence in an easterly direction to the mouth of the Kukapang.

2.—*Upon the East*:—The Whangpoo River from the mouth of the Kukapang to the mouth of the Yangkingpang.

3.—*Upon the South*:—The Yangkingpang from its mouth to the entrance thereinto of the Defence Creek, thence in a westerly direction following the line of the northern branch of the Great Western Road, and thereafter along that road to the Temple of Agriculture in the rear of the Bubbling Well village.

4.—*Upon the West*:—From the Temple of Agriculture in a northerly direction to the Hsiao Sha Ferry on the Soochow Creek.

The following table indicates how much the Settlement was enlarged by the extension:

	Before 1899.	After extension 1899.
Area in square miles	2.75	8.35
Area in English acres	1,768	5,584
Area in Chinese *mow*	10,606	33,503
Greatest length in miles	3.75	7.50
Greatest breadth in miles	1.30	2.27
Length of boundary line in miles (on land)	6.43	11.13
Length of boundary line in miles on Soochow Creek and Whangpoo River	3.50	9.76

Simultaneously the French Concession was largely increased, but did not include the British or American owned land, which had been in dispute.

In spite of the considerable increase in the area of the Settlement, the British authorities were not entirely satisfied. In a telegram dated May 12th, 1899, the Marquis of Salisbury, H.B.M.'s Secretary of State for Foreign Affairs, stated that H.B.M.'s Minister at Peking "may agree to the proposed arrangement, but should take care that nothing is said which would in any way pledge us to refrain from making further demands for extension in the direction of Paoshan or elsewhere in the future."

Owing to the large amount of capital invested in China by British subjects and to the growing importance of Shanghai as a centre for their trade, it was natural that the British Government should be greatly interested in future developments.

Considerable difficulty was encountered by the Council when it undertook to develop roads across the newly included territory. Opposition was made to the removal of graves, and to the filling-in of creeks, and it took time to adjust things satisfactorily. A Municipal Cadastral Office was established in 1900 for keeping a complete record of land owned in the Settlement and vicinity, so that its value might be assessed from time to time, as a basis for levying a land tax for the municipal revenue.

Establishment of the Chinese Post Office An important event belonging to this period is the establishment of the Imperial Post in 1896, at first under the supervision of the Maritime Customs.

Hitherto mails for foreign ports had been handled by six national post offices, British, French, German, Russian, Japanese and American.

The Shanghai Municipal Council conducted a Local Post Office for domestic mails as far back as 1866, although there was some question as to whether such a procedure was sanctioned by the Land Regulations. The

Local Post handled mails for places in the Settlements and in other Treaty Ports, and issued its own set of stamps.

When the Imperial Post came into existence, it began to handle mails for the Treaty Ports, and requested the Local Post Office to withdraw. Neither the Chamber of Commerce nor the Ratepayers would at first consent to this, but after the local steamship companies declared they could only carry Imperial mails for ports in China, the Local Post Office was discontinued.

China was admitted to the Postal Union in 1914, but the various national post offices were not finally withdrawn until after the Washington Conference, 1921-1922.

A large Chinese post office building was erected on Peking Road in 1907, and an efficient staff organized. Although there was some doubt at first as to whether China was prepared to undertake the supervision of postal affairs, yet experience proved that on the whole the mail service was better than it had been under the former system. The Postal Department was well run and brought in a small revenue to the Government. Even at times of internal disturbances in China, it continued to function in spite of many difficulties.

Shanghai Mutual Telephone Company The first telephone company in Shanghai was conducted by the Great Northern Telegraph Company, which was established in 1881. It was only on a small scale, having 338 subscribers exclusive of the Municipality, and later the business was handed over to the China and Japan Telephone Company.

On March 10th, 1898, at a Ratepayers' meeting, a resolution was passed authorizing the Council to enter into negotiations with the China and Japan Telephone Company, or with any other similar company, and, at its discretion, to grant a lease. Tenders were invited, and that of the Shanghai Mutual Telephone Company was accepted, partly because the company was formed locally with Directors in Shanghai, and partly because it offered to supply service at a cheaper rate than other companies.

Under the agreement, the company was to complete the lines by April, 1901, but by August 1st, 1900, a service was opened between a hundred of the principal stations, and on the day for the completion of the work of construction, the company was able to announce that it had connected all old subscribers, and added a considerable number of new ones. The work of the company has gradually been extended and is now being changed from the manual to the automatic system.

Lack of Traffic Facilities
By the introduction of the telephone, Shanghai put itself in line with other growing commercial cities, but it was still very backward as regards traffic. There were carriages and ricshas, but no trams and buses, and the day of the automobile was not to come until 1902.

At a Ratepayers' meeting on October 17th, 1898, a motion was made that the construction of tramways in Shanghai should be considered. The conservative residents, however, fearing interference with the existing traffic, rejected the motion.

The Reform Edicts of 1898
While the negotiations in regard to the extension of the Settlements were in progress, an important movement was taking place in which the residents of the Settlements, both Chinese and foreign, were deeply interested. The Emperor, Kwang Hsu, came under the influence of a group of young reformers, prominent among whom was Kang Yu-wei, a native of Kwangtung, a man of marked ability and strong personality. As a result, a series of reform edicts were published which aimed at modernizing the ancient system of government. The Empress Dowager, Tzu-hsi,

and the officials of the old type, regarding these innovations with consternation, gained possession of the person of the Emperor by a *coup d'état* and forced him into retirement. This left the Empress Dowager in control, and she proceeded to seize the reformers. Kang Yu-wei made his escape on a British vessel to Shanghai and at Woosung was transferred to the P. and O. steamer "Ballarat," leaving for Hongkong.

In regard to the reform movement of which so much was expected and which failed so lamentably, Cordier, the French historian, says, "The great fault of the reformers was to seek to transform China in too short a period, and to take in hand at the same time all the machinery of Government, to strike at one time at all abuses. In Japan there was a Feudal system to crush, but not the traditions of centuries to overcome."

Sir Robert Hart wrote in a private letter to a friend, "The Emperor's head was set in the right direction, but his advisers, Kang Yu-wei and others, had had no experience of work, and they simply killed progress with kindness. They stuffed it against its powers of assimilation and digesting, with food enough in three months for three times as many years; so it is killed for the present."

CHAPTER XVI.

SHANGHAI DURING THE BOXER OUTBREAK, 1900.

Signs of Unrest Ominous clouds appeared on the political horizon during 1899, and there was a general feeling of unrest throughout China. There were frequent reports of the growth of an anti-foreign spirit and of persecution of Christian converts. Rebellions broke out in different parts of the country and secret societies manifested considerable activity.

Shanghai was visited by Kangyi, Assistant Grand Secretary and President of the Ministry of War, who had been appointed High Commissioner for the purpose of investigating affairs in Kiangsu and of raising an increased revenue for the Imperial Exchequer. The foreign press facetiously termed him the "Lord High Extortioner." He was extremely anti-foreign and exercised a dangerous influence.

Rise of the Boxers At this time, a secret society, known as the "Boxers," became prominent in Western Shantung. In Chinese, the name might be written in two ways. In one way, it meant "The Association of Justice and Harmony," and in another way, "The Fists of Patriotic Union."

As the society made boxing and gymnastics its ostensible purpose, it obtained the name of "Boxers" and adopted as its motto "Preserve the Dynasty, exterminate the Foreigners." Its members passed through various stages of secret initiation, and believed that those who reached the highest stage became invulnerable to wounds by sword, spear, or bullet.   They became active in raids against Mission premises, and in the persecution of Christians, and as the provincial and local officials sympathized with their aims, little was done to check them.

Murder of Rev. S. M. Brooke   On October 31st, 1899, the Rev. S. M. Brooke, a missionary of the Church of England, while returning from Taianfu to his station at Pingyin, was murdered by a band of the Great Sword Society at Maokiapu, fifty miles southwest of Tsinanfu. Although the case was taken up by the British Government, and the culprits were brought to justice, the anti-foreign agitation continued.   The decree put forth at that time by the Empress Dowager was unsatisfactory to the foreign Powers, and was considered by the "Boxers" and "Great Sword Society" as favourable to their enterprise.

Protest Against Abdication of Emperor   It was known that the Empress Dowager had already decided on the policy of driving the foreigners into the sea, and that she looked upon the Boxers as valuable allies in carrying out her plans.   In order to maintain her power, she planned to force the Emperor, Kwang Hsu, to abdicate, and to place a child named Puchên on the throne.   Many of the officials of the Empire protested, and memorials opposing the proposal were sent to Peking.   One was telegraphed from Shanghai on January 26th, 1900, signed by Kin Lien-shan, Manager of the Imperial Telegraph Service, and 1,230 others, assuring the Emperor of the senders' loyalty and begging him not to abdicate.   The Empress Dowager, furious at the attempted frustration of her designs, ordered the arrest of Kin Lien-shan, who was able to escape only by fleeing to Macao.

Siege of the Legations   Although warnings were given of a terrible storm about to burst in North China and throughout the country, yet for the most part the foreign

Ministers in Peking were incredulous, and relied on the promises of the Chinese Government to quell the disturbances.

As the Boxers drew nearer to Peking and outrages were committeed in the neighbourhood of the Capital, the Diplomatic Body at last became conscious of the peril, and Legation Guards were sent up from Tientsin.

This is not a history of China, but of Shanghai, and so we must pass over a detailed account of the memorable siege of the Peking Legations, and must confine ourselves to a consideration of how Shanghai was affected by the cataclysm.

The Defence of Shanghai As the residents of Shanghai became aware of the dangerous situation in the North, it was realized that the conflagration might spread throughout the whole of China and that an anti-foreign uprising might break out in the Settlements. Shanghai was unprepared, as it depended for its defence almost entirely on the volunteer corps and the police force. It was not pleasant for those who understood the Chinese language to hear groups of servants and coolies speaking about the day of reckoning for the foreigners, and of the general massacre about to take place.

When Admiral E. H. Seymour of the British Navy visited Shanghai, after the failure of his attempt to reach Peking with a small relief force, the defence of Shanghai was seriously taken in hand. It was decided to make the line of defence on Defence Creek, and it was arranged to give rockets and flags to foreigners dwelling in the suburbs so that they could signal if their premises were attacked. Mounted Sikh policemen were detailed to patrol the outlying districts at night and to give warning of approaching danger, and an appeal for troops was sent to the governments in England and America.

Agreement with the Viceroys of the Central Provinces

The situation was somewhat relieved by the fact that the Viceroys of the central provinces refused to obey the order to rise and drive out the foreigners. They realized that China was not strong enough to throw down the gauntlet to all the Western Powers. An agreement was made by Chang Chih-tung, the Viceroy of Hunan and Hupeh, and Liu Kun-yi, the Viceroy of Kiangsu, Anhwei and Kiangsi, with the foreign Consuls in Shanghai, guaranteeing to preserve peace in their jurisdictions, provided the foreign troops confined military operations to the North. It was understood that whatever might happen to the foreigners besieged in Peking, these Viceroys were not to be held responsible. The Powers were satisfied, and the Viceroys issued proclamations to the people informing them of the agreement, which was faithfully observed on both sides, and was the means of saving China from wide-spread anarchy.

Edict of the Empress Dowager

Peking was soon cut off from the rest of the world, and surrounded by a hostile force, aided and abetted by the Empress Dowager.

On June 24th she issued an edict to the following effect: "Whenever you meet a foreigner, you must slay him; if the foreigner attempts to escape, you must slay him at once." Some one in Peking had the courage to alter the character "*sha,*" meaning "to slay," to "*pao,*" meaning "to protect," and thus the disastrous results of such an edict were partially averted. To the parts of China within the disturbed area, the written text of the edict was sent by courier, and foreigners were ruthlessly massacred at Paotingfu and Taiyuanfu.

On July 14th a deep gloom fell over Shanghai, when it was reported that Sheng Hsuan-hwai, Director-General of Telegraphs, had received a telegram from Yuan Shih-kai (Governor of Shantung) stating "Messenger from Peking, July 8th, arrived to-day, reports that the artillery of the Boxers and Tung Fu-siang's troops made a breach in the Legation walls, afterwards taking them by assault. Massacre followed, no one left alive. Chinese losses enormous, foreign ammunition exhausted." Although Sheng Hsuan-hwai denied receiving this telegram, it was telegraphed to all parts of the world and for a time was generally believed, so that even a day was appointed for holding a solemn memorial service in St. Paul's Cathedral, London.

In Shanghai there was much grief over what was supposed to be the tragic end of friends and relatives.

Arrival of Li Hung-chang in Shanghai Among the officials who understood the madness of the policy of the Empress Dowager was the veteran statesman, Li Hung-chang. Having received the appointment as Viceroy of Chihli and Peiyang Tachen (High Commissioner of North China), he left Canton for the North on July 16th. Upon arrival in Shanghai he attempted to negotiate with the Consular Body, but was informed that "if the Envoys were alive he must negotiate with them, and if they were dead he must deal with the Home Governments." Although not permitted to negotiate with the Consuls, he used his influence towards restraining the folly of those responsible for the uprising in the North.

Landing of Foreign Troops Throughout this period there was great apprehension in Shanghai, and it was not until the British authorities sent a force of 3,000 Indian troops from Hongkong that a feeling of security was restored. The Chinese authorities objected to the landing of these troops, and appealed to the American Government to uphold them in their protest.

Failing to get encouragement from this source, the Viceroys yielded and the men who had remained outside Woosung since August 12th were, much to the relief of the foreign residents, landed at Shanghai on August 17th.

The other Powers were unwilling to leave the duty of protecting Shanghai and the Yangtze valley entirely in the hands of one Power, and on August 18th the French landed a hundred sailors, and after a few days, 250 Annamese tirailleurs. These were followed in a short time by detachments of troops from all the nations concerned, and Shanghai took on the appearance of an armed camp.

Relief of the Legations   In the meantime, on August 14th, the Allied Force which had advanced on Peking from Tientsin, had succeeded in raising the siege of the Legations, and the Imperial Court had fled to Sianfu. Great was the joy in Shanghai when news was received of the relief of those who had been shut up in the beleaguered Legations for so many trying days and a solemn Thanksgiving Service was held in the English Cathedral.

German Overseas Expeditionary Force   At first Germany, having no troops in China and only a small naval force, had been unable to give assistance in suppressing the Boxer Outbreak. When the news of the murder of Baron von Kettler, the German Minister, on June 20th reached Europe, Germany at once took steps for organizing an overseas expeditionary force of 7,000 men, under the command of Count von Waldersee, who was recognized by the other Powers as Commander-in-chief of the International Force.

When Count von Waldersee arrived in Shanghai on September 22nd, a general review of all the foreign troops in garrison was held on the enclosure within the Race Course.

The force consisted of Rajputs, Sikhs, Baluchis, Ghurkhas, Volunteers, Artillery Companies A and B, Customs Company, Reserves, German Company, Japanese, French, Light Horse, Bombay Cavalry, Annamites, French Mountain Battery, and German Regulars.

Count von Waldersee arrived at eight o'clock in the morning, accompanied by Brigadier-General Creagh of the British Army, and carried in his right hand the baton presented to him by the German Emperor at the time of his departure.

In the march past the Germans led the way. The short, quick step of the little Ghurkhas aroused considerable interest, while the guns of the Royal Artillery, each drawn by six beautiful horses, excited general admiration.

It was the finest military display Shanghai had seen up to that time.

CHAPTER XVII.

THE PROTOCOL AND ITS EFFECT ON SHANGHAI.

Signing of the Protocol After peace had been restored in the North, a long period of negotiations followed, and it was not until September 7th, 1901, that the Protocol was signed.

In 1902 the foreign forces garrisoned at Shanghai during the troublous period, numbering about 8,000 men, were withdrawn by mutual agreement of the four Powers, England, France, Germany, and Japan.

Tariff Revision The final Protocol contained a provision that the specific duties of the tariff on imports should be raised to an effective five per cent. No change was to be made in the levies on opium. Duty was to be paid on important classes of goods formerly imported free, such as wine and spirits, foreign tobacco, soap, etc.

A joint commission worked at the new specific import tariff and based it on the market value of the last three years before the Boxer Outbreak. It was completed on September 31st, 1902. Thus the tariff at five per cent. based on the obsolete values of 1858 was amended in China's favour according to the value of imports between 1897 and 1899. This meant a great increase in duties collected on foreign imports. Whereas in 1899 according to the old scale of values, excluding opium, it amounted to Tls. 6,656,881, in 1915, according to the revised scale, it amounted to Tls. 14,233,801.

The two articles in the Protocol of the greatest importance to Shanghai were those which had to do with the revision of the treaties, and the formation of a Conservancy Board for the Whangpoo.

Revision of the Commercial Treaties In regard to the revision of the commercial treaties, China proposed that there should be a round table conference for its consideration, as it was of common interest. The general opinion of the Powers, however, was that the treaty revision should be negotiated with each Power separately.

In the negotiations Lu Hai-hwan and Sheng Hsuanhwai acted throughout as the Chinese plenipotentiaries and were assisted by Mr. A. E. Hippisley and Mr. F. E. Taylor of the Customs Service.

The first treaty to be negotiated was that with England, the British Special Commissioner being Sir James L. Mackay, who was assisted by Mr. (afterwards Sir) Charles J. Dudgeon, a merchant of Shanghai. The meetings were held in Shanghai and a treaty was signed on September 5th, 1902.

The American plenipotentiaries were Mr. Edwin H. Conger, Minister to Peking, Mr. John Goodnow, Consul-General at Shanghai, and Mr. J. F. Seaman, a Shanghai merchant.

The Japanese plenipotentiaries were Mr. Hioki Eki, Secretary of Legation, and Mr. Odagiri Masnoske, Consul-General at Shanghai.

The American Treaty for the most part followed closely that of the British. When negotiations opened with other Powers, difficulty was encountered, for they all demanded some *quid pro quo*, and hence negotiations were suspended and never resumed. The British and American treaties furnished the code to which China was expected to conform.

It contained a scheme whereby China might be enabled to abolish her system of *likin*, a tax paid at customs barriers by commodities in transit. It had been imposed at the time of the Taiping Rebellion and became a cause of international dispute for many years.

"All barriers collecting *likin* or such like dues were to be permanently abolished. . . . Foreign goods on importation, in addition to the effective 5 per cent., were to pay a special surtax of one and a half times that duty to compensate for the abolition of *likin*, of transit dues in lieu of *likin*, and of all other taxation on foreign goods." No change was to be made in regard to the duties on foreign opium, and there was to be no interference in "China's right to tax native opium." An excise on salt was to be substituted for the payment of *likin* in transit. China was to be allowed to revise her export duties to an effective five per cent. and a special surtax of "one half the export duty payable, in lieu of internal taxation and *likin*, may be levied on goods, exported either to foreign countries or coastwise." Native goods circulating in the interior might be charged with a "consumption tax," levied only at the place of consumption. An excise could be collected from "products of foreign type turned out by machinery." [1]

Thus the attempt was made to do away with *likin*, but it was doomed to failure.

First of all there was the condition "that all the Powers who are now or who may hereafter become entitled to most favoured nation treatment in China, enter into the same engagements as those undertaken by the British, American, and Japanese Governments." [2] This condition nullified the whole agreement as many of the smaller nations would not consent to the new arrangement. Furthermore *likin* was popular with provincial officials. It was a source of revenue to them, and if cut off, there

---

[1] H. B. Morse: *International Relations of the Chinese Empire*, Vol. III, p. 371.

[2] At present, 1928, there are some nineteen Treaty Powers.

would be difficulty in carrying on the provincial administration. The agreement never came into operation and *likin* exists up to the present time (1928).

Establishment of Whangpoo Conservancy Board The other matter of extreme importance to Shanghai was the improvement of the course of the Whangpoo. Annex No. 17 of the final Protocol provided for the establishment of a Conservancy Board.

For forty years the Shanghai mercantile community had agitated for the removal of the bars and the deepening of the channel in the river, but the Chinese authorities had continued to maintain a supine attitude. In 1882 a dredger had been set to work but with no enduring results. The future development in commerce and industry depended on Shanghai having an accessible waterway for ships of large draught.

According to the Protocol, the Chinese would have small representation on the Conservancy Board, not more than two appointees, and the representatives of the foreign community would have the predominating control.

This, of course, was unacceptable to the Chinese authorities, and was regarded as an infringement of the sovereign rights of China. In 1904 Mr. A. E. Hippisley, acting for the Viceroy of Nanking, brought forward a new proposal, designed to restore the control to China and to make use of the technical knowledge of the Marine Department of the Customs. The foreign contribution towards the work had been estimated at Tls. 230,000 a year, derived from tax on land or houses in the Settlement, tax on land on both banks of the river, tax on imports and exports, and from tonnage dues. This arrangement was dropped, and China undertook to assume the entire expense and to contribute annually Tls. 460,000 to cover the cost, continuing the appropriation until the work was completed.

The work was to be under the direction of the Taotai of Shanghai and the Commissioner of Customs, who would employ competent engineers. Quarterly accounts of receipts and expenditures were to be sent to the Consular Body in Shanghai. It took some time to get the foreign Powers to agree to the new proposal, but in the end, on September 27th, 1905, a set of twelve regulations, in accordance with the new proposal, was signed by the representatives of China, and the eleven Protocol Powers.

Mr. J. de Rijke, a distinguished Dutch engineer, who had wide experience of similar work in Holland and Japan, and who had made considerable study of the Whangpoo problem, was appointed to the post of Engineer-in-chief in January, 1906.

Jui Cheng, the Shanghai Taotai, and Mr. H. E. Hobson, Shanghai Commissioner of Customs, organized the work in an efficient manner, the secretarial staff being supplied by the Customs Service.

The work of improvement was carried on successfully and at the end of four years, the former junk channel, now known as the Astraea Channel, had acquired a considerable depth, and the Inner Woosung Bar had been practically eliminated.

Then difficulties arose owing to the fact that the sum appropriated for the work was almost exhausted, and there was no fund for additional work and for maintenance. The Board reported that a sum of eight million dollars was necessary for the further improvements. The Chinese authorities were in a quandary, as they had expected the whole scheme to be carried out for the amount already appropriated.

They refused to renew the contract of Mr. de Rijke, which expired in December, 1910, and engaged in his place a Swedish engineer, Mr. H. M. von Heidenstam, and created in 1912 the present Whangpoo Conservancy Board. To the new Board was given the balance of the government grant. The Board was composed of the Chinese Commissioner of Trade and Foreign Affairs for Kiangsu, the Shanghai Commissioner of Customs (Mr. H. F. Merrill), the Shanghai Harbour-Master (Captain W. A. Carlson), and three Chinese Government officials.

Eventually, in order to secure sufficient revenue for the work, it was agreed that instead of drawing a grant from the Government, the Board should obtain its funds from "wharfage dues" at the rate of one and a half *per mille* on the value of the goods, imported or exported. Later it was further agreed that the Board should use the proceeds of the sale of *sheng-ko* land—land formed by "tidal accretion or reclamation, which by the law of China is crown land." [1]

The Board's jurisdiction extended over the Whangpoo from the Yangtze to its tidal limit, that is, to a radius of more than 30 miles. It was stated that "the authority with which the Conservancy Board is invested is delegated to it by the Chinese Government." A consultative committee of five foreign and one Chinese member was appointed to safeguard the interests of the Shanghai community.

In report No. 8 of the Whangpoo Conservancy Board, the following statement is given of the work accomplished up to 1928.

"The improvement of a tidal river like the Whangpoo follows certain simple principles. To

---

[1] According to a statement in Whangpoo Conservancy Board General Series No. 8 at the present time the Board's income consists "of a Conservancy Surtax of three per cent. on the Shanghai Maritime Customs dues, one and a half *per mille* on duty free goods and 0.045 per cent. on treasure, and the proceeds from the sale of foreshore lands."

obtain a deep regular channel suitable for navigation the width between the low water lines must be
almost uniform, slightly expanding towards the
mouth. The Conservancy therefore laid down
Normal Lines within which the channel must be
kept. Those lines are about 1,400 feet apart at
the upper end of the harbour, expanding to about
2,400 feet apart at the mouth. . . . To guide
the water between these lines, training walls have
been built in many places, of various types, with
piles, brushwood, mattresses, caissons, stone, etc.,
etc., and where the channel was split by islands or
shoals, one of the two branches—the so-called ship
channel—was closed by heavy dams, and the other
one made into a first class waterway. In two places
the river was too narrow and was widened to the
normal width by dredging. Over 20,000,000 cubic
yards of mud has been dredged. . . . Very
large areas have been reclaimed by thus narrowing
the whole channel with the result that the deep
channel is wider and the tidal currents run unim-
peded from the Yangtze through the smooth gently-
curving course. At the points where the land
bulges out into the water the mud continues, however, to settle and at those places some 1,000,000
cubic yards has to be dredged each year.

"Thus the river has been converted from an
irregular and rapidly deteriorating creek into a
good shipway with a least navigable depth of 26 feet
at extraordinarily low water, except at the Wayside
Bar, which has only 24 feet in the middle of the
fairway.

"As the neap tide rises at least 6 feet, a through

high water depth of at least 30-32 feet is available every day of the year." [1]

The Whangpoo Conservancy is an encouraging example of the application of Western engineering skill and administrative methods to Chinese conditions, and is one of the many instances of efficient service rendered by the Maritime Customs to the Chinese nation.

The large mail steamers which formerly were obliged to anchor at Woosung, and transport passengers and baggage to and from Shanghai by launches are now able to proceed up river and dock at wharves in the Settlements.

In 1921 a committee of harbour and river experts of the first rank was convened to make definite proposals as to future programme and the necessary organization. The detailed report recommended improvement of depths on the Yangtze Bar, and the provision of public harbour facilities, public docks, wharves, moorings, etc., supplementing the existing accommodation.

Currency Reform   There was an article in the Japanese Treaty, made after the Boxer Outbreak, which, if it had been carried out, would have been a great boon to commerce. It was that China was to "establish a uniform national coinage and provide for a uniform national currency."

A short *résumé* of currency used in foreign trade in China may be interesting.

The Spaniards in the early days in their trade with China introduced the Carolus dollar, so named from Carolus III of Spain (1759), and sometimes called the "pillar" dollar, from the pillar of Hercules contained in its design. This was the standard familiar to the first

---

[1] The author is much indebted to Dr. H. Chatley for supplying him with information in regard to the work of the Whangpoo Conservancy Board. Dr. Chatley has recently been appointed as Chief of the Board in succession to Mr. H. M. von Heidenstam.

British traders in Canton.   Spanish dollars issued at a later date came into circulation, but were not considered by the Chinese with as much favour as the Carolus dollar, which came to have a fictitious value.

After the Taiping Rebellion, owing to the shortage of Carolus dollars, Mexican dollars were imported and put into circulation, but at first these were not acceptable, and compared with the Carolus dollar, were at a discount. In later days the Carolus dollar lost its early popularity, and was seldom seen on the market.

It became necessary to adopt the tael as the standard, in place of the Carolus dollar.   The tael was not a coin, but an ounce of silver by weight.   The value of the tael in different parts of the country varied considerably and this introduced the vexed question of exchange.   The merchant in China is still confronted with the uncertainty of fluctuating exchange, between the money of his own country and the tael, beween taels and Mexican dollars, and between the value of the tael in one part of the country and in another.   It is small wonder that the problems arising from exchange have occupied some of the keenest minds among bankers and merchants.

In the Customs Service a standard tael, known as the Haikwan Tael, has been adopted.

Of course one of the chief difficulties is that all the Chinese currencies are based on silver, while the currencies of Europe and North America are based on gold.

The fluctuations in exchange introduce an element of gambling into trading, and at times have led to serious consequences.

Mixed Court Rules of 1902   There had been considerable friction between the Mixed Court in the International Settlement and that in the French Concession, as to the matter of jurisdiction.   The whole matter was referred to the Consular Body, which

11

appointed a special committee consisting of the Consuls-General of Germany, France and Great Britain.

A code of Provisional Rules defining the respective jurisdictions of the two Mixed Courts was drawn up. This received the approval of the Consular Body and local Chinese authorities on June 10th, 1902, and on June 28th it was endorsed by the Diplomatic Body at Peking.

Tramway Service It was at this period, on August 21st, 1902, that the Shanghai Municipal Council accepted the tender of the Brush Electric Company to construct and operate electric tramways in the International Settlement, the whole scheme to be in operation within three years of the signing of the contract.

Unfortunately owing to the lack of width of the streets, the narrow gauge was adopted, reducing the carrying capacity considerably, and making it necessary to attach trailers to the cars.

At first some of the Chinese were suspicious as to the safety of riding in conveyances moved by the mysterious electric current, but convenience and cheapness soon overcame their scruples, and the tramway became a profitable enterprise. The overcrowding has made the trams more patronized by the Chinese than by foreigners.

First Automobiles The introduction of motor cars into Shanghai came in 1902, when two Oldsmobile cars made their appearance. The Licensing Department of the Municipal Revenue Office was puzzled in regard to the question of registration and at first regarded the automobile as a form of carriage. These vehicles caused much consternation and numerous runaways. At the time when they appeared there were carriages, ricshas, bicycles, wheelbarrows, and sedan chairs. Gradually the motors increased until at the present time (1928) there are over 7,000, and carriages have almost entirely disappeared.

Trade Statistics   The Boxer Outbreak of 1900 had as one of its consequences a depression in trade, but this was followed by a rapid recovery.

The Customs Report of 1901 shows that foreign imports were greater than for any previous year, even for 1899, which had been an exceptionally good year, and were more than double the figures for 1891.   The statistics for the Port of Shanghai were as follows:

	1899	190^	1901
Net Foreign Imports	Hk.Tls. 38,823,995	Hk.Tls. 38,729,112	Hk.Tls. 41,663,387
Net Native Imports	14,958,250	8,736,291	14,216,377
Exports	70,822,474	50,263,756	62,546,012
Total	Hk.Tls. 124,604,719	Hk.Tls. 97,729,159	Hk.Tls. 118,425,776

CHAPTER XVIII.

A MEMORABLE YEAR, 1905.

The year 1905 is a memorable one in the annals of Shanghai, as at that time a change in the attitude of the educated Chinese became evident, indicating that they were no longer willing to submit passively to what they regarded as an infringement of their rights. This, as we shall see, brought about a serious situation at the close of the year—the Mixed Court riot in the International Settlement.

War between Russia and Japan Before giving an account of that disturbance, a brief reference must be made to the war between Russia and Japan in 1904-1905. Much to the chagrin of the Chinese, the war was waged on Chinese territory, in Manchuria, and China was helpless to prevent the occupation of her own territory by the hostile forces of two foreign Powers. Indeed China had been compelled to declare her neutrality, while war was being carried on in the northeastern provinces. This was humiliating in the extreme.

On the outbreak of war, the Russian gunboat "Manjur" was afraid to leave the harbour, as the port was closely watched by the Japanese; and after the naval sortie from Port Arthur on August 10th, 1904, the "Askold" and the "Grozovoi" took refuge in Shanghai. China, acting in accordance with the duty of a neutral nation, finally took steps for disarming and interning these vessels.

Psychological Results of the War
The result of the war, however, had a marked psychological effect. The Asiatic for the first time for many years proved superior in warfare to the European, and Japan suddenly emerged as one of the great Powers. The exultation in her victory spread throughout all countries in Asia. It was easy to reason that if China followed in the footsteps of her island neighbour, by introducing Western scientific education, Western machinery, Western military methods, and governmental reforms, she could become even stronger than Japan. What one small Asiatic Power had done might surely be done by another, greater in area, in population, and in resources

Boycott of American Trade
The first manifestation of the new spirit was the boycott of American trade, as a protest against the restriction of Chinese immigration into the United States. The boycott was put in force in many places, but was most successful in Canton and Shanghai, producing its greatest effect in the latter city. The Chinese Government, anxious not to come into conflict with the United States, tried to suppress it, but as it was a popular movement, and was fomented by the students of the new era, especially by those who had studied in Japan, the authorities found themselves in a difficult position. The boycott finally subsided in September, 1905, chiefly because the Chinese traders who had bought American cotton piece goods on long time contracts, were unable to dispose of their holdings and consequently became lukewarm in regard to the agitation.

In old China, as we know, the *literati* exercised great influence on public opinion. In 1905 we have the first instance of the new student class exerting a similar influence.

Mixed Court Riot

This new attitude on the part of the Chinese will enable us to understand better the Mixed Court riot.

On December 8th, 1905, some women, one of whom was the widow of a Szechuen official named Li, and two servants, were brought up before Magistrate Kuan, the Assistant Magistrate, Mr. King, and the British Assessor, Mr. Twyman, on a charge of kidnapping girls for unlawful purposes, fifteen supposed victims being present in court. The case was remanded. A difference of opinion arose as to where the prisoners should be kept, pending trial. The British Assessor wished to hand over the accused and the girls to the Municipal police for detention *pro tem* under the control of the Municipal authorities, but the Magistrate directed they should be sent to the cells in the Mixed Court and instructed the runners accordingly. This led to a free fight between the police and the runners in which the police proved the stronger. The accused and the girls were put into the police van, but the runners locked the gate of the courtyard. When the police asked the Magistrate to have the gate opened, he declined, saying they might break down the gate, break up the whole court and kill him if they chose. The Magistrate then left the court, and shortly afterwards the gate was opened and the accused, with the girls, disposed of according to the orders of the British Assessor.

The Canton Guild called a meeting and made a protest in regard to the indignity to which the widow of a fellow provincial had been subjected. A telegram was sent to the Waiwupu, the Board of Foreign Affairs, reporting the matter and protesting against such treatment by the police of Chinese ladies of the official circle. It was stated that Mrs. Li was the widow of an official from Kwangtung Province and was returning to her home with the coffin of her late husband, servants and slave girls, and luggage consisting of over one hundred pieces.

A committee of Chinese merchants also protested against the conduct of the police in striking court runners while the court was in session. A demand was made for the dismissal of the police inspectors, detectives, and constables concerned in the case, and for the removal of the British Assessor.

As a result of the agitation, upon request of the Wai-wupu, the foreign Ministers in Peking instructed the Consular Body at Shanghai to order the Shanghai Municipal Council to release the lady without further trial, inasmuch as the Mixed Court had been closed by the Taotai, and it would be unjust to keep her in custody without an opportunity of proving her innocence.

The Municipal Council was obliged to yield to the wishes of the Consular Body, but resented the violation of the established procedure on the part of the Diplomatic Body in Peking.

Meanwhile the Chinese population was inflamed by exaggerated accounts of what had transpired in the Mixed Court. Threats were made of a general strike, a refusal to pay taxes, and a general exodus of the Chinese population from the Settlement.

As a result of the propaganda a mob was incited to attack the premises of the Municipal Council, and the police stations. The police, having been instructed not to use their firearms, were unable to defend themselves, and in the assault made on the Louza Police Station, were overpowered, and the station set on fire. Panic reigned throughout the Settlement, and the lives of foreigners were endangered.

Finally the riot was suppressed by the combined action of the police, volunteers, and landing parties from the foreign men-of-war in harbour. Captain A. M.

Boisragon, the Chief of the Municipal police in 1905, gave the following account of this serious incident:

Captain Boisragon's Report   "The Louza Station was made the scene of the most determined attack, the Foreign and Sikh Police were driven in, amidst a hail of bricks and stones, after having charged the attackers a dozen times.   The attack commenced at about 9.30 o'clock and lasted till 10 o'clock, when the latter obtained the upper hand, forced an entry into the station, turned out the fires in the grates of the various rooms on the ground floor, and thus set fire to the station in three or four different places.   The alarm for fire was sounded at 10 a.m. and the Brigade arrived on the scene some minutes after.

"In the meantime the attack on the Town Hall was being pressed with vigour, but the Police there fired on the mob, killing three men in the crowd, and two other innocent shop assistants sitting behind closed shutters on the opposite side of the road —an unavoidable misfortune.   This somewhat cowed but did not disperse the crowd, which was finally driven into side streets on the arrival of a landing party from the British warships in port. In addition to the three Chinese killed at the Town Hall, and one at the Kiangse and Nanking Road corner, three others were shot in the neighbourhood, making seven in all, but it is believed that others died from wounds received.   The total number of wounded could never be ascertained."

There is evidence to show that the uprising was organized by persons of a higher class than loafers and beggars, and that students educated abroad had a good deal to do with it.

Dispute
about
Procedure
in Mixed
Court

The Mixed Court had become unpopular with the Chinese community, inasmuch as it expressed very clearly the dominant position of the foreigner in the control of the Settlement.

There had been considerable discussion between the Chinese officials and the Council in regard to the conduct of affairs at the Mixed Court. The former had protested against the introduction of Municipal police into the Court Room. On April 15th, 1905, the Mixed Court Magistrate wrote to the Senior Consul as follows: "I was surprised to learn that the Sikh constable was sent here by the West Hongkew Police Station. As I have sole charge of the Court from the front door inwards, the Police have no right whatever to interfere therewith, and I should be entitled to expel the Indian at once, without writing to address H.B.M.'s Consul-General, with a request that he should forward a protest to the Police in the matter."

The Chinese contention that the precincts of the Court were excluded under the Land Regulations from Municipal control was debatable, for from the account we have given of the founding of the Court it will be seen that it was never intended to be a purely Chinese Yamen, and that in the beginning it was situated on the premises of the British Consulate. Its object was to bring about joint action of Chinese and foreigner in judicial proceedings. The reason given for the introduction of Municipal police into the Court Room was to guard against the miscarriage of justice and to see that the penalties awarded were duly executed. When the Mixed Court Magistrate objected to the presence of police in the Court, as a compromise, in place of a Sikh policeman a European member of the Municipal police force was appointed to attend at the Court.

Another bone of contention had been the custody of female prisoners. According to Article I of the Rules of the Mixed Court at Shanghai, a Chinese committing an offence in the Settlement was to be tried and detained in custody by the Magistrate of the Mixed Court. As a matter of fact, however, the male prisoners in all Chinese cases in the Mixed Court had generally been sent to the Municipal Gaol since its establishment, and on the average, 450 convicts per day were detained there. Female prisoners had not at first been taken to the Municipal Gaol owing to the lack of accommodation for women, but at the time of which we are writing this deficiency had been supplied.

The opinion had been expressed by the Council that the cells of the Mixed Court Gaol were not yet in a fit condition for the reception of women, and the Taotai had been asked to allow female prisoners to be taken to the Municipal Gaol. To this the Taotai strongly objected, the Chinese evidently having a strong prejudice against handing over female prisoners to the custody of foreigners.

The case was further complicated by the fact that the American Assessor, Mr. Julean H. Arnold, upheld the Chinese authorities and the Mixed Court Magistrate in their contention that according to the Rules of the Mixed Court, female prisoners should be remanded to the Mixed Court Gaol.

On December 19th an interview was held between Mr. F. Anderson, Chairman of the Municipal Council, Mr. Platt, a member of the Watch Committee, and the Taotai, in reference to the Mixed Court affair. It was agreed that in future female prisoners should be sent to the Mixed Court Gaol, which the Magistrate declared to be in a fit state for their accommodation, and which would be periodically inspected by the Health Officer.

The Taotai brought up the question of Mr. Twyman's removal from the office of Assessor, but Messrs. Anderson and Platt had no authority to discuss this point. It was agreed that an inquiry should be held in regard to the conduct of the police inspectors.

The matter was finally settled when the Viceroy of Nanking, Chou Fu, came to Shanghai by Imperial order, and the Chinese gave their consent to the presence of the Municipal police in the Court, while the custody of female prisoners was left in the hands of the Chinese Magistrate.

Shanghai-Nanking Railway Opened to Nanziang

During this memorable year, before the riot in Shanghai, one important event of an encouraging nature occurred. This was the opening of traffic on the Shanghai-Nanking Railway to Nanziang. A train conveying invited guests, foreign and Chinese, travelled on the line as far as this station, where a reception was given by the Chinese authorities. Congratulatory addresses were made on this significant sign of progress.

The Shanghai-Nanking Railway line was built by capital furnished by the British and Chinese Corporation. According to the agreement the construction and operation of the line were to be in the hands of five Commissioners—two Chinese, two English, and the Engineer-in-chief (English). The line and its plant were to be security for the loans of £3,250,000 and £650,000.

The short line between Shanghai and Woosung, already in operation, was purchased by the Corporation for the sum of Tls. 1,000,000 (£125,000) and became a branch of the Shanghai-Nanking Railway.

The whole line from Shanghai to Nanking was completed in 1908, and since that time the control has been vested in the Chairman of the Board of Commissioners, a Chinese.

CHAPTER XIX.

A PERIOD OF FRICTION, 1906–1911.

We have referred to the growing interest in national affairs manifested by Chinese foreign-educated students. The number of those who had studied in European, American and Japanese colleges was steadily increasing, and as they returned to their own country, they came with progressive ideas, and were anxious to "pour new wine into old bottles."

First Educational Mission to America It will be remembered that a party of Chinese students, numbering about a hundred, had been sent to the United States in 1872, under the direction of Dr. Yung Wing. Unfortunately, owing to conservative influences in the Government, and the raising of the cry that these young men were in danger of becoming denationalized and might become leaders of rebellion in their own country, they were all recalled just as they reached the stage of entering college. For a long time they were relegated to the background, and had no opportunity of helping to modernize China.

After the humiliation which came to the nation as a result of the Boxer Outbreak, when even the Empress Dowager saw that reforms must be instituted if Chinese national existence was to be preserved, these young men became prominent, and began to occupy positions of importance. Such men as Tang Shao-yi, Liang Tun-yen and Liang Cheng joined with the students of the post-Boxer period in advocating progressive measures.

The nationalistic spirit of the students found an outlet in two directions; first, in working for the reforms of China, and secondly, in opposing anything that looked like an increase in the authority of foreigners in the Settlements or Concessions.

In response to the demand for reform, the Empress Dowager issued the famous edict of 1905, abolishing the old examination system of China, and introducing in its place a system of modern education, from the primary school up to the university.

Suppression of Opium   Another popular manifestation of a new spirit, and one which concerned Shanghai to a considerable extent, was the revival of efforts for checking the evils of opium.

The students took the lead and young China imposed its will on old China. Those who had studied abroad realized that the addiction of the Chinese people to the opium habit lowered the prestige of their country in the eyes of other nations; and those who had been educated in Japan had been impressed by the strict prohibition of opium carried out in that country.

The student agitation swept the country, and the Government took action, with the result that on November 21st, 1906, an edict was issued ordering that the cultivation of the poppy should be gradually decreased, and finally cease altogether in ten years; that smokers must take out licences, and that those under sixty years of age must gradually reduce the amount they consumed; that restriction should be placed on the sale of opium appliances, and the opening of new opium divans; that smoking be prohibited in all government services; and that negotiations be opened for the gradual reduction of the amount of foreign opium imported, and its absolute cessation within ten years.

The British Government responded to the appeal made for her support in this moral movement and in December, 1906, consented to reduce the export of opium from India by one-tenth each successive year from 1908.

The offer was provisional for three years, but when it was found that China was really in earnest and more than carrying out her part in the programme, it was agreed on May 8th, 1911, to reduce annually the amount of opium exported from India to China, so that the exportation would cease entirely in 1917.

It was possible, however, for other countries to continue to send opium to China, and under existing treaties their nationals resident in the Far East were free to import it. In order to meet this situation an International Conference was held in Shanghai in February, 1909, at the invitation of the American Government.

It was presided over by an American, Bishop Charles Henry Brent, and passed resolutions urging the governments represented at the Conference to adopt regulations that would aid China in carrying out her purpose. It is unnecessary here to refer to the conferences on opium which have been held since that date, all trying to regulate the use and sale of this dangerous drug.

The opium dens in the native city of Shanghai were closed in 1907, and in response to the appeal made by the Chinese authorities, on March 20th, 1908, at the annual Ratepayers' meeting, it was decided to cancel semi-annually one-fourth of the opium den licences in the International Settlement. By December 31st, 1909, all were to be closed.

The sequel of the story of a movement characterized at first with great enthusiasm is somewhat discouraging and may briefly be narrated.

During the period of the Revolution in 1911, there was a recrudescence in the planting of the poppy. Under the Republic the evil of smuggling increased, and during the course of civil war, the cultivation of the poppy in many parts of China was encouraged rather than discountenanced by the militarists, as it was a source of revenue.

In recént years the National Anti-Opium Association has carried on a vigorous crusade, in the hope of rousing the whole country to the evils caused by opium.[1]

Other Reforms Many other reforms were projected at this period, and a promise of constitutional government was held out to the people.   In September, 1907, a National Assembly was constituted, and in the following month provincial Consultative Assemblies were created.   These were to be training schools for parliamentary government which was to have come into existence in 1917.

Death of Emperor Kwang Hsu and of the Empress Dowager In November, 1908, the Empress Dowager, Tzu-hsi, died at the age of seventy-three, her death being preceded twenty hours earlier by that of the Emperor, Kwang Hsu.   The removal of this strong and capable, but unscrupulous woman, left no one competent to steer the ship of state through the stormy days to come, and thus prepared the way for the Revolution.

Opposition to Settlement Extension We will turn now to the consideration of another way in which the new spirit of nationalism displayed by the students, manifested itself—namely by blocking all measures for the further expansion of the Settlements.

They did not want to increase the authority of the Municipal Council, but to curtail it as far as possible.

The attention of the Chinese became fixed on the gradual and irresistible penetration of foreign influence into Chinese territory, which in the eyes of foreigners was justified on the ground of necessity.   Foreign mills, factories and residences had been erected outside the settlement boundaries with the tacit consent of the

---

[1] The Nationalist Government in Nanking in October, 1928, issued stringent laws for the suppression of opium.

Chinese authorities, and roads had been constructed, connecting them with the Settlement.

Dispute over Roads outside Settlement

The question arose of supplying these localities with water and electricity, and of policing the roads and keeping them in repair. The Council had granted the Shanghai Waterworks Company authority to extend its mains into the outlying districts, but at the same time had made a regulation that those using the water supply should pay rates and taxes.

The Chinese objected vigorously to the extension of Municipal jurisdiction, and gave as their reasons that "a Chinese Works Bureau for Chapei was to be established, which would be competent to supply the residents of that district with water and electricity, and would take over the policing and repairing of the roads."

When the authorities in Chapei, in pursuance of the plan to establish a Chinese Works Bureau, trained a constabulary, and stationed police on the roads, occasions for conflict between the Municipal and Chapei police became frequent.

Council Seeks for Further Extension of Settlement

Finally the relations between the Municipal and the local Chinese authorities became so strained that the Council formally addressed the Consular Body, asking it to support the Council's proposal "that all the lands lying between the Settlement and the railway line be incorporated within municipal limits and made liable to administration under the Land Regulations." Among the reasons given by the Council for this extension were the following: "the nominal boundary of the Settlement on the north is for practical purposes eliminated, merely threading its way through continuous house property and if the authority of the municipal police were limited by this, the difficulties of detective and patrol work would be almost insuperable, and a large proportion of the land in question has been registered under the Land Regulations," the fact that land outside the Settlement boundary cannot be taxed, while land within can be, puts an unequal burden on the shoulders of the residents in the Settlement.

The Shanghai-Nanking Railway line was proposed as the most suitable boundary for the extension, owing to the absence of any natural barrier.

The Consular Body addressed the Nanking Viceroy on the subject, asking him to appoint the Shanghai Taotai or some other official with whom it could enter into negotiations. The Viceroy refused to discuss the matter and pointed out that the area of extension granted in 1899 amounted "to over 21,500 *mow,* which in comparison with the English and American Settlements as originally fixed, amounted to an addition of twice the size. The object of fixing the extension on this exceptionally liberal scale was that the measure might be an entirely permanent one, and that therefore there might be no further extension."

Furthermore the Viceroy reiterated the unwillingness of the Chinese to contemplate the possibility of even a portion of the Paoshan *hsien* being included in the Settlement.

On August 21st, 1909, the Consular Body addressed the Viceroy a second time, adding further arguments for extension, showing that it would be advantageous not for the foreigners alone, but also for the Chinese. It was stated that out of 53,000 houses in the International Settlement, only 3,000 were owned by foreigners, while 50,000 were owned by Chinese.

The Viceroy remained firm and declined to discuss the matter further, and the Consular Body decided to appeal to the Ministers in Peking, but all negotiations were for

12

a time brought to a standstill by the Chinese Revolution, which broke out in 1911.

Continued Friction over Construction of Roads

Meantime the causes of friction continued, especially in regard to the construction and control of roads outside the settlement limits.

The Council based its right of unlimited construction of roads beyond the settlement limits on Land Regulation VI of 1898, which reads as follows: "It shall be lawful for the land-renters, and others who may be entitled to vote as hereinafter mentioned, in public meeting assembled, to purchase land leading or being out of the Settlement, or to accept land from foreign or native owners upon terms to be mutually agreed upon between the Council and such foreign or native owners, for the purpose of converting the same into roads or public gardens and places of recreation and amusement, and it shall be lawful for the Council from time to time to apply such portion of the funds raised under Article IX of these Regulations, for the purchase, creation, and maintenance of such roads, gardens, etc., as may be necessary and expedient. Provided always that such roads and gardens shall be dedicated to the public use, and for the health, amusement and recreation of all persons residing within the Settlement."

Foreign Policing of Roads outside the Settlement

The foreign policing of the roads goes back to 1884, when, on account of the disturbed condition of the country during the war between China and France, the Council determined to give some protection to the residents outside of the Settlement. Sixteen Sikh constables were engaged to police the Bubbling Well and other roads, and these measures did not at that time meet with opposition on the part of the Chinese, and the policing of the roads after the country had quieted down was continued for some time without protest from the local authorities.

Chinese Police on the Roads outside the Settlement
The Taotai in 1907 claimed that the Chinese police had the right of functioning on the outside roads constructed and owned by the Council according to Land Regulation VI, and the Chinese authorities laid particular stress on the fact that "in localities outside the Settlement all matters affecting law uniformly revert to the control of the Chinese Police Bureau, and the Mixed Court, and the Municipal Council cannot encroach or interfere. If therefore there is land owned by foreigners, it enjoys, together with the native population, the advantages which accrue from the Chinese Police Bureau within the powers of which it is situated, and must therefore, in like manner acknowledge the police regulations of the place."

This position theoretically was strong, in spite of the claim that the protection of foreign property by the Chinese police was inefficient and unreliable.

In 1908 the Taotai protested against the filling of the Shanghai-Paoshan boundary creek and construction thereon of a road, although the construction of such a road was for the public benefit.

Protest and counter-protests were the order of the day.

Friction in Regard to Rights of Native Press
There was still a further cause of friction, full of interest, especially when we compare its earlier and later developments. This was in regard to the Native Press.

The first Chinese newspaper published in Shanghai was the *Shun Pao* (the *Shanghai Journal*), which appeared in 1872. It was succeeded in 1880 by the *Hu Pao*, the Chinese edition of the *North-China Daily News*, which soon discontinued publication, the *Sin Wan Pao* (the *New News Journal*) in 1893, and the *Shih Pao* (the *Eastern Times*) in 1904. The first three papers were founded originally by foreigners, and registered as foreign companies.

They all enjoyed the freedom of the press and naturally were unrestrained in their utterances in regard to political affairs. During the period 1902-1907, when the anti-monarchical movement in China assumed serious proportions, they exerted a powerful influence on public opinion, and the Central Government made strenuous efforts to suppress them.

In their endeavour to close up the premises of certain newspapers printing seditious and libellous articles, the Chinese authorities acted contrary to the Municipal Regulations and attempted to carry out their purpose without holding a trial of the accused at the Mixed Court. Against this method of procedure the Council vigorously protested, and would not allow the premises of the newspapers to be sealed, until the cases had been given a proper trial in the Mixed Court.

In one instance, the *Shun Pao* case of 1903, six editors might have been summarily executed, without an opportunity to prove their innocence, had it not been that the Council insisted on the legal method of procedure.

The Council realized that in affording protection to newspaper editors it incurred the danger of making the Settlement a place where the liberty of the press might be greatly abused, and saw the necessity of a bye-law for licensing the native press, so that it might be brought under a reasonable amount of control. This early effort was, however, unsuccessful. At a later period, as we shall see, the Council endeavoured again to obtain authority to license the native press, not because of the printing of seditious articles and attacks on the Chinese Government, but because of its agitation against the Municipal Council, and its anti-foreign propaganda.

During the period we have been describing, the following events of importance to the Municipality occurred.

Establishment of the United States Court   On December 15th, 1906, the United States, following the example of Great Britain in founding a Supreme Court, established in Shanghai the United States Court for China.   L. R. Wilfley was appointed as the first Judge, and as soon as he assumed office, a determined effort was made to close up the houses of prostitution on Kiangse Road, conducted by American women.   The existence of these houses, carrying on business contrary to the laws of the United States, had injured the reputation of Americans in the Far East, and had become a matter of national reproach.   Judge Wilfley's vigorous crusade against these houses, and his programme of moral reform, was of course unpopular with certain vested interests, and consequently he became the mark for severe criticism.   Others were alienated by the fact that he acted more as a prosecuting attorney than as a judge, and were of the opinion that he might have produced the desired results in a less sensational manner.

He became so unpopular that libellous articles were printed about his personal character in one of the Shanghai dailies, the *Shanghai Gazette*.   This led to a suit for libel, and Shanghai had the novelty of seeing the Judge of the United States Court bringing a charge against the editor of the *Shanghai Gazette* before the Judge of H.B.M.'s Supreme Court.   Although he won his suit, it was felt by American citizens that the prestige of the United States Court had for the time been somewhat lowered.

Chinese Company of the S. V. C.   In 1906, two new Companies, the Portuguese and the American, were added to the Volunteer Corps, and in the following year a Company of Chinese Volunteers was incorporated.   This last named Company has won an excellent name for efficiency in drill and in marksmanship, and under difficult circumstances has proved loyal to the interests of the Settlement. It is an example of successful co-operation between the foreigners and Chinese, and it is to be regretted that experiments of this character have not been tried more frequently.

Centenary Conference of Missions An event of importance to the missionary community occurring in 1907, was the holding of a large Conference in Shanghai. It was known as the Centenary Conference in recognition of the fact that one hundred years had elapsed since Dr. Robert Morrison arrived in Canton, as the pioneer of Protestant Missions in China.

Threat of Bubonic Plague Shanghai in the year 1910 was threatened with the spread of the bubonic plague which was carried to Shanghai by rats from the ships. If it had obtained a footing in some of the congested districts in which the Chinese dwelt, the consequences would have been disastrous. Strict precautionary measures were taken by the Municipal Council, but at first it was difficult to get the Chinese to co-operate. They objected to the house-to-house inspection carried on by the health authorities, and to the introduction of means to make the native houses rat-proof. When the Council wished to put in force strict regulations in regard to members of the family not being allowed to conduct the usual funeral ceremonies, in cases where the deceased had died of plague, it came into conflict with the strongest religious sentiment of the Chinese people, and was obliged to modify its ruling. The Chinese, however, became aware, after an educational propaganda, of the seriousness of the danger, and their obstructive attitude to a large extent disappeared.

In June, 1911, a Chinese Isolation Hospital was opened in Chapei under the auspices of the Chinese gentry, the chief reason for its establishment being to care for cases of bubonic plague.

Famine Relief The residents of Shanghai have always been noted for their generosity in times of distress, and in the years 1910 and 1911 we find them responding liberally to appeals put out by the Central China Famine Relief Committee for funds to meet the dire need caused by the famine in North Kiangsu and North Anhwei. China is a country of periodic famines, due to frequent floods or droughts.

Opening of the Shanghai Club, and Municipal Development The early part of the year 1911 was marked by the opening of the new Shanghai Club on January 6th by Sir Pelham Warren. The difficulties encountered in the early days, to which we have referred, had long been surmounted, and the Club had become one of the strongest institutions in Shanghai. The new building was one of the finest erected on The Bund up to that time. Its total cost was about Tls. 450,000. The erection of this heavy structure was rendered possible by the introduction of a new feature in construction, the use for the first time of a concrete raft for the foundation.

The soil of Shanghai is of delta formation, and water is met at the depth of about eight feet. On this account, in the early days, foundations were laid on wooden piles driven into the ground. And for a long time it was considered impracticable to erect high and heavy buildings. The new method of using concrete rafts has made it possible to put up buildings approaching in appearance the sky-scrapers in Western lands.

In the same year a new fire station was opened at Sinza by the Council, and land was purchased on the corner of Foochow and Kiangse Roads in anticipation of the erection of a new Municipal Building and Headquarters for the Volunteers

The
Rubber
"Boom"
In the years 1909-1910 Shanghai passed through what is known as the "rubber boom." During the six or seven months the boom lasted, some thirty-five local rubber companies, absorbing capital of some twenty million taels, were added to the list of the Shanghai Stock Exchange, and a further large amount was paid locally for shares in London companies. It was a period of wild speculation. The crash came with the June settlement of 1910, and some of the leading Chinese banks in Shanghai and other centres were forced to close their doors.

There was also considerable speculation in opium, owing to the restriction of the amount imported into Shanghai, and the consequent enhanced value of the drug.

Trade
Statistics
Notwithstanding the disasters owing to over-speculation, we find that the imports and exports of China in 1910 reached a higher figure than in 1901, which up to that time had been the highest recorded.

Imports . . .	Hk.Tls. 462,964,894
Exports . . .	380,833,328
Total . . .	Hk.Tls. 843,798,222

The higher values of opium and cotton help to account for this increase, in which Shanghai had, of course, a large share.

CHAPTER XX.

SHANGHAI DURING THE REVOLUTION, 1911.

The Revolution in China, resulting in the overthrow of the Manchu Dynasty in 1911, was a turning point in the history of China, with far-reaching consequences.

Before speaking of the Revolution, and its effects upon Shanghai, we must refer briefly to some events of the earlier part of the year 1911.

First Aeroplane in Shanghai The interest of the residents was attracted to the advances made in the navigation of the air by some exhibitions of flying given in April by M. Vallon at Kiangwan. His successful flight over Shanghai in an aeroplane was considered at that time as a remarkable feat. Unfortunately, this bold airman lost his life the following month while giving an exhibition of fancy flying over the Recreation Ground during the Spring Race Meeting.

Celebration of the Coronation of King George V. On June 22nd the coronation of King George V. was celebrated with great enthusiasm. The ships in the harbour were dressed, solemn services were held in the churches, and sports were held on the Recreation Ground. At night there were a torchlight procession, and fireworks. It was another occasion of the display of international goodwill, as all Shanghai united in the festivities.

National Schools This year also saw the development of national schools in Shanghai. A German School was opened on April 23rd on Weihaiwei Road, and a French Municipal School for foreign children on Avenue Joffre on September 25th.

Shanghai is a cosmopolitan city, and its residents sometimes refer to themselves as "Shanghailanders."

Nevertheless, national spirit is strong, and parents able to afford it prefer to have their children educated in schools where a national influence can be exerted. The British led the way, as the Cathedral School from the beginning was practically a national school. The Germans and French followed, and later, national schools were developed by Americans and Japanese.

A commission, appointed by the Shanghai Municipal Council in 1910 to study the whole matter of education in the Settlement, rendered its report on June 16th, 1911. One of the questions considered was that of assisting national schools by municipal grants. On this point there was some difference of opinion, and the Council adhered to its former policy of helping only those schools open to children of all nationalities.

Golf An undertaking of much interest to a large section of Shanghai residents at this time was the decision of the Shanghai Golf Club to lease land from the International Recreation Club at Kiangwan. Hitherto golfers had been limited to a nine-hole course on the Recreation Ground within the Race Course, but the new agreement permitted the laying out of an eighteen-hole course. To anticipate a little, the links at Kiangwan were formally opened on Saturday, November 30th, 1912, the President of the Club, Sir Haviland de Sausmarez, at that time Judge of H.B.M.'s Supreme Court for China, driving the first ball. Later, other golf courses were opened—one at Hungjao in the western district, and another at Seekingjao, two miles beyond the links at Kiangwan.

The Revolution Coming to the subject of this chapter, great excitement in Shanghai was caused in October by the unexpected news of the outbreak of a revolution in Wuchang, which had as its aim the overthrow of the Manchu Dynasty.

There were many causes contributing to this violent upheaval, among which may be mentioned—the weakness and inefficiency of the Regent, who guided the country during the minority of the young Emperor, Hsuan Tung, the poverty and distress caused by the continued famine in Central China, the plottings of secret societies, and the propaganda carried on by the emissaries of Dr. Sun Yat-sen. Among the immediate causes were the unpopularity of the Four-Nation Loan, and the policy of nationalizing the railways.

The Revolution broke out prematurely on October 9th, 1911. This was due to the fact that by an accidental explosion, a secret bomb factory was discovered in the Russian Concession in Hankow, and the revolutionists were forced to act quickly. They were supported by public opinion and by a mutiny of local troops, and without encountering any determined opposition, gained control of Wuchang, Hankow, and Hanyang. General Li Yuan-hung was persuaded, against his own will, to put himself at the head of the movement. Troops were despatched from the North to put down the uprising, and in the latter part of October, Hankow was recaptured by the Imperialist forces, and partly destroyed by incendiary fires. The fall of Hanyang followed, and it looked as if the Revolution would be crushed in its cradle.

In the meantime, however, the movement spread throughout the country, and city after city declared its independence. Fourteen out of the eighteen provinces threw off the Manchu yoke.

Shanghai went over to the Revolution without any fighting on November 4th. The outward evidence was the sudden appearance of white flags on all houses and shops, especially on Nanking Road.

Delegates gathered in Shanghai on November 22nd to take steps for the formation of a new government.

As an offset to the loss of Hankow and Hanyang, Nanking was captured, after severe fighting, by the revolutionary army on December 1st.

The Manchu Government was obliged to recall Yuan Shih-kai, who had been living in retirement, as the one man strong enough to cope with the situation. It was finally arranged that a conference should be held in Shanghai, and Tang Shao-yi was appointed as representative of the Peking Government with full powers. He arrived in Shanghai on December 18th, 1911, and the Peace Conference began. The principal representative of the Revolutionary Government was Dr. Wu Ting-fang. After long deliberations and contrary to the wishes of Yuan Shih-kai, the chief demands of the revolutionary party were granted, and a national convention was summoned to meet in Nanking.

Dr. Sun Yat-sen, who had been the head of the movement against the Manchus for many years, and in consequence had been exiled from his country, returned to assume the leadership of the Revolution at the psychological moment. He arrived in Shanghai in company with his military adviser, General Homer Lea, and his staff, on December 24th, and on January 1st, 1912, was inaugurated in Nanking as the first President of the Provisional Government of the new Republic.[1]

Political Importance of Shanghai   Shanghai, as we have pointed out, began as a commercial city and then became a manufacturing centre, and at the time of the Revolution increased in importance from the political point of view.

Owing to the fact that it was governed by the representatives of foreign Powers, and during internal troubles adopted the policy of strict neutrality, it became a place of

---

[1] Later on, in order to bring about union between the North and the South, he resigned in favour of Yuan Shih-kai.

safety for political refugees, and also neutral ground where representatives of different factions could meet for conferences. The Chinese sometimes bring forward as an argument for the return of the Settlement to the Chinese Government the fact that it affords an asylum for political refugees, but they fail to bear in mind that it has also been a harbour of safety for a multitude of peace-loving people during times of disorder and confusion.

Among the reasons for the growing political importance of Shanghai are the great wealth of its Chinese merchants, who can be taxed to contribute to government funds; the location of the arsenal on its outskirts, and the revenue that can be derived from the illicit smuggling of opium into China, through Shanghai as a doorway.

The Effects of the Revolution on Shanghai In attempting to measure the effects of the Revolution on Shanghai, we must bear in mind that while it indicated a spirit of progress among the Chinese, at the same time it made possible the outbreak of a spirit of lawlessness. All authority for a time broke down, and the disorderly elements of society took advantage of this state of affairs.

As might have been expected, the leaders of the Revolution, filled with the ambition to restore the rights of China, adopted a more obstructive policy towards the extension of the Settlements than their predecessors. **Dispute between S.M.C. and Chapei Authorities** There was further friction in regard to the Municipal policing of the roads outside the Settlement, and the numbering of the houses, and several conflicts took place between the Municipal and the Chapei police.

The Chapei Water and Electricity Works Company, which had been established by the Chinese in October, 1911, made application for permission to lay mains across North Szechuen Road Extension, both sides of the road being Chinese territory. Inasmuch as the Council had entered into an agreement with the Shanghai Waterworks Company for the supply of water throughout "all the roads and other lands under the control of the Council within and without the Settlement," the Council was obliged to comply with the request. The Council was sued in the Court of Consuls, and the following judgment was given. "In the opinion of the Court, the furtherance of monopoly is directly contrary to the provisions of the treaties between China and the Powers and could not be legally countenanced by the Court, nor should be by the Chinese authorities. On these grounds the judgment was entered against the Council, which was bound by the Court to issue the necessary permit, while the Chapei Water and Electricity Works Company was ordered to enter into an undertaking with the Council, not to prevent, hinder, or interfere with in any way, except by legitimate competition, the operation of the Shanghai Waterworks Company, to the east of North Szechuen Road." [1]

Reorganization of Mixed Court Another very important result of the Revolution was in regard to the administration and reorganization of the Mixed Court.

When the Revolution broke out in Shanghai, the Mixed Court was closed. Two of the Magistrates fled, taking with them all the funds deposited by the litigants with the Court, and leaving the Mixed Court organization

---

[1] The Council in refusing to grant the permit was moved by another consideration, namely, the taxation of the houses beyond the limit of the Settlement was effected by means of the terms of the Waterworks Concession agreement.

In regard to the contention that the strip of land across the Municipal road belonged to the Chinese authorities, the following judgment was given, "neither party having satisfied the court of absolute ownership or of right to exercise the same over the crossing of the two roads, the dispute must be decided on broad grounds of equity." See *Shanghai—Its Municipality and the Chinese*: A. M. Kotenev, p. 66.

in a chaotic condition.   It was necessary that something should be done promptly to re-establish the Court, and it was decided that it should be taken over by the Consular Body, and a notification to that effect was issued on November 10th, 1911. In regard to the financial support of the Court, the Consular Body requested the Council to pay all Mixed Court expenses, wages, and salaries, exclusive of the Magistrates' salaries; to receive all fines for the above purpose; to create a separate financial office at the Mixed Court under the direction of a special officer of the Council's staff.

Further it was determined that Assessors should sit in Civil as well as in Criminal Cases, inasmuch as it was felt that the former, as well as the latter, had a bearing on the welfare of the Settlement.

The powers of the Court were extended, and jurisdiction was asserted over the roads owned by the Municipal Council.

Naturally the Republican authorities were not pleased with this arrangement. Exception was taken especially to the sitting of Assessors in Civil Cases, and considerable difficulty arose over the fact that there was no Court of Appeal from the judgments of the Mixed Court.

Increase in Kidnapping With the breakdown in authority to which we have referred, we find at this period a great increase in kidnapping and in the number of young girls sold into slavery. The Mixed Court in dealing with these cases, as a means of saving some of the children, continued the practice of handing them over to the "Door of Hope." This institution had been founded in 1900 by some missionary ladies of the International Settlement for the care of girls who wished to give up life in the brothels. It had its first house on Chekiang Road and a home for children in Kiangwan.

The name of Miss C. Bonnel will long be remembered with this charitable work of mercy.

At the same time an institution, known at first as " The Slave Refuge," was founded by Mrs. F. R. Graves and some of the community ladies of the Settlement. It had as its object the rescue of slave girls rather than of prostitutes. For some time it was under the charge of Deaconess M. T. Henderson. After it was amalgamated with the "Door of Hope," Deaconess Henderson founded "St. Faith's Settlement" on Jessfield Road.

Disappearance of Queues Among other changes which came with the Revolution we may mention the disappearance of the queue. It was considered as a badge of submission to the Manchus and a Presidential mandate ordered its removal. Many of the country people, however, were most unwilling to part with this appendage, and strenuously resisted the regulation. At the city gates of Shanghai, barbers with shears were stationed, and those wearing the queue were forcibly seized and shorn. The reform was carried out in much the same way as Peter the Great disposed of the long beards in Russia.

Demolition of City Wall The demolition of the city wall was decided on, as it was looked upon as a relic of mediavalism, out of keeping with modern China. The work was immediately taken in hand, but at first went on haltingly, owing to lack of funds. The whole wall disappeared during the course of the year and was replaced by a broad boulevard. It is now difficult for a stranger to distinguish the boundary between the French Concession and the native city.

Other Changes The solar calendar was adopted, but did not displace altogether the old lunar calendar, and the attempt to do away with the old China New Year was not a success. It was difficult for the merchants to anticipate by about a month's time the date of their final settlement of accounts. Moreover it was not easy to change by an official proclamation a custom which had existed for centuries.

With the Revolution there sprang into existence a very large number of publications, newspapers and magazines, for the purpose of spreading modern ideas.

A tramway was constructed in Nantao, an Industrial Exhibition was held in Chang Su Ho's Garden in August, 1912, and an Engineering Department was established in connection with Nanyang College—all testifying to the dawning of a new day.

The old picturesque dragon flag entirely disappeared and in its place the streets were gay with the new five barred flag adopted by the Republican Government, symbolizing the union of the five peoples, the Chinese, Manchus, Mongols, Turkestanese, and Thibetans.

Some Other Things of Importance Occurring at this Time The educational facilities for the Chinese were increased by the opening of the Ellis Kadoorie Public School on November 25th, the land being furnished by the Council and the money for the building by Mr. (afterwards Sir) Ellis Kadoorie.

A change of considerable interest to the community took place in connection with the General Hospital. The Sisters of Charity of St. Vincent de Paul decided in 1912 to withdraw from service, partly on account of the difficulties created by religious troubles in France, and partly because it was felt by the Heads of the Mission that the time given to the Hospital had been to the detriment of the missionary work of the Sisters. The community was indebted to them for their fifty years of devotion to this work of caring for the sick of Shanghai. It was promised that l'Institute des Soeures Franciscaines should carry on, and the Mother Superior in Rome expressed her willingness to send out thirty Sisters within two years, and nine afterwards—if necessary—to undertake the work.

Plans for the alteration and extension of the Hospital were made and the work taken in hand.

Some Philanthropic Movements There are many blind in China and little or nothing has been done by the Chinese people to alleviate the misery of their lot. For the most part, fortune-telling is their only means of earning a livelihood.

On March 11th, 1911, there was founded in Shanghai an Institution for the Chinese Blind, by the generosity of the late Dr. John Fryer, who furnished a permanent endowment of Tls. 50,000, and gave an additional Tls. 10,000 for buildings and equipment. The institution was first located in temporary premises on North Szechuen Road Extension and opened with eight students. Later it was moved to Edinburgh Road where the work is now carried on very efficiently by Mr. and Mrs. George B. Fryer.

The first missionary work for the blind in Shanghai —the Chinese Blind Asylum—was started by the Rev. Edward W. Syle, one of the early missionaries of the American Episcopal Church Mission, as long ago as 1858, and has been continued up to the present time. It is, however, more of the nature of a charitable than of an educational enterprise.

In June, 1913, a meeting was held at the residence of Dr. J. M. W. Farnham to devise means of helping the ricsha coolies. Mr. George Matheson reported that at that time there were more than 30,000 ricsha coolies plying for hire in the Settlements, and that the conditions under which they lived were pitiable in the extreme. They were crowded in small houses, from 10 to 15, at one time, sleeping in a room. As the men were exposed to all kinds of weather, their occupation was full of hardship, and often resulted in the shortening of their lives. The investigation carried on by a committee appointed at this meeting, led to a Mission to Ricshamen being formed, and Mr. George Matheson became the Honorary Secretary. Under his efficient management, religious, educational and social activities of great value to this class of workers have been conducted in various localities. The generous response made annually to the Christmas appeal in the *North-China Daily News* for the ricsha coolie is an evidence that the undertaking has gained the confidence of the community, and has become a popular charity.

CHAPTER XXI.

THE SECOND REVOLUTION, 1913.

What is generally referred to as the second revolution broke out in the summer of 1913. It might better be called a rebellion, as it was a revolt against the government established by Yuan Shih-kai.

Dissatisfaction with Yuan Shih-kai The members of the Kuomintang, or Citizen's Party, were dissatisfied with President Yuan and accused him of planning to make himself dictator.

Seditious articles appeared in the Chinese newspapers, calling on the people to rise and to overthrow his government, and it became necessary for the Shanghai Municipal Council on May 2nd to issue a warning to the native press.

One of the causes of dissatisfaction was the arrangement for a loan by the Government with the Sextuple Group (reduced to five after the withdrawal of the United States). It was claimed that according to the provisional constitution this loan should first have received the approval of Parliament, but that it had never been submitted to that body for consideration.

The murder of Sung Chiao-jen on March 20th in the Shanghai North Station of the Shanghai-Nanking Railway, was regarded as an act of treachery on the part of the Government. Mr. Sung, a young Hunanese, was an active member of the Kuomintang, and was destined by his supporters to become Premier. There was strong evidence that his murder was instigated from Peking so as to remove him from the political stage.

The hand of Peking was also seen in the removal of Mr. Y. C. Tong from the directorship of the Chinese

Telegraphs in Shanghai, in order that the control might be obtained by the authorities in Peking.

Outbreak of Rebellion at Wuchang

The rebellion, like the first Revolution, broke out in Wuchang, but was suppressed at that centre by General Li Yuan-hung, Vice-President of the Republic. At the same time it spread along the Yangtze, and Huang Hsin, one of the leaders in the Revolution of 1911, raised the standard of revolt in Nanking, which led to a long siege of that city by the troops from the North.

Trouble in Shanghai

On July 20th an attempt was made within the Settlement on the part of the revolutionists to seize the Telegraphs. This was resisted by the Municipal police, as military operations within the Settlement were a violation of its neutrality.

As early as May 29th a futile attack was made by 70 men on the arsenal at Shanghai, with the expectation that the troops at Lunghua would mutiny and come to their assistance. When this did not happen, the attempt collapsed.

In marked contrast with the first Revolution, the Chinese mercantile community of Shanghai withheld financial support, as it was anxious for peace, and unwilling to pass through another long period of confusion.

Admiral Tseng Ju-cheng was appointed by the Peking Government to control the Shanghai district and to hold it against the rebels. He succeeded in ousting from the arsenal 1,000 Chekiang troops of whom he felt doubtful and in replacing them by 1,500 of his own men, and proceeded to put the arsenal into a state of defence.

Bombardment of the Arsenal

On Wednesday, July 23rd, at three o'clock in the morning, the rebels began the bombardment of the arsenal from three points, Nantao, St. Catherine's Bridge, and Lunghua, and this was resumed on Wednesday, Thursday, and Friday nights.

There was a cessation of hostilities Saturday and Sunday nights, but on Monday night of the following week the bombardment was renewed with double fury.   One of the Chinese cruisers on the Whangpoo was struck.   As the firing from the ships was somewhat wild, some of the shells fell in the Settlements and on The Bund, and caused considerable consternation.   A lighter in the harbour was sunk and a Portuguese boy in the Public Gardens was wounded.

The week was a nerve racking one for Shanghai. The nightly bombardment started at eight o'clock and continued till the early hours of morning, and the screaming of shells passing overhead, with the noise of the machine guns and rifles, made sleep impossible.

Taking over of Chapei by the Council   The Shanghai Volunteers were kept under arms and had but little rest.   On July 26th the Municipal Council made a declaration of the strict neutrality of the Settlement, Chapei, and the Soochow Creek.   Chapei was included, although Chinese territory, because a number of Chapei residents appealed to the Council to take temporary control of that area.

This became necessary after General Chen Chi-mei, in command of the attacking forces, moved his headquarters from Nantao to Chapei, for if Chapei had been used as the base of hostilities, the International Settlement would have been in great danger.

When Col. C. D. Bruce, Lt.-Col. A. S. Barnes and the Volunteers marched in to take possession, General Chen Chi-mei was forced to leave his headquarters in Chapei. He retired to Woosung and shortly afterwards disappeared.

There was considerable irresolution on the part of the Council over the occupation of Chapei, but finally the Police Station in that district was put under the control of 150 bluejackets from H.M.S. "Monmouth," who remained in possession until the district was formally returned to Admiral Tseng on August 17th. The occupation was resented by the Chinese as it was considered a prelude to annexation, inasmuch as they were aware that, in the proposed extension of the Settlement, a part of Chapei had been included.

Landing of Men from Ships in Harbour   During this critical period strong forces of British, German, Austrian and Italian sailors were landed and made a ring around the Settlement, joining hands with the French at Siccawei.   British bluejackets patrolled the Soochow Creek, to keep the rebels from coming into Shanghai by water.

Hostilities at Woosung   After the attempt on the arsenal failed, the scene of operations shifted to Woosung. The Commander of the Woosung Forts had been willing to surrender to Admiral Tseng, but the rebels had obtained possession of the forts and hoisted the rebel flag.

On August 2nd, the forts were unsuccessfully bombarded by the cruisers "Hai-chi" and "Hai-yung," and on August 6th the "Dare-to-die" regiment, although originally on the side of the rebels, attempted to seize the forts and hand them over to the Government. It was repulsed with great slaughter.

Battle at Kiangwan   When the government forces advanced to Kiangwan, the rebels from the Woosung Forts made a daring sortie and delivered a vigorous attack.   A battle was fought, in which the operations extended from the Kiangwan Railway Station to the International Race Course.   Some foreigners who came to see what was happening were caught between the fires and obliged to take refuge under the grand stand on the Race Course.   Others sought safety in the first bunker on the golf links which they found already occupied by some of the Northern troops.   After a struggle the rebels retired to Paoshan, and melted away into the surrounding country.

One of the last acts in the drama was an explosion on the government yacht "Lienching," which had been seized by the rebels at Woosung and loaded with bombs. Five men were killed and seven injured.

Fall of Nanking   Although the rebellion had been suppressed in Shanghai, the siege of Nanking continued.   It lasted from August 14th to September 1st. With the fall of that city into the hands of General Chang Hsün, this attempt to overthrow Yuan Shih-kai's government came to an end.

On the whole the sympathy of the residents of Shanghai was with the Government.   They could see no evidence of the ability of the rebels to establish a better *régime* than the one they plotted to overthrow, and feared that their success would result in an increase of turbulence rather than in a period of peace.

CHAPTER XXII.

SHANGHAI DURING THE FIRST YEARS OF THE GREAT WAR, 1914–1916.

At the beginning of the year 1914, the residents of Shanghai had no intimation of the storm brewing in Europe. Still less did they realize that a war would be waged for four long years, which would affect the whole world, politically, socially, and industrially.

Shanghai felt the great struggle in many ways, but it was among the few places where outwardly the direct influences of the war were but little in evidence, and where life on the whole went on much in the same way as if the peace of the nations had not been disturbed.

We must first review some of the events of the early part of the year 1914.

Municipal Building The final completion of the plans of the new Municipal Building and their exhibition to the public, and the laying of the corner stone of the S.V.C. Drill Hall on April 4th, were of civic importance.

Jubilees The occurrence of certain jubilees during the year, such as those of the Shanghai Gas Company, the Mixed Court, and the *North-China Daily News*, witnessed to Shanghai's advance in years, and moved some of the older residents to reminiscences regarding early days.

The completion of fifty years of service by the *North-China Daily News* suggests a brief reference to the history of foreign journalism in Shanghai. The *North-China Herald* existed before the *North-China Daily News*. Its first number came out on August 3rd, 1850, and was a folio sheet of four pages, and gave a list of the fifty-nine foreign residents living in Shanghai at that time. The *North-China Daily News* appeared in 1864, and at first was intended to contain little more than shipping and commercial news, but it gradually developed into a newspaper, the *North-China Herald* becoming the weekly edition.

Among the early editors who had much to do with making the *Daily News* the leading paper in the Far East, may be mentioned Mr. R. S. Gundry, Mr. F. S. Balfour, and Mr. R. W. Little.

Other papers published at an early date, which had more than a transient existence, were the *Shanghai Recorder* and the *Shanghai Mercury*. The latter, which is still published, was issued first on April 17th, 1879, and for a long time was the only evening paper.

Two Murders In the early part of the year there were two ghastly acts of crime which aroused the Settlement to the existence of a dangerous element in its midst. The first was that of Mrs. Neumann on January 23rd, who was murdered by Chinese robbers in a most brutal manner in her home in Hongkew, and the second was that of Mr. Z. F. How, Manager of the Commercial Press, who was assassinated on Honan Road while stepping into his car. Mr. How had been among the residents in Chapei who had asked for protection from the Shanghai Municipal Council for that district, during the turbulent period of the second revolution, and, in the opinion of some, this led to his death.

A Statue to Sir Robert Hart The official unveiling on The Bund of a statue in memory of Sir Robert Hart took place on Monday, May 23rd. The statue has now (1928) been moved to a more suitable location opposite the new Customs Building. It is an excellent piece of work, and bears the following inscription:

"Sir Robert Hart, Bt., G.C.M.G., 1835-1911. Inspector-General of the Maritime Customs; Founder of the Chinese Lighthouse Service; Organizer and Administrator of the National Post Office; Trusted Councillor of the Chinese Government; True friend of the Chinese people; Modest, patient, sagacious and resolute, he overcame formidable obstacles and accomplished a work of great beneficence for China and the World."

A Great Municipal Improvement — At last after many years of controversy, it was decided at the Ratepayers' meeting held on June 11th to culvert the Yangking-pang, the creek between the International Settlement and the French Concession.   For many years the French authorities had advocated doing away with this waterway, but the Council of the International Settlement had been lukewarm, and had been inclined to dredge it instead of doing away with it entirely.   It was only navigable at high tide, and as it was a receptacle for sewerage, was both unsightly and offensive.   The Ratepayers voted a sum of Tls. 200,000 for the share of the International Settlement in culverting it and turning it into a broad boulevard, the present Avenue Edward VII.   The work was completed in 1916, and furnished the Settlements with another main artery of traffic running east and west, which to a certain extent has relieved the congestion on Nanking Road.   This fine boulevard connects with Avenue Foch and the Great Western Road.

Another municipal improvement of a different nature, was the rebuilding of the Hongkew Market in this same year.

Fall of Markham Road Bridge — On account of the dangerous condition of Markham Road Bridge, spanning the Soochow Creek, the Municipal Council in March closed it to vehicular traffic.   A controversy arose in regard to its reconstruction between the Chinese authorities on the Chapei side and the

Council. The proposal was made by the Council to co-operate with the Chinese authorities, each to pay half the cost of a new bridge. The Chinese were not satisfied with this arrangement and began to make plans for undertaking the work by themselves, giving as a reason, the protection of their sovereign rights. To this the Council replied, " that they would call the attention of the Chinese authorities to the fact that the bridge was the property of the Council, and that its repair by unauthorized persons will not be sanctioned."

The work of taking down the old structure was begun by the Council on June 28th, but during the course of the demolition the sag of the bridge increased, and the lower portion of the eastern girders snapped, with the result that half of the bridge fell into the creek, and three men were thrown into the water, one of whom was drowned.

A temporary bridge was erected by the Chapei authorities which later also proved unsafe, resulting in another accident caused by its collapse on July 23rd, 1927. Since that time another temporary bridge has been erected.

A previous collapse of a bridge in Shanghai occurred on May 1st, 1907, when the so-called Stone Bridge, which crossed the creek at the settlement boundary, gave way, precipitating a large number of people into the water. On that occasion some fifty persons were drowned. It will be remembered that this was the bridge over which the British troops crossed on their approach to Shanghai in 1842.

The Last Mail Gun On July 27th, 1914, the last mail gun, announcing the arrival of foreign mails, was fired from the Pootung Point. From that time this out-of-date custom ceased, and thus another old institution passed away.

Outbreak of the World War As we have said, the chief event of 1914 was the outbreak of the World War. When the news reached Shanghai on August 4th there was great excitement. At first considerable alarm was felt in regard to shipping, but this was considerably allayed when Japan, acting in accordance with the terms of the Anglo-Japanese Alliance, issued an ultimatum to Germany and demanded the evacuation of Kiaochow. As soon as the Japanese fleet was mobilized and began to patrol the China Sea, the menace to merchant ships disappeared. The German cruiser "Emden," however, managed to make its escape from Tsingtao and for many months committed ravages on British shipping in the South Seas until it was finally captured at Keeling Island.

The Japanese forces, aided by a small British contingent, began operations against Tsingtao. As the city was invested both by land and sea, its fate was inevitable, and after some resistance it capitulated on November 7th, and was occupied by the Japanese.

In Shanghai, as in other parts of the world, it was thought at first that the war would be of short duration, and no one imagined it was to be waged on a titanic scale and to continue until the belligerents were well-nigh exhausted.

When later it was realized that the war would last for some time, many young men left their business and volunteered for the front, and the women took up the work of making hospital supplies and comforts for the troops.

A difficult situation was created in a cosmopolitan Settlement like Shanghai, containing quite a large number of Germans and some Austrians. German trade and influence in China had gradually increased and Germany had become one of England's keenest competitors. One member of the Council was a German, and German

doctors were on the Board of the General Hospital.   It
became impossible under the circumstances for English
and Germans to work in harmony with one another, and
thus we find the Ratepayers refusing to elect again a
German on the Council or German doctors on the Board
of the General Hospital.   Social relationships became
strained, and clubs took steps to eliminate their German
members, ignoring sometimes strict legality.   The sinking of the " Lusitania " caused the same revulsion of
feeling against German methods of warfare in Shanghai
as in other parts of the world, and put an end to all
friendly relations between English and Germans.

Numerous war funds were started for the alleviation
of the suffering caused by the war, such as the Patriotic
Fund, the Prince of Wales' Fund, and the Fund for British
Mothers, and money was liberally contributed.

Settlement Extension   One of the results of the outbreak of the
war was, as we have stated, to side-track
once more the desired extension of the Settlement.

The French had succeeded in obtaining a considerable extension, taking in the land enclosed by the roads
they had constructed, and the Municipal authorities of
the International Settlement had been hopeful in regard
to taking in the Chapei district and Jessfield.   As all
such matters required the sanction of the Diplomatic
Body in Peking, an *impasse* occurred with the outbreak
of war.

Railless Cars   Railless cars were introduced into Shanghai
at this time, to care for the traffic across
town, and in this way to extend the service carried on by
the Shanghai Tramways.   From the beginning the cars
were popular, especially among the Chinese.

The Twenty-one Demands, 1915   The year 1915 was a critical one for China.
In the early months there was the long
discussion between representatives of the

Japanese Empire and the Chinese Government in regard to the "Twenty-one Demands." Japan was anxious to ensure that she should have the dominant control in China and took occasion, while the Great Powers were at war, to make this perfectly certain. As a result she stirred up much enmity, and lost the prestige she had secured. Her aggressive policy led to a boycott which seriously injured her trade.

Trade and Commerce The World War had considerable effect on the commercial life of Shanghai, and led to a rapid decline in business. Imports were affected more than exports. The principal difficulty in regard to the latter was the question of shipping, as merchant vessels of the Allies were needed for war purposes, and it was hard to arrange for the transportation of freight. Rates rose on account of the scarcity of shipping, and both Japan and America had an excellent opportunity for reaping a golden harvest by supplying the need.

British Chamber of Commerce In many ways the most important happening, commercially, as it affected foreign interests, was the formation of the British Chamber of Commerce on May 31st. In promoting co-operation among British merchants it supplied a need that had been felt for many years, and helped to stimulate British enterprise.

Railway Building Railway building came to a standstill, as the nations of Europe were unable to furnish the necessary capital, but one important line was finished by Chinese capital—that connecting Shanghai with Hangchow.

The main object of railway building in China was, of course, to promote commerce, but, in later years, the railways played an important part in civil warfare.

Municipal Undertakings The work on culverting the Yangkingpang proceeded throughout the year. Connected with it was the filling in of the Defence Creek, on the eastern boundary of the Race Course. It is interesting to recall the history of this waterway. It existed as a sluggish stream at the time of the Battle of Muddy Flat. Later, when Shanghai was in danger of being attacked by the Taipings, in 1861, it was decided to dig it out and make it a creek which might be defended, so that it would be difficult for the enemy to gain access to the Settlement from the west. After being filled in, it was converted into a wide road, and the old bridge known as Loongfei disappeared.

Looking to the future, the Council very wisely decided to purchase the property belonging to Mr. E. Jenner Hogg, opposite St. John's University at Jessfield, for the development of a new park for the western district. This park has become the most beautiful in Shanghai, and is noted for its landscape gardening and botanical features. In many ways it reminds one of Kew Gardens, laid out on a smaller scale.

Shanghai is fairly well supplied with public parks. In addition to those already mentioned, there are the attractive Hongkew and Wayside Parks, and several playgrounds for children.

Chinese Interest in Sports As an evidence of the change in the psychology of the Chinese, there was an increased interest in sports and athletic competitions. This new spirit had been fostered first in the Mission and later in the Government schools.

What is known as the Far Eastern Olympics was organized, at which selected teams from Japan, the Philippine Islands, and China competed in Field and Track and in other forms of sport. When it was arranged to hold the meet in Shanghai in 1916, the Council gave permission for the use of Hongkew Park. The competitions lasted from May 15th to 22nd, and attracted great crowds of spectators.

Unrest in
Shanghai

The latter part of the year 1915 was distinctly one of anxiety for Shanghai. There were signs of unrest in the Settlements, and indications that it was becoming more and more a haven for desperate characters, and a hatching ground for political plots. There were several bomb outrages, and a building was discovered in the French Concession in which bombs were stored. Importation of arms and ammunition was carried on on a large scale.

A strike occurred on December 3rd among ricsha coolies, caused by the policy adopted by the Shanghai Municipal Council of cutting down the number of ricsha licences. Ricshas were more numerous than necessary and many of them were in a dilapidated condition. The grievance of the ricsha coolies was due to the fact that the ricsha companies owning the ricshas, which they rented to the coolies, finding their income somewhat decreased, wished to charge the coolies more for hire than before. The strike lasted three days, and was accompanied by several acts of violence.

Nothing showed more clearly than the assassination of Admiral Tseng Ju-cheng on November 8th, the harbouring of undesirable characters in the Settlements. Admiral Tseng, it will be recalled, was in charge of the defence of Shanghai during the rebellion of 1913. Later, he had been appointed Defence Commissioner of Shanghai and Woosung, and Director of the Kiangnan Arsenal. While proceeding in his car to the Japanese Consulate on the occasion of the celebration of the coronation of the Emperor of Japan, a bomb was thrown, and immediately afterwards two men jumped on the footboards of the car and fired at him with their revolvers. His assassination

14

in the open daylight caused a good deal of excitement in the Settlement.

Shanghai was again stirred by an attack on the arsenal on December 6th and 7th. Some desperadoes on a launch sailed up the Whangpoo and by a clever ruse managed to board and take possession of the cruiser "Chao-ho" anchored off the arsenal. They then commanded the gunners on the ship to fire on the arsenal. The gunners, probably with intention, aimed high and some of the shells, instead of hitting the arsenal, fell in the Settlement, with the result that several houses were struck. Admiral Li, who was in command of the arsenal, ordered the rest of the fleet at anchor to manœuvre in such a way that they could fire on the "Chao-ho," and a few well placed shots caused the desperadoes to abandon their prize and take to boats in order to make their escape before the day dawned. It was probably expected that a general rising would take place in Shanghai at that time as the government of Yuan Shih-kai was unpopular among a large section of the people.

Other Events Looking back over 1915 we find several other events meriting at least a passing mention.

The last of the old bungalows facing The Bund, that belonging to Dent and Company, was sold and torn down at this period. It stood near the corner of Kiukiang Road and The Bund.

The death of a well-known lawyer, Mr. W. V. Drummond, who had resided in Shanghai for more than forty years, occurred on March 20th, at the age of seventy-three. Mr. Drummond had always taken an active interest in municipal affairs, as well as in the affairs of China generally. Under the *noms de plume* of "Sinophilus" and "Cosmos" he wrote several able pamphlets in regard to the political situation after the Chinese Revolution.

Census

Early in the year 1916, the returns of the census taken in October 1915 were published, of which the following is a summary.

The total number of Chinese in the International Settlement was 620,401. The total number of foreigners was 18,519, making a grand total of 638,920. The figures for the French Concession were, Chinese residents 146,595, and foreign residents 2,405. The grand total for the two Settlements was 787,920. It is difficult to estimate the exact number of Chinese living in the adjoining districts, but if these are added, it would make the population of the port of Shanghai at that time approximately 1,500,000.

A census is taken about once in five years, and when we compare the figures of 1915 with those of 1910, we find that there was an increase of 170,433, or a little over 34,000 per annum, the Chinese population having increased 164,521, and the foreign, 5,912. These figures include both the International Settlement and the French Concession.

Among the foreign residents, more than thirty nations were represented. The figures for the largest were as follows:

1.	Japanese	7,387
2.	British	5,521
3.	American	1,448
4.	German	1,425
5.	Portuguese	1,352

The following facts are significant. The Japanese doubled during five years, increasing from 3,466 to 7,387. In 1890 there were only 386 Japanese in the International Settlement. The British population increased only slightly during the five years, but this may be accounted for by the War, some 500 having gone home to join the colours. The Americans gained substantially, the figures being 959 in 1910, and 1,448 in 1915.

Of the Chinese population, 36,398 were in foreign employ in houses, offices, mills, etc. This figure does not represent the actual number engaged in such a way, as a very large proportion of the mill workers live outside the settlement boundaries.

Japanese Police   In connection with the rapid increase of the Japanese residents, mostly located on North Szechuen Road Extension, forming what was virtually a Japanese settlement, the Municipal Council was led to agree to the appointment of a certain number of Japanese constables on the Municipal Police Force, and in November, 1916, thirty Japanese police arrived in Shanghai, and, after a period of training, were appointed to service on North Szechuen Road Extension.

New Loop Railway   The War perforce put a stop to further railway building. One small piece of work, however, was carried out at that time which was of importance to the expansion of Shanghai. That was the completion of a loop to connect the Shanghai-Nanking Railway with the Shanghai-Hangchow-Ningpo Railway. A line ten and a quarter miles long was built from the Shanghai North Station of the former railway to the Lunghua Junction on the latter. The inaugural ceremony of opening the new line was held on December 9th, and the Engineer-in-chief, Mr. A. C. Clear, under whose direction the scheme had been carried out, received congratulations on the successful accomplishment of this important work.

It was thought that one of the results of the building of the line would be the further development of Jessfield as a residential district, and a good station was built at Jessfield of neat appearance and attractive design. Owing to the inadequacy of the train service, and the inconvenient situation of the North Station, the railway has not proved of much use to residents in this district.

Two Jubilees   In 1916 there were two jubilees. One of special importance was that of the Fire Brigade on Saturday, June 17th. The Brigade had become a modern and efficient force for fighting the fires, so frequent in the Settlement and vicinity, and it was fitting that the development of fifty years, with the splendid record of volunteer firemen during that time, should be celebrated by an inspection drill and a torchlight procession.

Another was that of St. Luke's Hospital in Hongkew, on November 25th. Started in a very small way, it had grown to be one of the two large hospitals under foreign auspices, for the benefit of the Chinese, the other being the Shantung Road Hospital (now the Lester Chinese Hospital).

Purchase of Ground for the U. S. Consulate   The fact that for many years the United States Government did not permit the purchase of land in a foreign country for the erection of embassies or consulates made it necessary for its representatives to rent premises, and they often found it difficult to secure quarters that were adequate and in keeping with the dignity of their country. These regulations were modified in such a way as to make it possible to purchase a site for the American Consulate in Shanghai in August, 1916, and the present very fine piece of property on Whangpoo Road was bought from Mr. Edward Ezra for the sum of Tls. 425,000. The buildings contained on it were remodelled to serve as the Consulate-General, the United States Court, and residences for the Consul-General and staff.

CHAPTER XXIII.

SHANGHAI AND THE LAST YEARS OF THE GREAT WAR, 1917–1918.

During the year 1917, several prominent
**Deaths of
Noted Chinese**
Chinese passed away. The death of Sheng
Hsuan-hwai (Kung-pao) occurred at his
residence on Bubbling Well Road on April 25th. He was
a man intimately connected with some of the most
important events of modern Chinese history. He had
a great deal to do with the development of the China
Merchants Steam Navigation Company and the Chinese
Telegraph Administration. Just before the Revolution,
he had been appointed Director-General of Railways, and
his policy of state control of railways had been one of the
immediate causes of the revolt in Szechuen and Central
China. In consequence of the failure of his policy he had
been cashiered by the Government and deprived of all his
offices and became one of the most unpopular men in China.
It was under his management that the Hanyang Iron and
Steel Works, Tayeh Iron Mines, Pinghsiang Collieries, and
Chuchow-Pinghsiang Railway had come into existence,
and he was also the founder of Nanyang College. He
accumulated enormous wealth, and it is estimated that the
elaborate funeral held in the following year, when the
coffin was sent to Soochow, cost Tls. 300,000.

One of the revolutionists, Chen Chi-mei, was assassinated in the French Concession on May 18th. He had been
Military Governor of Shanghai in 1911, and had been one
of the leaders of the rebellion of 1913, when the Kiangnan
Arsenal was attacked. After defeat, he sought safety in
Japan, but returned to Shanghai about two months before
he was murdered.

The last death happening at this time was that of Yuan Shih-kai on June 6th, his end probably being hastened by his chagrin over the failure of the plan to restore the monarchy and make himself Emperor of China.

Burning of the Opium
A spectacular event occurred toward the close of the year, in December, in Pootung, opposite the Public Gardens. The Chinese authorities, anxious to convince the world of their sincerity in dealing with the suppression of opium, committed to the flames 150 piculs of the drug, valued at half a million dollars, which had been seized by the Customs. Special furnaces were put up for the purpose and the holocaust was witnessed by officials and a small number of Europeans.

The United States Enters the War
The outstanding event connected with the Great War during this year was the entrance of the United States on the side of the Allies. During the first years of the struggle, the neutrality of the United States had created to a certain extent a feeling of estrangement between the British and American communities. It was difficult for Britishers to meet with what appeared to be a spirit of lukewarmness on the part of their American cousins, some of whom were suspected of having pro-German sympathies. After April, 1917, however, the atmosphere cleared, and the fact that American and Briton were fighting shoulder to shoulder on the battlefields of France was a source of mutual satisfaction.

Rupture between China and Germany
Then followed the breaking off of diplomatic relations between China and Germany, and the entry of China into the war on the side of the Allies against the Entente Powers. As a consequence all German and Austrian residents in Shanghai were obliged to register in the Town Hall, and their rights of extraterritoriality came to an end. The

Deutsch-Asiatische Bank on The Bund was closed, and placed in the hands of liquidators.

Three Austrian ships, the "China," "Bohemia," and "Siberia," were seized in the harbour of Shanghai. These, with the five German ships which had already been interned, made eight enemy vessels in all, and permission was granted for their employment by the Allies for war purposes.

The German Minister to China, Count von Hintze, and his staff passed through Shanghai early in the year, and after the declaration of war the Chinese Government contemplated sending all enemy nationals back to their homelands. The German Medical and Engineering School, situated in the French Concession, was closed, but was reopened at Woosung with a staff of 50 teachers and a student body of 600. This caused much dissatisfaction to the British residents of Shanghai, as they considered it a dangerous centre of propaganda, and a possible source of military danger.

Effects of the War

Week by week the war came home more closely to the people of Shanghai, especially as they scanned the list of Shanghai men killed at the front, which appeared from time to time in the *North-China Daily News'* Roll of Honour.

The various war funds continued to grow and the subscriptions to the China and Japan War Saving Association reached £578,798. 13. 4.

The Shanghai Volunteer Corps was able to keep up its enrolment by taking in fresh recruits to replace those who left for the front, but the foreign police force decreased from 284 to 180, and there was also a falling off of volunteers for the Fire Brigade.

The British Women's Work Association

The British Women's Work Association was opened in Shanghai on October 1st, 1914, and closed in December, 1919, and carried on a very remarkable work.

As time went on, the British women in twenty-four Treaty Ports joined the Association. Shanghai was the main centre of the work and all materials supplied by the Association were cut here and sent to the different outlying centres.

All contributions other than those of the Sock and Volunteer Supply Department were regarded as gifts to the Queen Mary's Needlework Guild and sent first to London, then to Mesopotamia and finally to Siberia, according to instructions given by Her Majesty.

The Sock and Volunteer Supply Department had a separate fund and gifts were sent direct to volunteers gone from China.

The Association was generously supported in Shanghai and elsewhere by subscriptions, donations and the proceeds of entertainments, etc. The total in Mexican dollars appearing in the Treasurer's accounts for the five years ending October, 1919, was $423,452.37. Of this approximately $70,000 was subscribed by the Treaty Ports and other places outside Shanghai. The Shanghai Race Club alone contributed $26,500.

In view of the very high silver rate prevailing during the last two years, when about two-thirds of the amount was raised, the value of the grand total in sterling could not have been much less than £100,000. The total expenses of the Association other than the purchase of material were $28,902.73, of which nearly two-thirds were expended on payment of Chinese work. It is thus obvious that a very large and incalculable amount of help was furnished gratis. There were no charges for premises, storage, insurance, shipping, clerical and other work.

The grand total of work accomplished amounted to 1,630,760 articles, more than one-third being garments, and the rest, bandages and surgical dressings.

At the close of the war, His Majesty, King George V., manifested his great appreciation of the Association's work by bestowing the honour of Dame of the Grand Cross of the British Empire on the President, Lady de Sausmarez, who had held the post throughout the five years.[1]

American Red Cross The American War Relief Association gave place to a chapter of the American Red Cross which was established at a meeting held in the Palace Hotel on March 8th. The American women vied with their British sisters in useful forms of war work.

Two work rooms were established, the output of which from March 8th, 1918, to May 1st, 1919, was as follows:

Bandages	203,177
Hospital Garments	29,722
Gauze Dressings	87,414
Hospital Supplies	21,102
Refugee Garments	10,757
Under-clothes	5,000

A Tea Room was opened, which added to the Red Cross Funds about a thousand dollars a month.

Shanghai contributed about $85,000 Mexican in the war drive conducted in the Settlements.

Shipbuilding The shipbuilding industry received great impetus from the War, about twenty-four ships being under construction. The Kiangnan Docks had a contract for four 10,000 ton ships for the American Government. The Old Dock had four standard ships of 5,000 tons each. The New Engineering Works had two in hand, and the Nicholas Tsu Engineering Works were completing two, starting a third, and expecting to secure contracts for three more of 5,000 tons each.

---

[1] The account of the work of the British Women's Work Association was courteously supplied by Lady de Sausmarez.

Epidemics and the Health Department

A serious epidemic of scarlet fever broke out in the early part of 1917, and in five months 70 cases among foreigners, and 423 among Chinese were reported. Scarlet fever had scarcely been known in Shanghai before the year 1900, and as the Chinese had been immune before that time, they made a fertile field for the culture and propagation of the disease. It may be considered one of the diseases brought to China by foreigners.

Just before the outbreak, Dr. Arthur Stanley, the Health Officer of the Shanghai Municipal Council, had called attention to the fact that the International Settlement had an enviable record as far as health statistics were concerned, and that the death rate was exceedingly low, 15.4 per thousand among foreigners, and 13.2 per thousand approximately among the Chinese population.

Anti-kidnapping Society

The preservation of order in Shanghai became a bigger problem as the population increased, and as the undesirable elements made it their headquarters. We now come to the period when armed robberies became frequent, many of the robbers being disbanded soldiers. The duties of the police became more dangerous and they carried on their duties with considerable risk to life. The first instance in this connection of a foreign constable being killed was on October 23rd, when Sergeant Hamilton was shot on Yates Road while engaged in searching men suspected of carrying concealed weapons.

The Chinese themselves were alive to the evils to which they were exposed, especially that of kidnapping, and formed an Anti-kidnapping Society. This society was established in 1912 by a number of merchants and had as its object the stamping out of kidnapping and trafficking in children of both sexes. It was a very worthy philanthropic enterprise and was the means of rescuing many unfortunate children stolen from their homes in the country, some of whom were sold for immoral purposes. A refuge was built at Kiangwan in which were housed several hundreds of rescued children.

The Wheel Another social evil was the establishment of a gambling hell on North Honan Road Extension (now Paoshan Road), known as "The Wheel." Large sums of money were lost at this place and many young men ruined. Although there was a great outcry, it was difficult for the Council to do anything in the matter, as the casino was situated in Chinese territory. It required long negotiations with the Chinese authorities before the place was finally sealed up in November, 1918.

Unfortunately in later years the same trouble arose, gambling houses with roulette wheels being established in the Settlement on Bubbling Well Road and on Yates Road. These were raided and closed in April, 1928.[1]

Last of the Opium Shops The year 1917 saw the last of the opium shops in Shanghai. The resolution passed at the Ratepayers' meeting in 1915 required the withdrawal of one quarter of the licences of these shops by means of half yearly drawings. The first drawing took place in June, 1915, the second in December, 1915, and the third in June, 1916, leaving the remaining quarter to be withdrawn on March 31st, 1917.

The passing of these shops recalls the time of the opium houses or dens, in which opium was sold and smoked on the premises. In 1904 a clear distinction was drawn between an opium shop and an opium house. In the former the sale was permitted but not its consumption on the premises, in the latter both were allowed.

After 1907 no further licences had been granted to

---

[1] Up to the present time the evil has not been entirely eradicated and gambling establishments are still secretly carried on.

opium houses and those in existence at that time were closed in 1909.

The opium shops did a roaring trade to the last, as habitués were anxious to lay in a good stock of the drug.

To its credit the Municipality, contrary to its financial interests, co-operated with the Chinese Government in the suppression of the sale of opium.

The Maloo or Nanking Road

The "Maloo" or more properly the "Ta Maloo," meaning the "great horse road," at this period began to take on its present appearance. The Maloo in the early days, which began at the old Barrier Road (Honan Road) and ended at Defence Creek, was known as Park Lane. This was the section of Shanghai on which cheap Chinese shanties had been built for the accommodation of the large number of people flocking into the Settlement, at the time of the Taiping Rebellion. This condition lasted well on into the "seventies" and then there came a better class of buildings, which with their ornamented and brightly gilded hanging signboards gave the road a character of its own. Then a great change was introduced by a general modernizing process and the erection of large department stores. The first of these to make its appearance was Sincere's, opened in October, at the corner of Chekiang and Nanking Roads. It was followed in the next year by the completion of the building of the Wing On Company, on the opposite side of the street. Both these buildings are reinforced concrete structures, with modern equipment and high towers. At night they are illuminated by thousands of electric lights, and help to make the upper part of Nanking Road a "great white way." In connection with each of them is a hotel which does a flourishing business. Most significant of all, they answer to a demand, and are crowded by a throng of shoppers, many of whom are visitors to Shanghai from other cities. They mark both the gradual

process of the modernization of China and the growing
prosperity of Shanghai.   Some years later another large
department store, Sun Sun, was erected in the same
locality.[1]

Pleasure Palaces
Still another change in Shanghai was the
building of Pleasure Palaces.   Along the
Maloo, there had always been a great number
of tea-houses, where visitors on pleasant afternoons sat
on the verandahs, sipping their tea and watching the
traffic and scenes in the street.   These were now largely
supplanted by places of general amusement.   The first of
importance was the New World on the corner of Bubbling
Well and Thibet Roads.   At first it was exceedingly
popular, so much so that an annex was built on the other
side of the street.   In order to connect the two buildings,
the proprietors obtained permission to make a tunnel
beneath Bubbling Well Road.   It is the only subway of
the sort that has been attempted in Shanghai, but owing
to faulty construction, was not an unqualified success,
more or less water seeping into it.   The next large place
of public entertainment to be built was the Great World on
Avenue Edward VII.

Contrasts in Shanghai
Perhaps one of the things making Shanghai
one of the unique cities in the world is that
it contains so many striking contrasts.
There has been an evolution from former days to the
modern period, but vestiges of the old China are apparent
on every side.

On some of the streets we may see at the same time
the wheelbarrow crowded with passengers and the automobile, the old fashioned Chinese shop with its front open
to the street, and the modern counterpart with its plate
glass windows.

---

[1] Plans are now on foot for the erection of another large Department Store on the site of the present Town Hall.

On the river we can still see the old junks with their high sterns, the two large eyes at the bows, and brown sails, and, in close proximity, the modern steamship.

On the Soochow Creek some of the old craft have entirely disappeared. In days gone by the fastest boat was the mail boat rowed by the feet of a man who sat in the stern and steered with his hands. Then came a large boat with a huge paddle wheel at the stern, worked like a treadmill by shifts of men, and then came the steam launch, towing a string of six or more boats, each fastened to the stern of the boat in front.

Political Events of the Year 1918
The year 1918 was a troublous one for China, politically and economically.

There was civil war between North and South and the Southwestern provinces declared their independence of the central government. There were frequent changes in the administration, and the election of a new President, Hsu Shih-chang.

For a short time there was considerable excitement over the attempt made by General Chang Hsun to restore the young Emperor, Hsuan Tung, to the throne, and there was fighting in Peking. The *coup d'état* failed miserably because it received no support from the country at large.

China became further entangled in the meshes of loans, some legal, and some illegal; and floods in the Province of Chihli brought suffering and destitution upon several hundred thousands of people.

Conditions throughout the country produced a general feeling of unrest and uncertainty in Shanghai, and an increasing desire on the part of the merchant class for peace and security.

During the year the Customs Tariff Revision Commission was again in session in Shanghai with the object of securing an effective five per cent. duty on imports. After long negotiations the end was obtained, and it resulted in a large addition to this source of revenue.

The Statistical Secretary of the Customs reported that, notwithstanding adverse conditions, due largely to the War, the year 1917 had been a record one for foreign trade. Its value was Hk.Tls. 1,012,450,404 which was an increase of Hk.Tls. 14,246,043 over the trade of 1916.

Turning to municipal affairs we find special
Municipal
Affairs
attention paid to health matters.   This was partly due to the fact that in the early part of the year Shanghai was again threatened with an invasion of plague.   This was the pneumonic plague, which had spread from Manchuria as far south as Nanking on March 18th.   Its further advance was only stayed by the suspension of train and steamer traffic between Shanghai and Nanking until the end of the month.

Considerable work was done in further culverting of the creeks, which were the breeding ground for mosquitoes, and thus a cause of disease.

At the Ratepayers' meeting held on March 28th the freedom of the city was conferred on Mr. (afterwards Sir) Edward C. Pearce in recognition of his long and valuable services as Chairman of the Shanghai Municipal Council.

The peace of the Settlement was disturbed
Ricsha Riot
by two riots.

The first on April 17th was in connection with a strike of the ricsha men, who objected to the traffic regulations put out by the Council, which confined the ricsha men to stands, and forbad them wandering about the streets touting for hire.   This seemed to them to interfere with their earnings.   One of their grievances was the taking away by the police of the licences of those who refused to obey the orders in regard to waiting for hire at the stands.

In some way the rumour spread that the Shanghai Tramways, a rival concern in the eyes of the coolies, had been instrumental in bringing the new regulations into force, and this still further roused their ire.

The trouble began early in the morning at about half-past eight. Inspector Aiers noticed a large crowd at the junction of Avenue and Carter Roads attacking a stationary tram with stones, sticks and iron bars, and when he endeavoured to interfere, he was handled roughly and received a severe blow on the back of the head. While he was trying to escape from the crowd, Chief Inspector Aiers appeared on the scene, and gave chase to those who were pursuing Inspector Aiers. At about the same time another car, containing passengers, was attacked, while passing over the Avenue-Carter Road junction, by 200 rioters with cross-bars, sticks and bamboos, and similar attacks took place in Sinza Road.

The number of rioters increased to about 700, but with the arrival of the police in sufficiently large numbers, the trouble subsided. Only a few arrests were made, it being difficult to distinguish between rioters and spectators. In the evening some of the Volunteers were mobilized and held in readiness at the Town Hall and elsewhere, but no further trouble arose. Fortunately the loss of life was slight, only one man being killed.

Japanese Riot in Hongkew Another serious riot broke out in Hongkew. At this time there was bitter feeling between Chinese and Japanese, owing largely to the presentation of the Twenty-one Demands by the Japanese Government. The beginning of the trouble was the arrest by Chinese constables of a Japanese sailor who was making trouble at a watchmaker's shop. Some Japanese compatriots came to his assistance and a free fight ensued. A few days later, on the morning of Friday, July 19th, a large body of Japanese, armed with daggers and sword-sticks, gathered in Woosung and Quinsan Roads. They were much excited and obsessed with the idea that the

15

Chinese were about to make a general attack on the Japanese community. When the police tried to disperse the crowd, two Chinese constables were injured. On the night of the same day trouble broke out again near the Hongkew Market, and two Japanese were killed, one a Japanese constable and the other a Japanese shopkeeper who was watching the fray from a verandah. The Chinese police had been stirred up against the Japanese, by receiving threatening letters, and had been on the point of mutiny, owing to the fact that the police authorities wished to send them out on duty unarmed. The issue soon crystallized into open warfare between the Japanese rowdy element and the Chinese police. It became necessary to withdraw the Chinese police for a time from the disturbed area, and to substitute others, and to call out some of the Volunteer Companies. Feeling ran high for several days, but the display of force by the Volunteers had the desired effect, and by Tuesday of the following week all was quiet.

The Japanese pressed some demands, asking for an indemnity for the Japanese killed, an increase in the number of Japanese police, and the disarming of the Chinese police in the Settlement. The Chinese on their part threatened to institute a boycott on the Japanese shops.

When it was decided to introduce Japanese police into the Municipal force, some had anticipated the danger of serious friction with the Chinese, and this riot shows that these fears were not altogether unfounded. The riot had a serious aspect, as it might have led to a racial conflict, and might have aroused feelings in the interior, leading to disastrous consequences. It also manifested the unwisdom of having one district policed exclusively, or nearly so, by men of the same nationality as that of the majority of residents, as tending to suggest undesirable distinctions.

First Chinese Bishop

Wednesday, October 2nd, 1918, will be a memorable day in connection with the work of the Christian Church in China, for on that day the first Chinese Bishop of the Anglican Communion was consecrated as Assistant Bishop of Chekiang. The service was held in the Church of Our Saviour on Dixwell Road. The new Bishop, Archdeacon T. S. Sing, had been connected with the work of the Church Missionary Society for many years, first in Ningpo and afterwards in Hangchow. Seven Bishops were present at the Consecration Service. Only one Chinese had ever been elevated to the office of Bishop in China before the consecration of Bishop Sing, and that was Bishop Lo, a Dominican monk of the Roman Catholic Church. on April 8th, 1685.

The Armistice

At last, after four years of anxiety and suspense, the tidings of the armistice reached Shanghai. Great was the relief, and the whole community joined in giving free expression to its joy. The news of the signing of the Armistice on November 11th was received early on the 12th, and the city was decorated with the flags of all the Allied Nations. The first to celebrate were the members of the Fire Brigade, who dashed about the Settlement in motors, with bells clanging and horns hooting, as a notice to all that the day of peace had dawned.

At a meeting held on Thursday afternoon, November 14th, of representatives of the Allied Consulates, and the Shanghai Municipal Council, an executive committee was appointed to arrange a programme for the celebration of the Allies' victory on Thursday, Friday, and Saturday, November 21st, 22nd and 23rd.

On November 17th, Thanksgiving Services were held in all the churches, and there was a special American Song Service in the afternoon at the Palace Hotel.

Shanghai gave itself up to jubilation for three days. The official programme began on Thursday, the 21st, on the Cricket Ground by the firing of a salute of twenty-one guns by the Artillery of the Shanghai Volunteer Corps, and as the last gun was fired a fanfare was blown by the Tonkinese buglers. Then followed a brief service of Thanksgiving, conducted on the steps of the Cricket Club Pavilion, some three thousand persons being assembled on the lawn.

In the afternoon there was a procession of school children, seventeen schools including Chinese and Japanese being represented. It formed on the Race Course, and proceeded down Nanking Road, along The Bund and Foochow Road to the Drill Hall where the children listened to an address, sang national songs, and witnessed an entertainment.

In the early evening there was a special Chinese students lantern procession arranged by the Y.M.C.A. In the procession were a number of decorated cars, symbolizing the defeat of the Entente Powers.

Shanghai had never been so profusely decorated with flags and bunting and triumphal arches as on this occasion, and with the illuminations at night it was a blaze of light, especially on Nanking Road.

Across at Pootung the Dock Company gave the reason for all this festivity in the immense word picked out in red lights, "Victory," with the equivalent characters in Chinese.

On the following day, Friday, at noon there was a great reception at the Shanghai Club, and in the afternoon there was a civilian parade, in which all nationalities of the Allied cause participated, the Japanese community being especially prominent.

On Saturday, the 23rd, at ten o'clock in the morning, there was a military parade on the Cricket Ground.

Troops representative of ten nationalities in Shanghai gathered to the number of several thousands, including sailors, soldiers, police, Sikhs, Chinese regulars, Volunteers and Specials, under the command of Captain Marryat, Senior British Naval Officer. The route of the march was down Nanking Road, along The Bund, up Rue du Consulat, Rue Montauban, Avenue Edward VII, Thibet Road and thence to the Cricket Ground, where the march past took place.

At night when Shanghai with its illuminations was being transformed into fairy land, the last act of the programme was performed, consisting of a Torchlight Procession. It started on Avenue Edward VII, and when organized it extended from The Bund to Boulevard de Montigny. There was a large number of floats, cars, torch bearers and people in fancy costume.

When the procession reached the Recreation Ground those taking part gathered around a structure erected to represent the House of Hohenzollern, which was committed to the flames with unrestrained glee and wild rejoicing.

Thus ended Shanghai's commemoration of one of the greatest events in history. It is remarkable that although multitudes were attracted from the adjoining country to see the celebration, and the streets were thronged with visitors, no serious disorder took place. It was an evidence of the general good nature and peaceableness of a Chinese crowd.

Pulling down the Iltis Monument War stirs up the spirit of hatred and rancour, and the resentment felt at German atrocities is not to be wondered at. Even so, there were some acts committed at the close of the war of which succeeding generations will not feel proud. One of these was the destruction of the Iltis Monument. It had been put up by the German community in memory of some sailors who lost their lives when the "Iltis" was wrecked off the Shantung promontory in 1896, and permission for its erection on the foreshore had been granted by Jardine, Matheson and Company. It was a memorial to the dead, in the form of a broken mast in bronze, with a flag and wreath of laurels, and not even by the wildest stretch of imagination could it be supposed to have had any connection with the war. An attack was made on it shortly after midnight on December 2nd, when it was torn from its pedestal by a party of foreigners whose identity was never revealed.

CHAPTER XXIV.

THE AFTERMATH OF THE WAR, 1919–1920.

During the war period, assurances were made by the rulers of the Allied Powers, and especially by President Woodrow Wilson, of the beginning of a new era after victory had been secured. Among the benefits promised would be the right of self-determination for small or weak nations, and the doing away with all racial discrimination.

After the signing of the Versailles Treaty, there was a great feeling of disappointment throughout the world at the non-fulfilment of many of these promises.

At the same time, as the result of this disillusionment, there grew up a determination on the part of peoples, who considered they were oppressed, to secure complete independence and to remove racial inequality.

This has been especially evident in Oriental countries, and in order to understand recent movements in China, this new desire for complete independence, and the regaining of full sovereign rights must be borne in mind.

Political Conditions in China Political conditions in China in 1919 became more and more chaotic, and the split between North and South more strongly accentuated. The attempt to bring about reconciliation led to the holding of a Peace Conference in Shanghai between representatives of both sections in the spring.

Mr. Tang Shao-yi was the delegate from the South, and Mr. Chu Chi-chien from the North. The Conference had a stormy career, and accomplished nothing. Another attempt was made later in the year, when Mr. Wang I-tang was appointed in place of Mr. Chu Chi-chien. He arrived in Shanghai on September 17th, but as Mr. Tang Shao-yi refused to meet him, and resigned, negotiations came to an end.

Burning of the Opium
In the spring of the year, there was another opium holocaust. The Chinese Government purchased from the opium combine all the stocks in Shanghai, consisting of 1,200 cases of prepared opium, valued at Tls. 25,000,000, and committed them to the flames in the specially erected furnaces in Pootung. At about that time, the International Anti-Opium Society renewed its activities and appointed representatives to witness the examination and destruction of the opium.

This expensive bonfire, however, did not accomplish a great deal in the way of freeing China from the opium evil, inasmuch as the cultivation of the poppy had been resumed in many provinces. Furthermore, a more insidious form of the drug was having direful results, due to the smuggling of morphine into the country, and to its illicit sale.

There was another large seizure of opium in 1921, and on October 12th of that year more than one and a quarter million dollars worth of opium and other drugs went up in flames at the Pootung furnaces.

Deportation of Enemy Aliens
One of the immediate effects of the defeat of the "Entente" was her complete humiliation in the eyes of the world. During the war the Allies had brought pressure to bear on the Chinese Government, after the latter joined the Allied cause, to repatriate the Germans. China had shown reluctance to take this step, and the mandate for the deportation of the Germans and Austrians was not issued until two days before the signing of the Armistice. Although the war was over, the Allied Powers insisted that the mandate should be enforced, on the ground that the Germans might still carry on baneful propaganda. Throughout the whole

of China there were about 3,500 Germans and Austrians. In Shanghai, the numbers were 673 men, 404 women, and 383 children.

There was considerable discussion as to who should be exempted from deportation on account of health or advanced age, but the sharpest controversy arose over the desire expressed by a few influential members of the community that some German doctors should be allowed to remain in the Settlement, because of their professional skill. These were days when feeling ran high, and when, if anyone ventured to say a good word for a German, he was looked upon as a traitor to his own country.

In order that China might finance the deportation of this large number of aliens, she was obliged to raise a loan of $500,000 from the banks of the Allies. After considerable delay, the embarkation of the Germans and Austrians was successfully carried out between March 6th and 10th, 1919.

Connected with it there was necessarily a good deal of hardship, but on the whole it was accomplished in a humane manner.

There will always be doubt as to whether such an extreme measure was justifiable after the war was over, or whether any real harm would have resulted in allowing the Germans to remain.

Connected with the deportation of enemy aliens there was the question of the liquidation of alien property, and the Chinese Government appointed a special commission for this purpose.

Student Movement and Japanese Boycott
In the year 1919 the Student Movement, which had played a large part in arousing public opinion at the time of the American boycott, became more articulate.

When it was known that Kiaochow was to revert to Japan by the decision of the Great Powers at the Versailles Peace Conference, the students and the people generally expressed great indignation.

During the latter years of the Great War, the Chinese Government, in order to obtain funds, contracted large Japanese loans.   Tsao Ju-lin, Lu Chung-yu and Chang Chung-hsiang, who were instrumental in the negotiations, became very unpopular with the students and were accused of selling their country.   Tsao Ju-lin's house in Peking was attacked and burnt.   The attempt to curb the students by imprisonment only resulted in causing the agitation to spread throughout the whole country.   A Students Union was organized, with branches at various centres, and in a short time a student strike was declared, that is, students abandoned their studies and gave themselves up to political propaganda.   The people were called upon to boycott Japanese goods, and Japanese trade for a time was entirely at a standstill.

In Shanghai all the students of Government and Mission schools went out on strike on May 26th.   To express sympathy with the student agitation, the merchants of Shanghai also declared a strike, and all shops closed their doors on June 5th.

Backed by public opinion, China's representatives at the Peace Conference refused to sign the Treaty.

Later in April, 1920, the students united in declaring a second strike, to protest against the Chinese Government entering into direct negotiations with Japan in regard to the return of Kiaochow, inasmuch as the pro-Japanese clique was in power at Peking.   It became nation wide, and for a time threatened to be as effective as the first had been.

In Shanghai it led to a clash between the soldiers and the students, when the latter tried to force an entrance into the Arsenal at Lunghua, for the purpose of stirring up the workmen, and five students were severely injured.   In the end, owing to lack of public support, the strike was abandoned, and this led to a temporary loss of student prestige, and to an effort on the part of the officials to suppress the unions.

The End of the Volunteer Fire Brigade The Shanghai Fire Brigade had been a volunteer organization for over half a century, and had made for itself an enviable record.

Difficulties arose after the engagement of a professional chief officer for the Brigade in 1912. Owing to the growth of Shanghai, and the decline in the number of volunteers, it became necessary to employ a paid Chinese force, but it was not easy to harmonize in one organization a volunteer foreign force and a paid Chinese force. More and more the foreign volunteers realized they were in an impossible position, and finally the whole force consisting of 44 men resigned *en bloc* on April 30th, 1919.

Mr. Edward C. Pearce, when inspecting the volunteer members of the Fire Brigade for the last time, before their disbandment, reviewed the services of the Brigade to the community during the preceding 50 years. He recalled that in the years 1886 to 1894, when he was a member of the Fire Brigade, the firemen themselves had to run the hose reels and ladder trucks to fires, and that reels were first drawn by ponies in 1890. It was not until 1908 that the first motor was introduced. After that changes became more rapid until the most up-to-date motor equipment was secured. He pointed out "that to meet present more exacting requirements and those of the near future, we must rely more fully on a paid fire staff whose whole time can be devoted not only to the extinction of fires but to their prevention."

Municipal Finance Turning now to Municipal affairs of the International Settlement, there were some important happenings in 1919 to which reference must be made.

During the war period, the Council found it difficult to float debentures, and to secure the money necessary for extraordinary expenditure, and this furnished considerable concern as the Municipal debt was increasing. The ordinary expenditure of the Municipality had grown as is shown in the budget of 1918.

	Tls.		Tls.
Police Force	1,088,000	Fire Brigade	106,000
Public Works	1,058,000	Finance	84,000
Health	238,000	Public Band	49,000
Education	205,000	Volunteers	45,000
Secretariat	186,000	Public Library	3,000

Trouble over the Increase in Municipal Rates

The Municipal rates were increased owing to this serious financial condition, but the Chinese took the stand that they would not pay these rates unless representation on the Council was granted, and this brought about an awkward situation. The Council explained that it was not at liberty to change the Land Regulations, and that Chinese representation must first be voted by the Ratepayers, and then referred to the Diplomatic Body in Peking. Only the latter body, in consultation with the Chinese Government, could sanction this change in the Land Regulations.

Of course, the Chinese were not satisfied with this answer, but the agitation gradually subsided, and the leaders of the Street Unions and the Chinese Chamber of Commerce issued a circular in the name of both organizations, advising the people to pay the rates. From this time on, however, the question of Chinese representation on the Council became an important issue.

Street Unions

As an evidence of the growing demand on the part of the Chinese community for a voice in the affairs of the Settlement, Street Unions were organized and meetings were held for the purpose of obtaining equality of treatment for the Chinese community. A new set of Land Regulations was drawn up by the local Chinese leaders, and forwarded through the Special Commissioner for Foreign Affairs to the Consular Body. According to these Regulations the Chinese residents in the Settlement were to be granted the franchise, and a rental of $10 *per mensem* was to confer a vote. There were other radical proposals of so extreme a nature that they received but scant attention.

Community Affairs

Immediately after the close of the war, in Shanghai, as elsewhere, there was a marked reaction to the feeling of anxiety and suspense which had continued so long. Shanghai broke out into an unparalleled round of festivity, marked by collective and individual extravagance.

Increased Cost of Living

At the same time the residents of Shanghai began to feel the increased cost of living, and the dearer price of food caused by the general unsettled conditions of the world. The housing problem became quite acute, especially for those living on moderate salaries. This was due to high rents. It was claimed that these high rents were not entirely the result of landlords taking advantage of the fact that the supply was less than the demand, but to the increased cost of building, caused by the higher price of materials, and the advance in workmen's wages.

There were many proposals as to the way in which more housing accommodation could be secured at moderate rentals, among them being the suggestion of the advisability of the erection of flats, and the development of a Garden City in the western suburbs. The former plan proved more practicable, and resulted later in bringing apartment houses or flats in increasing numbers to Shanghai. It is still, however, a fact that the salaried man in

Shanghai has to pay a much higher ι rcentage of his income in rent than he would in the homeland.

Formation of Union Club   In order to foster friendly intercourse between the foreign and Chinese merchants of Shanghai, a Union Club was founded. It was inaugurated on October 2nd, 1919, in quarters in the former Chartered Bank Building. Mr. H. H. Girardet (Acting Chairman of the British Chamber of Commerce) presided, and in his address called attention to the importance "of closer and more intimate social relations between Chinese and foreigners."

The establishment of this Club has proved to be of considerable value, inasmuch as it has provided a meeting ground for the two sections of the community. In 1924 the Club moved into more commodious quarters on Avenue Edward VII.

War Activities   Even after the Great War, help was still needed for the soldiers, especially for the White Russians fighting against the Bolshevists in Siberia, and for the Czechs who had come into conflict with the "Reds" and been reduced to serious straits in their endeavour to return to their own country by crossing Siberia and taking ship at Vladivostok for Europe. The British Women's Work Association and the American Red Cross continued their good work for many months after the signing of the Armistice and the Treaty of Versailles.

An Appeal to Charity   The large number of Russian refugees from Siberia made an appeal to the sympathy and charity of the whole community. Most of these people were in dire necessity both for food and clothing, as they reached Shanghai in a penniless condition, and were practically stranded. Not only were they unable to raise the funds for returning to Russia, but they feared to put themselves and their families under the reign of

terror in the homeland. It was difficult to find employment
for these immigrants, and for the first time the Chinese
beheld white men undertaking menial work, and becoming
hawkers, and sellers of newspapers on the streets. Shanghai responded liberally to the call for help and much was
done to relieve the situation.

The American School   A vigorous campaign was conducted in 1919
for raising $100,000 for the purchase of land
for the Shanghai American School. It met
with success, and the fine property on Avenue Petain was
bought for the site of the new school buildings. Two years
later another successful effort was made for raising an
additional Tls. 150,000 for the school buildings.

Fortieth Anniversary of St. John's University   In the educational world of Shanghai one
of the interesting events was the celebration
of the fortieth anniversary of the founding
of St. John's University on November 15th, 1919. The
occasion brought together a large number of friends and
former students of the University to express their congratulations on the completion of forty years of successful
work in advancing the cause of modern education in China.

Farewells   Shanghai is essentially a place of "comings"
and "goings" and most years bring their
quota of farewells. In 1919 there was one departure that
left a big gap in the life of the community. It was that
of Lady de Sausmarez, who had carried on in a very able
manner the British women's work in connection with war
relief. At a meeting held in November a presentation,
consisting of a very beautiful ring and an address, was
made to her as a token of the affection and esteem in which
she was held by those who had been privileged to work
under her leadership.

Commerce and Trade   Contrary to expectations, according to the
report of the Statistical Department of the
Inspectorate-General of Customs, the port of

Shanghai showed during 1918 unmistakable outward signs of increasing material prosperity.

The big staple industries—cotton mills, docks, shipping—had never had a more prosperous year.   Piece goods importers, however, were severely handicapped by shortage of stocks.   Japanese merchants reaped the biggest harvest, and on account of the proximity of the market, found Shanghai a veritable El Dorado.

The scarcity of cotton throughout the world, and the great demand for it, created a cotton boom and the number of cotton mills increased rapidly.   Twenty-one mills were in operation and there was considerable speculation in the purchase of cotton shares.

In Shanghai, the Japanese acquired two more large cotton mills, the International and the Yu-yuan, and purchased three wharf frontages, two at Pootung and one at Yangtszepoo, and the number of Japanese banks increased.

The high rate of exchange which ordinarily stimulates imports and discourages exports, in this instance did not have a deleterious effect on exports.   This was due to the fact that Chinese exports brought exceptionally high prices in the foreign market.   The gross value of the trade in 1918 was 627 million Haikwan taels, an increase of nearly 47 million over the 1917 total.   In 1919 the net value of foreign trade in China amounted to Hk. Tls. 1,277,807,092, a great advance on the preceding year.   The gross value of trade in Shanghai reached the record total of Hk. Tls. 768,000,000.   There was a revival of British piece goods and large importations were made of motor cars and cigarettes.

In the report of the Maritime Customs, we find the year 1920 referred to as another record year, eclipsing that of 1919.   Volume of trade, Customs revenue, and tonnage of shipping using the port, all established new

THE BUND, ABOUT 1889.

THE CUSTOM HOUSE, 1893.

figures.   Although the gross value of the trade of Shanghai which amounted to Hk. Tls. 841,000,000 and was an
advance of Hk. Tls. 73,000,000 over the 1919 record,
seemed to indicate quite an unusual state of prosperity,
yet actually during the greater part of the year this was
not the case.   The year opened with a great boom in trade,
but by May it became evident that the foreign markets,
already glutted in 1918, had reached the limit of their
powers of absorption, and consequently exports began to
decline, especially in silk and tea.

Furthermore, after the Great War, many new firms,
inexperienced in Chinese trade, had been established, and
large quantities of goods were ordered from England and
America, in excess of the legitimate requirement of the
China market.   Under disturbed conditions in China the
demand for goods from the interior became weaker and
business at the end of the year was at a standstill.   In
consequence many Chinese dealers closed their doors and
disappeared.

The summer months brought a serious commercial
crisis, due to the rapid fall in exchange.   Chinese piece
goods merchants had ordered large supplies when exchange
stood at 8 shillings or $1.40 gold to the tael.   When the
goods arrived and they were called upon to pay for them,
the tael was only worth four shillings and sixpence or
89 gold cents.

There was a desire on the part of many of the
Chinese merchants that the orders might be cancelled, and
there were some threats of repudiation.   The foreign
Chambers of Commerce naturally were not inclined to
agree to the cancelling of contracts.   The situation became
so serious that a good many of the Chinese merchants went
into bankruptcy and large losses were sustained by the
foreign merchants.

Notwithstanding this trade depression, optimistic

16

views were entertained in regard to the future, and it was significant that just at this time the foundation stone of the new building of the Hongkong and Shanghai Banking Corporation was laid. It was the largest building enterprise undertaken in Shanghai up to that time, and the erection of the proposed massive structure was made possible by the method, to which we have referred, of laying, as the foundation, enormous concrete rafts.

A new bank was opened in September 1919—the Chinese-American with a capital of $10,000,000.

At this time the Banque Industrielle de Chine was obliged to close its doors and to suspend payment. There was an extended delay in winding up its affairs, which entailed great hardship upon the creditors, especially those with limited incomes. Later the creditors of the Banque were somewhat relieved by the news from Paris that the Banque was to be reconstructed, and that the debts amounting to £14,000,000 would be partly met by the use of the Boxer Indemnity Fund for this purpose. The amount of this fund still due to France was £7,000,000.

A new company was formed, known as the Société Français de Gérance de la Banque Industrielle de Chine, with the object of managing the business of the Banque Industrielle until the latter settled all claims of its creditors and recovered full liberty of action.

The Chinese opened the Chartered Stock and Produce Exchange at No. 1 Szechuen Road, for convenience in business transactions. Unfortunately this resulted in considerable gambling in stocks, and brought about several financial crises.

Conference of British Chambers of Commerce The British Chambers of Commerce of China and Hongkong held their first joint conference on November 5th, 6th, and 7th, and Sir John Jordan, H.B.M.'s Minister to China, came from Peking to preside at the meetings.

He was given a warm reception, not only by the foreign community, but by the Chinese as well.

As a result of the conference, several resolutions were formulated and sent to the British Government in regard to matters affecting commercial relations between China and Great Britain.

Meeting of Ratepayers At the meeting of Ratepayers held on April 7th, 1920, several important actions were taken. It was decided, in spite of the large expenditure involved, to allow the further expansion of the Electricity Department, and to raise the capital needed by another sale of debentures, adding considerably to the debt of the Municipality. The Council received permission to borrow up to Tls. 4,800,000, of which Tls. 2,800,000 was to be used for the expansion of the Electricity Department. The total debt of the Municipality at that time was thus raised to Tls. 18,847,500.

Mr. Edward C. Pearce, in an address delivered during the same year, pointed out that this was not quite as bad as it looked, as against this debt might be placed the assessed value of the land owned by the Municipal Council amounting to Tls. 6,000,000, and the value of buildings amounting to $3,250,000, and the assets of the Electricity Department valued at Tls. 12,870,000.

There had been some criticisms raised in regard to the increased expenditure of the Electricity Department, on the ground that it was largely for "power" purposes, and that Shanghai should not aim at becoming a great manufacturing centre, but should abide by its original object, which was the development of commerce. The attempt, however, to prevent the increase of modern industries in Shanghai would have been similar to King Canute's attempt to stay the incoming tide.

Another important resolution was that of the adoption of the report of the special Vice Committee,

which had been appointed for the study of the social
evil in Shanghai.   According to the recommendation, the
number of licensed brothels in the International Settlement was to be diminished gradually, until they were
completely abolished.   On December 21st, at 8 p.m. the
first drawing took place for the closing of one-fifth of the
brothels.

Chinese
Advisory
Committee
In reply to the demand that the Chinese
should be represented on the Council the
following resolution was passed:

"That this meeting approves of the creation
of a Chinese Advisory Committee and that the
constitution and powers of such a committee be
limited to those set forth in the letter from the
Chairman of the Council, to the Senior Consul
dated October 24th, 1919, and published in the
Municipal Gazette of January 8th, 1920."

The constitution of the committee referred to was
"that it should have a membership of five, to be nominated
annually by the Chinese, that the nomination be subject
to the veto of the Consular Body, that the nominees
reside in the Settlement for five years immediately
preceding nomination, that they should have paid
General Municipal rates during the whole of this period
on an assessed rental of not less than Tls. 1,200 per annum,
that they shall not, at the time of nomination or whilst
on the membership of the Committee, hold any other
office under the Chinese Government."

Mr. E. S. Little proposed the following amendment:
"That the meeting hereby instructs the Council to take
such steps as are necessary to procure the alteration of
the Land Regulations for the purpose of increasing the
number of Councillors from 9 to 12, of which three shall
be Chinese Ratepayers, with the same qualifications as
Foreign Councillors, and to be elected as may be sub-

sequently determined." This amendment was lost by a majority of about three to one.

Although the Chinese were far from satisfied with the measure passed by the Council, yet they accepted it for the time being. Later in the year a Chinese Rate-payers Association was formed which had as one of its functions that of electing the Advisory Committee. The Municipal Council could not at first see its way to accepting this method of appointing the Advisory Committee, inasmuch as it appeared that the Chinese Ratepayers Association might try to exercise control over those they elected, and it was not until May 11th, 1921, that the Chinese Advisory Committee began to function.

Census of 1920

A census of the foreign and Chinese population was taken in 1920 which showed a still further increase over 1915. The foreign population was 23,307 and the Chinese 759,839. In the foreign community the principal increase was in the number of Japanese and Americans.

Famine in the North

The Shanghai community, in addition to the relief work for Russian refugees, was called on to show its usual generosity for those who were suffering from one of the periodic famines in the North. Continued drought over a large area brought great distress upon the people of Shantung, Chihli and Honan. It was estimated that as many as 12,000,000 were threatened with starvation.

A Chinese-Foreign Famine Relief Committee was formed and relief funds were raised both in China and in foreign countries, and the Treaty Powers consented to the Chinese Government charging a surtax for famine relief. An attempt was made to provide productive labour for the people in the famine district, such as the making of roads. In the course of the year the Committee raised a total of $863,491.79 and Tls. 182,908.86.

In the final report of the North China International Society for Famine Relief, dated December, 1921, the total receipts for famine relief are given as $3,457,899.64.

Unfortunately as soon as the famine began to abate, another severe calamity followed, caused by great floods in various parts of the country.

There was considerable criticism of the continuation of the surtax after the famine was over.   The excuse given was that it was for the purpose of accumulating a famine prevention fund, but it was generally known that this tax on industry and imports was used for the purpose of assisting the Government to meet some of its liabilities, and that it amounted to what in common parlance is called "squeeze."

The Retirement of Dean Walker During the year occurred the retirement of Dean A. J. Walker, who had served the Cathedral for twenty years.   A farewell meeting was held in the Cathedral School for Boys on April 8th, at which time a handsome casket, containing an address signed by the members of the congregation, was presented to him.   As Dean, he had done much for the Cathedral and for the people of Shanghai.   He had built up the Cathedral Schools, introduced a boy choir, improved the fabric of the Cathedral, and raised a fund for the purchase of the new organ.

Passing of Some Prominent Citizens The deaths of some prominent citizens in 1920 call for more than a passing mention. First was that, on January 18th, of Mr. George Lanning, who for many years had been headmaster of the Shanghai Public School.   After his retirement he had been occupied in writing a voluminous history of Shanghai, but did not live long enough to complete it.

Then came the death of Mr. E. Jenner Hogg, February 26th, at the age of 83.   He came out in 1857, and had been in Shanghai for 63 years. His memory went back to the early days of the Settlement, and the time of the Taiping Rebellion. During the latter eventful period he was one of the Mounted Rangers who scoured the country around Shanghai to gather information as to the movement of the rebels.

He purchased and developed the spacious grounds at Unkaza, which now form a part of the campus of St. John's University. For many years he was Chairman of the Parks Committee of the International Settlement.

The death of Mr. T. R. Jernigan occurred on November 1st. He came out to Shanghai as United States Consul-General in 1893, and at the close of his term of office took up the practice of law and continued to live in the Settlement. He was interested in all civic affairs, and was also a sportsman and the author of several interesting books on China.

Labour Unrest

Signs of unrest were noted among the labouring classes, and there were evidences of Bolshevistic propaganda. The following table in regard to strike movements for the years 1918-1924, is an indication of the new economic problems introduced into the industrial life of Shanghai.

Year.	Strikes.	Strikers.	Work days lost.
1918	13	15,000	90,000
1919	25	24,000	245,000
1920	45	57,088	325,401
1921	36	22,000	195,800
1922	71	65,000	728,010
1923	51	23,500	118,939
1924	60	37,435	289,630

Among the chief causes we may note the high price of rice, the depreciation of copper coins, the revolt against discipline in the factories, and labour agitation carried on by the Trades Unions and the Students Unions.

Visit of
Mr. T. W.
Lamont

Mr. Thomas W. Lamont, of J. P. Morgan and Company, visited the East during 1920 in the interest of the Consortium formed by an International Banking Group of Great Britain, the United States, France and Japan. His object was to make a survey of the financial conditions of China, with a view to ascertaining how far the Consortium could be of use in furnishing China with loans for constructive purposes. The Consortium was not popular in China, as it was feared that the Government would secure loans for military purposes, and that loans, over which the Consortium would exercise a measure of control, would violate in some way the sovereign rights of China.

At the end of the year Mr. F. W. Stevens arrived in Shanghai as representative of the American Banking Group. Mr. Stevens tried to remove misunderstandings in regard to the real object of the Consortium, but was unable to arouse any great enthusiasm. Largely owing to the disturbed conditions in the country, the Consortium was unable to carry out its well-devised plans of furnishing China with financial assistance for internal development.

CHAPTER XXV.

GROWING OPPOSITION TO THE COUNCIL.

The Washington Conference of 1921 By invitation, China was represented at the Washington Conference for Armaments Limitation held in November, 1921. Her representatives went there hoping to gain from the Conference the removal of all existing restrictions upon the political, economic, juridical and administrative activities of their country, but in this they were disappointed.

Agreements were reached in regard to doing away with the foreign post offices. A Commission was to be appointed to take up immediately the matter of tariff revision, and another Commission was to be appointed to visit China, for the purpose of studying the judicial system of the country with a view to determining when extraterritoriality might safely be abolished. Japan definitely withdrew Group V. of the Twenty-one Demands, and Great Britain agreed to return Weihaiwei.

The delegates from China and Japan met separately to consider the question of the return of Kiaochow. Japan finally agreed to give back the leased territory, but asked payment for the improvements made in Tsingtao, and the redemption of the Kiaochow-Tsinan (Kiao-Tsi) Railway.

The real power behind the Chinese delegates at Washington was not the Government, which was disunited, but Chinese public opinion which had been created by the student class in the Treaty Ports, and especially in Shanghai. This was a new factor in international politics, which had first become articulate in Peking in 1919. Shanghai was becoming a centre of new political life in China, and of a new national movement.

Municipal Affairs The proposal to widen The Bund and to throw into the roadway a section of the Public Gardens met with much criticism from the foreign Ratepayers. The objectors were right in regretting the sacrifice of some beautiful trees and a portion of the garden, but were unwise in resisting what, with the rapid increase of traffic, had become a real necessity.

The Council found itself stirring up a hornet's nest when it proposed to license the rice shops of the Settlement. It was led to take the step, owing to the attempt on the part of the native dealers to corner the rice market and charge exorbitant prices. As a result of the proposal, the rice shopkeepers instituted a strike, and of the 450 rice shops in the Settlement about sixty per cent. were closed. One of the objections to the licensing measure was that it involved inspection by the Municipal police. There was no disorder in connection with the movement, and as it was not backed by the people, it soon collapsed. The Council agreed to an arrangement by which the licences might be taken out through the guilds, and by which the police inspection might be dispensed with, provided certain conditions were observed.

Continued Opposition The Municipal Council advocated the passing of bye-laws by which some control might be exercised over the press and by which there might be an increase in the wharfage dues. In regard to both these measures it encountered strong hostility on the part of the Chinese community, as well as with apathy on the part of the foreign Ratepayers.

Licensing of the Press The proposal in regard to the licensing of the Press was briefly as follows: "Printers and publishers shall register with their Consul if they have one, or with the Council, if they have not. Having registered, printers must print their names and places of business on their publications. Nobody must publish or disperse any printed matter which does not bear the name and place of business of the printer."

The object of the registration was to suppress the dissemination of libellous, seditious, and Bolshevistic literature. Whether, if passed, it would have had the desired effect, is doubtful, as it would have been comparatively easy to print such literature outside the Settlement limits and smuggle it in for secret distribution.

The Chinese residents regarded it as interfering with their rights, and as too far-reaching in its scope. They feared, if it were passed, all concerned in printing "would find themselves constantly entrammelled in the meshes of the law."

The Chinese General Chamber of Commerce and other associations brought the matter to the attention of the Waichiaopu (Ministry of Foreign Affairs), who addressed the Consular Body on the subject, through the Commissioner of Foreign Affairs, asking that the proposed bye-law be cancelled.

A protest was also signed by the Booksellers Guild, the Booksellers Association, the Press Association, and the Booksellers and Journalists Union of Shanghai.

At the special meeting of Ratepayers held on April 15th, 1921, a quorum was lacking, and the Council was unable to pass a bye-law for licensing the press.

Further attempts were made in 1923, 1924 and 1925 to pass the same measure with the same result.

In 1924 the Chinese Advisory Committee passed a resolution in opposition to the proposed bye-law.

Increase of Wharfage Dues

In regard to the proposed bye-law increasing the wharfage dues, the right to levy such a tax was obtained from the Land Regulations

promulgated in 1845 and 1854, and amplified in the subsequent Land Regulations of 1869 and 1898.

The amount of the wharfage dues levied on imports
was fixed in 1854 as one-tenth of one per cent. of the
value of the goods passing the Imperial Maritime Customs
at Shanghai.

There had been much difficulty in collecting the
wharfage dues from the Chinese merchants doing
business in the Settlement, and an arrangement had been
arrived at by which the Taotai undertook to manage the
collection, and to pay a certain definite sum annually to
the Council in commutation for wharfage dues.

In course of time the fixed sum of commutation came
to Tls. 10,000. The Council realized that the sum had
become too small, owing to the great expansion in trade,
and that it furnished only 1.56 per cent. of the total
Municipal revenues, and in 1897 made the following
proposal, "That the entire collection of wharfage dues
on all classes of trade be undertaken by the Imperial
Maritime Customs, and from the proceeds thereof one
half of the amount realized on the ' domestic trade ' be
payable to the Taotai as cost of collection, the remainder,
i.e., all the dues on foreign trade together with one half
the dues on native trade, being remitted quarterly to
the Council."

The Taotai gave his consent to the arrangement.

The French Municipal Council became a party to the
proposal on condition that "of the total sum handed over
by the Customs authorities, after deduction of the Taotai's
share of native trade dues and cost of collection, 25 per
cent. of the balance should be handed over to the French
Council as its dues."

This arrangement was approved by the Ratepayers,
and worked satisfactorily. In 1899 the Council derived

from this source of revenue Tls. 135,762.65, as compared with Tls. 69,900.75 in 1898.

The Council, however, needed a larger revenue as the Settlement grew. It was difficult to increase it by direct taxation, inasmuch as the general Municipal rate had already been raised from 12 to 14 per cent. Such being the case, the solution of the problem seemed to be in increasing the indirect taxation, or in other words, the wharfage dues. It was proposed therefore to amend the bye-law stating that such dues shall not exceed one-tenth of one per cent. of the value of the goods, so that it would read three per cent. of the five per cent. *ad valorem* Customs duty. The Council did not anticipate any great objection to the change, and estimated it would result in a very considerable increase in Municipal revenue. The plan was endorsed by the French Municipal Council on March 17th, 1921.

Contrary to expectations, the bye-law met with the same reception as the bye-law concerning the Press. It failed to pass in 1921, for want of a quorum at the special meeting of Ratepayers, and again at the Ratepayers' meeting in 1922 for the same reason. In 1923 considerable agitation had been stirred up among the Chinese against it, and the Commissioner of Foreign Affairs had forwarded to the Senior Consul a protest by the Chinese General Chamber of Commerce.

The bye-law met with the same fate in 1924 and 1925, making it impossible for the Council to raise additional revenue in this way.

Licensing
Exchanges
A third bye-law in regard to licensing the Chinese Produce and Stock Exchange was not intended for increase of revenue, but for the purpose of protecting the Chinese community from bogus speculation.

The French Concession had already adopted a regulation for the licensing of Exchanges, and as a result many of the financially unsound Exchanges had been eliminated.

Even the Peking Government had telegraphed the Commissioner of Foreign Affairs instructing him to consult with the Consular Body with a view to securing its co-operation in controlling the Exchanges in the Settlement. The Council framed a measure against unrestrained speculation and gambling and amended bye-law XXXIV so as to include the words "Stock and Produce Exchange."

This was submitted at special meetings of the Ratepayers in 1922, 1924 and 1925. It met with vigorous opposition from the Chinese community, and one can only interpret this as meaning that the Chinese were more and more inclined to take an antagonistic attitude to any new proposals of the Council. The foreign Ratepayers manifested no interest in the matter, and the amendment was never carried from the usual lack of a quorum whenever it came up for consideration at the special meetings.

Legislation in Regard to Child Labour   The Council found it necessary to take some action in regard to the problem of Child Labour in factories and mills. The conditions of labour since the introduction of steam industries into Shanghai had been far from satisfactory, but the blame for this must not be attributed entirely to the foreign employers. The Chinese had established factories and mills before the foreigners obtained the right to engage in such industries by the treaty made between China and Japan in 1896. In Chinese owned factories and mills, child labour had always existed and it was not introduced for the first time by the foreign mills. This point is sometimes overlooked.

It is true, however, that the conditions of labour in Shanghai, with the possible exception of some of the factories in the Settlement, were worse than in many other parts of China. This produced a good deal of criticism in Europe and America, and caused discontent among the working classes.

The conditions were brought to the attention of the Chairman of the Shanghai Municipal Council in 1922 by Miss A. Harrison of the Y.W.C.A. At that time, the Chairman expressed the view that "the Council should give a lead in the matter by adopting a sympathetic attitude towards actions to limit some of the abuses with which the employment of child labour is fraught."

When the matter came before the Chinese General Chamber of Commerce and the Cotton Mill Owners Association, they stated that they had already taken steps urging the Peking Parliament and the Ministers of Interior, and of Agriculture and Commerce to take action for the passing of bills on the subject in Parliament. There the matter rested for a time.

It was taken up again by the Women's Clubs of Shanghai, both foreign and Chinese, and as a result the Municipal Council decided to appoint a Commission "to go into the whole question and to report thereon in due course, with recommendations for the Council's consideration."

A very representative committee was appointed, and had the advantage of obtaining the co-operation of the well-known social worker, Dame Adelaide Anderson, as a member of the Commission, with the approval of the Municipal Council.

An exhaustive investigation of the local conditions of labour in general and of child labour in particular was carried out, and a thorough study was made of the Chinese Government's Provisional Regulations in regard to child labour, which had been promulgated on March 29th, 1923.

As the Central Government of China at that time

was unable to enforce its decrees throughout the country, it seemed hopeless to place confidence in government regulations for bringing about any improvement in the local situation. Accordingly, the Municipal Council decided to submit a bye-law concerning child labour to a special meeting of Ratepayers. The object of the bye-law was to prohibit for a period of the next four years, the employment of children under 10 years of age, and after that, of children under 12 years of age. The period of work was limited to 12 hours a day, one hour being allowed for rest. All children under 14 years of age were to be allowed 24 hours of continuous rest every 14 days, and were not to be employed in any dangerous work likely to cause serious injury to body or health, or to be exposed to dangerous or hazardous conditions.

This resolution was presented to the special meeting of Ratepayers on April 15th, 1925, along with resolutions concerning the increase in wharfage dues, licensing of printed matter, and licensing of Stock and Produce Exchanges, but failed to be acted upon owing to lack of a quorum.

The final chapter in regard to this measure is well known. A special meeting of Ratepayers was called on June 2nd, 1925. It came just after the excitement caused by the May 30th incident.[1] Although the meeting was better attended than previous ones, a quorum was lacking and legislation on this important matter had to be postponed *sine die*.

This continued indifference on the part of the Ratepayers in regard to these measures may be partly accounted for on the ground that, owing to the hostility of the Chinese public to these regulations, the foreign community feared that, by insisting upon them, condi-

---

[1] See Chapter XXVIII.

tions might be created harmful to peaceful relations in carrying on business.

It remains to consider why the Chinese community was opposed to measures evidently beneficial to both the Chinese and foreign communities. Perhaps a sufficient answer is that a section of the Chinese was opposed to anything which appeared to be an extension of Municipal authority.

Before any such further extension took place, it considered that as a *sine qua non,* there must be Chinese representation on the Municipal Council. Until that could be obtained, it was inclined to adopt an obstructionist attitude.

It is also probable that Bolshevistic agencies were at work, having as their aim the destruction of British prestige and trade in the Far East. This may help to account for the fact that the antagonism showed itself much more in the International Settlement than in the French Concession, some of the measures so bitterly opposed in the International Settlement being actually put into force in the French Concession, such as the licensing of printed matter, and the licensing of the Stock and Produce Exchanges.

In considering these bye-laws we have followed their history through to the end, and have thus been obliged to anticipate somewhat. We now return to the chronicle of cther events in 1921–1922.

Shanghai Waterworks Company   Although negotiations were in progress looking forward to the Municipal Council obtaining the ownership and control of the Shanghai Waterworks Company, the outlay of capital demanded was so large that the matter was delayed.

In Shanghai there are several public utilities, such as water, gas, telephone, tramways, conducted as private

17

companies, the exception being electricity, which became a department of the Municipal Council in 1893.

In the meantime, with the growth of the Settlement, it had become necessary to extend the waterworks by the addition of new pumps, the construction of western district reservoirs, and the laying of new mains.

The following figures are interesting. In 1920 the company distributed 6,881,225,230 gallons of water, and in 1921, 8,292,069,769 gallons, an increase of 1,410,844,539 gallons. The maximum delivered in any one day was in 1921, 30,426,490 gallons against a maximum of 24,894,315 gallons in 1920.

Mr. A. P. Wood, for 36 years Secretary and Engineer-in-chief of the Shanghai Waterworks Company, retired in April, 1921, and returned to the homeland in June. Under his direction the Waterworks Company had made extraordinary progress.

Bolshevists at the Far Eastern Olympics The Far Eastern Olympics were held for the second time in Shanghai, in 1921, at Hongkew Park. During the meet, an attempt was made to distribute Bolshevist literature. Some young men were arrested, one of whom was armed with a pistol. While being pursued, he fired seven times before being caught by Dr. H. H. Morris.

Opening of New Municipal Building The new Municipal Building was formally opened on November 16th, 1922, by Mr. H. G. Simms, Chairman of the Municipal Council. The Chairman in his address referred to the fact that as far back as 1904 the need of a new building had become apparent. In 1912 the Council had appointed a committee to study the matter and draw up a schedule of requirements for the projected building. Upon this schedule was prepared a series of designs which were submitted to the Ratepayers in 1913. When a final design had been adopted, it was placed before the

President of the Royal Institute of British Architects in London, who advised that it be executed in granite instead of artificial stone, as originally intended.

For various reasons, principally owing to the Great War, it took nearly eight years to complete the building. The area covered by it is 12 *mow*, and it contains 400 offices capable of accommodating all the departments of the Council. In connection with it, as already described, is the new Drill Hall for the Shanghai Volunteer Corps. The total cost was one and three-quarters million taels.

The building met with enthusiastic approval from those present at the opening ceremony. It furnishes a fitting home for the administration of the great International Settlement. As was said in an editorial in the *North-China Daily News*, written on that occasion, "the building is a parable in stone commemorating the past, and prophesying of an even better future."

The S.V.C. Club   In the part of the building devoted to the activities of the Volunteer Corps, rooms were set aside for the S.V.C. Club, and these were formally opened on December 18th by Mr. H. G. Simms and Col. R. Marr Johnson, Commandant of the Corps. At that time a presentation was made to Col. T. E. Trueman upon his retirement as Commandant, in recognition of his valuable services, especially during the period of the Great War.

Opening of the Ewo Building   On November 15th another new building was formally opened, that of the old firm of Jardine, Matheson and Company, known by its Chinese name as "Ewo." The edifice is an imposing granite structure and adds much to the fine line of buildings along The Bund. At the time of the passing away of the monopoly of the East India Company, trading to China, the firm of Jardine, Matheson and

Company had been established at Canton, as far back as 1832. Gradually other trade centres were established, as new ports were opened up, and this firm was among the earliest to come to Shanghai. Thus at the opening of the new building it could look back upon a history of over eighty years.

Szechuen Road Bridge The new Szechuen Road Bridge was finished and opened to traffic during this year, and gave Shanghai a bridge greatly superior to the Garden Bridge from an architectural point of view.

Strike at Chinese Post Office Although Shanghai had become more or less accustomed to industrial strikes, it was a new feature to have labour troubles in connection with the public services. Some 300 postmen employed by the Chinese Post Office in Shanghai went out on strike on April 24th, and for a time threw the service into confusion. As the demands were not complied with immediately, a majority of the sorters employed at the central and district offices decided to join the strikers, and this resulted in further disintegration of the service. By yielding to some of the demands of the strikers, the matter was finally adjusted. This movement on the part of government employees to join in strikes caused considerable apprehension in regard to the future, and later events showed that these apprehensions were not altogether groundless.

Strike of Women Workers With the passing years, strikes in mills and factories became more frequent, but it was not until 1922 that women workers participated on a large scale. There was a strike of women connected with the silk filatures in Chapei in the month of August. Nearly 10,000 of the workers went out, when the employers refused to grant their demands for a ten-hour day and a daily increase of five cents in wages. At that time, they were working thirteen and a half hours a day, for forty cents. More than 24 mills in Chapei were affected by the strike, and when some of the employees of the filatures in the Settlement joined them, the numbers on strike increased to 20,000. The strikers paraded the roads in Chapei carrying banners to "make the world know of their harsh conditions."

One of the results of the strike was an appeal, representing 900,000 women workers, to the Civil Governor of Kiangsu, imploring him to reduce their hours of labour. They pointed out that though their hours were nominally eleven, yet in practice they were usually fourteen, and that although at the Washington Conference in 1921, an eight-hour day and a 48-hour week had been approved, the proposal had been entirely ignored by the silk filature authorities.

Proposed Road around the Settlement Owing to the deadlock in connection with settlement extension, the Shanghai Municipal Council continued its policy of opening up new roads leading out of the Settlement. The Chinese looked upon this as a precursor of further claims for extension so that foreign property and residences on these roads might be brought under the control of the Municipal Council. In order to check this supposed policy, some of the Chinese authorities advocated the building of a boundary road around the Settlement and its environs which would serve as a clear line of demarcation and prevent the construction of any further roads by the Council outside the area thus delimited.[1] It would also serve the further purpose of facilitating communications between Chapei and Lunghua.

Increase in Crime Shanghai in recent years has become altogether too familiar with acts of violence.

---

[1] In 1928 work on this road was taken in hand.

Now and again it has been aroused by some sensational shooting affair of an unusual nature, such as the attempt on the life of Baron Tanaka on March 28th, when he was leaving for Japan. Two Coreans threw a bomb among the crowd on the Customs jetty, but it failed to explode. In their effort to escape, they fired indiscriminately into the crowd so as to prevent pursuit, with the result that one of the passengers, Mrs. W. J. Snyder, an Indian watchman, and some coolies were struck. Mrs. Snyder was fatally wounded and died shortly afterwards in the General Hospital.

Associated American Chambers of Commerce The American Chambers of Commerce in Shanghai, Tientsin, Peking and Hankow, following the example of the British merchants, decided to form an Associated American Chambers of Commerce, and representatives from these local associations met in Shanghai on October 23rd for the organization of this body.

It had become increasingly apparent that the merchants throughout the country had many common interests, and that it was greatly to their advantage to come together so that they might act unitedly in presenting to their Government statements in regard to matters affecting American trade in the Far East.

Community Affairs More interest in settlement matters was evidenced by the establishment of a Civic League, for the discussion of Municipal affairs. For the most part Ratepayers have been content to allow the Council to conduct the affairs of the Settlement without interference. Once in a while there has been vigorous agitation when some unpopular measure has been proposed, but generally speaking the public has been indifferent. The Civic League gave opportunity for those who were critical to express their views, and to do something in the way of creating public opinion.

Shanghai was still troubled by the increase in house rents, and by the evidence of profiteering on the part of landlords. The slump in business began to show its effects, and for the first time in its history, the problem of unemployment among the foreign residents assumed serious proportions.

War Memorials

On February 8th, a war memorial was unveiled in the Shanghai Club by the British Consul-General, Sir Everard Fraser, on which were inscribed the names of members of the Club who had given their lives in the War. Sir Everard in his address referred to those, who dying, "gave us rarer gifts than gold."

Another memorial was the Cathedral War Memorial Chapel, dedicated on Sunday, December 10th, by the Rt. Rev. H. J. Molony, D.D. The Chapel is a fitting shrine for over 200 men, who gave their lives in the Great War, and whose names are commemorated in letters of gold. Above the names on three sides of the Chapel is the inscription:

> "To the Glory of God and in honour of the memory of those connected with the Cathedral and Shanghai who fell in the Great War, 1914-1918, this Chapel is dedicated."

The Chapel also contained a memorial to the Rev. W. H. Price, former Sub-Dean of the Cathedral. Two memorial windows were presented by Sir Edward Pearce in memory of his son who fell on "Flanders' field."

Recently a memorial tablet has been erected to the late Dean C. J. F. Symons who died on January 19th, 1928.

National Christian Conference

Of great interest to the missionary community, was the holding of the National Christian Conference in Shanghai on May 2nd. Heretofore the membership of Missionary Conferences had been almost entirely composed of foreign missionaries, but in this case the membership was predominantly Chinese.

Out of the National Christian Conference came the appointment of a National Christian Council of one hundred members, whose function was stated to be that of acting as an advisory body in regard to the Protestant Christian enterprise in China.

New Pasteur Institute
A new Pasteur Institute was opened on December 27th, at Hospital Ste. Marie in the French Concession on the centenary day of the great scientist. Its object was not to compete but to co-operate with the Pasteur Service established by the Municipal Council of the International Settlement. The need of such an institute was amply shown by the fact that in the preceding year, 1,500 stray dogs, the majority of them infected with rabies, had been captured and destroyed in the French Concession.

Noted Visitor
The French Concession was *en fête* for several days in March, 1922, in honour of the visit of the distinguished French soldier, Marshal Joffre. He was entertained lavishly, and the Chinese residents displayed much interest in seeing the man who played so prominent a part in the opening days of the Great War.

Deaths of Prominent Citizens
During the year under review, 1922, several old China hands joined the "great majority." On February 25th the death of Mr. H. E. Hobson occurred in England. He was Senior Commissioner of the Chinese Maritime Customs at the time of his retirement. He came to Shanghai in 1861 to join the Customs, and during the Taiping Rebellion was staff interpreter to General Gordon. He opened several of the new treaty ports for the Customs and had resided in no fewer

than eighteen. His last term of service was in Shanghai where he endeared himself to a large number of friends.

On March 21st occurred the sudden death of Sir Everard Fraser, K.C.M.G., British Consul-General in Shanghai for eleven years, and his country's representative through the trying war period. He had won the respect and admiration of the whole foreign community by his devotion to duty, marked ability, and high character. Memorial services were held in the English Cathedral and Union Church, and there were many expressions of appreciation, especially from the American officials and organizations.

A tablet in his memory was placed in the War Memorial Chapel of the English Cathedral.

The Rev. Samuel Couling, for many years a missionary educator in China, died in June. He was an eminent Chinese scholar and the author of the *Encyclopaedia Sinica*, a work highly commended by Sinologists throughout the world. Upon the death of Mr. George Lanning, the Shanghai Municipal Council asked Mr. S. Couling to continue the official history of Shanghai, but like his predecessor, he died before completing the task.

The death of Mr. J. D. Clark on October 26th, took away another well-known resident of Shanghai. He had been in the East since 1865, first in Japan, and then in China. In 1879 he established the *Shanghai Mercury*, for a long time the leading evening paper.

CHAPTER XXVI.

A YEAR OF UNCERTAINTY, 1923.

Political Events of 1923 The breach between different political factions continued to widen, and the political situation became more confused. In the Capital, President Li Yuan-hung's Government was overthrown by a *coup d'état* and he was compelled to flee to Tientsin.

Brigandage was rife throughout the country, and on May 6th, 1923, an outrage occurred of a sensational character. The famous Blue Express, from Pukow to Tientsin, was derailed by bandits at Lincheng, near the southern border of Shantung. They looted the train and carried off into the mountains thirty-five foreigners, as well as some Chinese, many of whom were well-known residents of Shanghai.

It is generally supposed that the affair was more than a daring attack of bandits, and that the latter were in the employ of a high official anxious to get possession of one of the foreign travellers. Owing to the difficulty of picking out the person wanted, the bandits took the whole party of foreigners into their net.

However this may be, great delay was experienced in obtaining the release of the captured party. The majority were set free in driblets, but eight were removed to the high peaks of Paotuku, and held until negotiations for their ransom had been completed.

On June 1st, a mass meeting was held in the Town Hall in Shanghai to record its protest, and to strengthen the hands of the Diplomatic Body.

Before the release of the eight men could be secured,

the Chinese officials were obliged to agree to a general pardon and the enrolment of the bandits in the army.

The Diplomatic Body presented its claims for compensation and retribution on August 10th, asking for monetary compensation for those who had been captured, the cashiering of Tien Chung-yü, Tuchun[1] of Shantung, and the appointment of railway guards, organized and officered by foreigners. The Chinese Government was unwilling to comply with the demand in regard to railway guards under foreign control and organized a special force to give protection to those travelling on the line.

Signs of a rupture between the Provinces of Chekiang and Kiangsu became more evident. When General Hsu Kuo-liang, chief of the Shanghai and Woosung constabulary, was assassinated in Yunnan Road, off Avenue Edward VII, on November 11th, General Ho Feng-ling, Defence Commissioner of Shanghai and Sungkiang in charge of the Kiangnan Arsenal, lieutenant of the Chekiang Tuchun, immediately appointed a successor, much to the chagrin of the Kiangsu Tuchun, who contended that as Shanghai was in his province, the appointment rested with him. The peace between the two provinces was seriously endangered, but the break was postponed for a time.

After the *coup d'état* in Peking, a large number of the members of Parliament fled to Shanghai, where an attempt was made to convene a session. Later on by extensive bribing, many of the M.P.'s were persuaded to return to Peking, so that a quorum could be secured for the election of Tsao Kun as President, and for the adoption of a constitution.

Russian Cadets   A Russian fleet of 27 ships under the joint command of Admirals Stark and Bezoire

---

[1] A Tuchun was the Military Governor of a province.

left Vladivostok toward the close of 1922, on the incoming of the "Reds." They had on board some 8,000 people, whose main idea was to flee from the Red Terror. At first they took refuge at Gensan, but were requested by the authorities to quit Japanese waters. Some of the vessels, owing to lack of coal and food, were obliged to remain at the port, with 6,000 on board. The remaining 15 vessels had sufficient coal and food to reach Fusan, but were not allowed to anchor. After encountering a violent storm, in which one vessel was lost, they sought refuge in the Yangtze and anchored off Woosung.

The ships carried a number of orphans, who had no means of support whatsoever. They were the sons of Russian officers killed in the war, and Admiral Stark was anxious to find some place where they could be landed and taken care of. The Chinese authorities were unwilling to have these ships remain in harbour, but offered to provide them with sufficient coal to reach the next port.

As Christmas was approaching, the hard fate of these people, and especially the needs of the young Russian cadets—350 in number—made a strong appeal to the sympathies of the residents of Shanghai.

Finally twelve of the ships left *en route* for the southern ports, but of the 1,800 people on board at the time of their arrival at Woosung only 650 remained with their ships, the rest having gained permission to land. The Bureau of Russian Affairs, which had been established in Shanghai, had the difficult task of arranging for the refugees left on its hands. The 350 cadets, the majority of whom were orphans, were quartered for a time in a house at 4 Jessfield Road, and were supported largely by public charity.

In succeeding years the Russian refugee problem

continued to cause considerable anxiety. The arrival off the Chusan Archipelago of the " Eldorado " from Gensan on July 1st, 1923, with 700 fighting Russians on board, and quantities of arms and ammunition, caused a sensation. It was found that the real purpose of the " Eldorado " was gun-running. Captain Kearny, an American, was arrested for complicity, tried and sentenced to pay a large fine.

On September 19th three more ships under Lieutenant-General Gleboff put in an appearance at Woosung, carrying some hundreds of fighting men, but the Chinese authorities refused them permission to enter the harbour.

Signs of Decline in Prosperity In the year 1923 it became evident that the rapid development of Shanghai which took place in 1921 and 1922 could not be continued at the same pace.

Owing to the fact that during the war period everything had been retarded, there naturally followed, when peace was restored, a time of feverish activity. Old buildings on The Bund gave place to handsome modern ones whose cost ran into millions. In some cases the funds were derived from excess profits made during the war. Cotton mills were started, on account of the cotton boom, and blocks of new foreign and Chinese houses went up, to supply the demand for living accommodation. The plans passed by the Public Works Department in 1921 were for buildings of an estimated cost of Tls. 21,000,000, in which was included the new Hongkong and Shanghai Bank, the cost of which was between five and six millions. In 1922 there was still an endeavour to make up for lost time, but the new buildings projected that year were not as numerous, and the total cost was probably not more than fifteen millions. Especially was this true of Chinese house property, which was less than that of the two preceding years, indicating that this demand had nearly been satisfied.

Office accommodation had been well supplied, being greatly increased by the large buildings erected on The Bund and elsewhere.

The cotton industry failed to be the successful enterprise it had been during the war period, and many of the mills, unable to carry on, were sold.

Among the new buildings under contemplation were the new Custom House, and a new Community Church[1] for the American community.

It appeared as if some of the development was due to too great optimism in regard to the future of trade, and the slowing up was probably an indication of a spirit of greater discretion.

Municipal Affairs   Nothing extraordinary transpired in the year 1923 in regard to Municipal affairs. The increase in expenditure began to cause anxiety, and aroused discussion as to the way in which reductions might be made.   For the first time the growing cost of the Municipal Orchestra was adversely criticized.

The Council pushed forward the matter of road extension, especially that of the Great Western Road, and in spite of protest and opposition on the part of the Chinese authorities, this work was carried to completion. The Chairman of the Council, Mr. H. G. Simms, in the correspondence on the subject made the interesting statement " that excluding the Great Western Road Extension, the Council at present owned 19½ miles of roads in the Western Districts beyond the Settlement boundary acquired and laid out under the powers granted by Land Regulation VI."

---

[1] The Community Church was the outgrowth of the American Song Service inaugurated in Shanghai during the Great War.

On Thursday, March 22nd, the War Mem-
Municipal
Council's War orial to the Municipal Council's employees
Memorial was unveiled.   It was placed at the top of
the stairs in the main entrance hall of the
new Administration Building.   It is a handsome tablet
upon which are inscribed the names of the dead, twenty
in all.   The ceremony of unveiling was conducted by
Mr. Simms.

Serious charges were brought against two
Charges of members of the Municipal police force by
Torture
Against the a man named Loh Tse-hwa, who claimed
Municipal he had been subjected to severe torture in
Police one of the police stations.   The case was
tried before Judge Skinner Turner in H.B.M.'s Supreme
Court for China.   Although the jury brought in a verdict
of " not guilty " in regard to the two men who were
accused, yet they added the significant rider that they
were convinced that " Loh Tse-hwa received his injuries
whilst he was in the hands of the police."   The case
brought to light the unjustifiable practice sometimes
resorted to of extorting confessions from men who were
arrested, and resulted in steps being taken to do away with
this evil.

One of the most important events in the
Opening of
the Hongkong commercial world was the formal opening
and Shanghai of the Hongkong and Shanghai Bank on
Bank June 23rd.   The building, which had taken
two years for its erection, in size and architectural beauty,
is probably the finest commercial house in the Far East.
As was well said in the *North-China Daily News* of June
25th, "The building of ' Way-foong ' (the bank's Chinese
name) reflects the highest credit on all concerned in its
erection, on the daring of the men who authorized the
stupendous plan, the creative genius of the architects who
designed it, and the triumphant organization that made

its completion possible in the short space of little more than two years."

As the traveller approaches Shanghai by water, one of the first sights to attract his attention is the well proportioned dome that fitly crowns the edifice.

Sir Ronald Macleay, K.C.M.G., H.B.M.'s Minister to China, was the Master of Ceremonies. When he opened the central gates, a vast crowd poured into the building, indicating the great place occupied by the Hongkong and Shanghai Bank in the interests of the commercial world of the Far East.

The erection of the building at such a time was an evidence of the faith in China's financial future, and of her future development as a great country. It was an evidence, too, that in some ways Shanghai might fittingly be called the Venice of the Eastern World.

Bank of China Another interesting event in banking circles was the conversion of the German Club on The Bund into new offices for the Bank of China.

Earthquake in Japan On September 1st, 1923, occurred the appalling earthquake in Yokohama. Much sympathy was manifested for the people of Japan, and this increased as the news came through showing that the calamity was greater than at first had been supposed. Steps were at once taken in Shanghai to start relief measures and Yen 20,000 were cabled to the foreigners relief committee in Japan. The British Women's Association and the American Women's Club exerted themselves especially on behalf of the foreign women victims of the earthquake. Many residents were in suspense for a long time in regard to the fate of friends and relatives spending the summer holidays in the Island Empire.

Riverside Power Station Calamity A very unusual and serious accident occurred at the Riverside Power Station of the Electricity Department on Thursday,

November 15th.   An explosion took place in one of the new 20,000 k.w. turbines which was being run on trial for purposes of balancing.   The three engineers who were in charge of the trial were killed, making it difficult to discover the real cause of the disaster.   Four Chinese workmen were killed and many others injured, and the turbine house was completely wrecked.

Anti-Japanese Boycott   During the year the anti-Japanese boycott had serious effects on trade.   The students stirred up an agitation because Japan was unwilling to return Port Arthur and Dairen and, as they claimed, still insisted on the Twenty-one Demands.

The Japanese Chamber of Commerce protested against the interruption of trade, and appealed to their Government for support.

The Customs revenue for Shanghai, in spite of the effective five per cent. import tariff, showed a decrease in the month of July of nearly Hk. Tls. 180,000.   This was largely due to the anti-Japanese boycott.

Distinguished Visitors   Several distinguished visitors were in Shanghai during the course of the year, among them being Dr. Einstein, who gave an address on the theory of "Relativity," Miss Jane Addams, the well-known welfare worker of Chicago, who gave a talk at the Community Church, and Dame Adelaide Anderson. The latter came at the invitation of the National Christian Council, to investigate the condition of child labour in the factories.

Death of Rev. Dr. Fitch   The death of one of the most respected and well-known missionaries in Shanghai, Dr. G. F. Fitch, occurred on February 7th, after 53 years of service in the Mission field.   Largely owing to his efforts, the Presbyterian Mission Press developed into an important agency for the publication and printing of missionary literature.

18

CHAPTER XXVII.

CIVIL WAR IN THE NEIGHBOURHOOD OF SHANGHAI.

The latter part of the year 1924, and the beginning of 1925 was a period of anxiety for the residents of the Settlements, owing to the fact that Shanghai city and its environs were fought for as a prize in the war between rival political factions in Kiangsu and Chekiang.

In the opening part of the year there was little anticipation of the stormy days ahead, and the Municipality and community, except for the disturbance to trade caused by the turmoil in China, pursued the even tenor of their way.

Before giving an account of the war and its effect upon the Settlements, we will briefly review other events of 1924 which were of importance to the community.

New Shanghai American School Buildings, and New American Club On January 2nd the handsome buildings erected for the Shanghai American School on Avenue Petain were dedicated with impressive ceremonies, and on January 10th the corner stone of the new American Club on Foochow Road was laid. These events were indicative of the growth of American interests in Shanghai.

Round-the-World Cruises It was at this time that round-the-world cruises became popular, large steamers being chartered to convey passengers on a circumnavigating tour, and as Shanghai was one of the points of call, the residents became familiar with the incursions of globe trotters from the Western World.

The Cunard liner "Franconia," chartered by the American Express Company, arrived at Woosung on

Monday, January 7th, as one of the pioneers in this new enterprise.

At the time of the arrival of the "Franconia," large steamers were still obliged to anchor at Woosung, and to send up their passengers on launches. Shortly afterwards, owing to the improvement in the harbour and the further deepening of the channel made by the Whangpoo Conservancy Board, it became possible for large ships to come up the Whangpoo River and to dock off Shanghai. The first large steamer to accomplish this successfully was the "Empress of Russia" of the Canadian Pacific Steamship Company, which tied up at her berth on the China Merchants Eastern Wharf on the Pootung side on Saturday, February 9th. After this venture, the way was opened, and it became the usual thing for even the largest vessels to come up and berth at Shanghai.

Dedication of the Shanghai War Memorial As long ago as 1919 the people of Shanghai had begun to make plans for a War Memorial, and after many years of waiting it was at last completed. The solemn dedicatory service and the unveiling ceremony took place on February 16th in beautiful weather, and were witnessed by a vast throng. The Bund was crowded from Avenue Edward VII to beyond Canton Road. Those taking part in the ceremony were drawn from every section of the Settlement's many-sided interests, and included representatives from religious, civic, diplomatic, naval, and military organizations. Commander G. de Rossi, the Senior Allied Consul, performed the unveiling. The Memorial is a beautiful piece of work, simple in construction and striking in its general effect. It represents the Angel of Victory with her hand upon the head of a little child and bears the inscription *"Ad mortuorum gloriam."* Erected on a stone terrace facing the entrance to Avenue Edward VII, it is in full sight from the harbour.

On Sunday preceding the unveiling of the Shanghai War Memorial, some beautiful stained glass windows were unveiled in the Union Church as a memorial to those connected with the church who made the supreme sacrifice in the Great War. The ceremony of dedicating the main window was performed by H.B.M.'s Consul-General, Sir Sidney Barton, and that of dedicating the two small windows, presented by the Sunday School, by Col. W. F. L. Gordon.

Union Jack Club To meet the need of men of the British Navy in port, the Union Jack Club on Myburgh Road was formally opened on May 12th by Admiral Sir Arthur Leveson, K.C.B., Commander-in-chief of the China Station. It was erected and equipped by the Navy League and the Shanghai Race Club, and is largely supported by the latter.

Missions Building Another building completed at this time was the Missions Building on Yuen-ming-yuen Road. Put up for the National Christian Council, and for the housing of various mission agencies and associations, it was intended to symbolize the underlying unity of the Protestant Missions in China. The project was made possible by a generous grant from the American Presbyterian Mission, a gift of $150,000 from Dr. F. J. Tooker and his sisters, and a contribution of $120,000 from the Laura Spellman Rockefeller Fund.

New Buildings Among other new buildings opened during the year was the splendid new home of the *North-China Daily News*. The ceremony was performed by Sir Ronald Macleay, K.C.M.G., on February 15th. At that time the *North-China Daily News* had been published for sixty years and the *North-China Herald* for seventy-four. The front is of granite and makes the building a handsome addition to The Bund.

The new building of the Yokohama Specie Bank was opened on July 19th.

The present imposing Chinese Post Office on the corner of Szechuen and Soochow Roads was completed at this time. For its spaciousness and completeness of design, it ranks as one of the finest administration buildings in China. It took two years to construct and cost Tls. 2,250,000.

The handsome McBain residence on Bubbling Well Road with its beautiful grounds was purchased and converted into what is now known as the Majestic Hotel.

Of special importance to the Chinese community was the opening of a new Chinese Textile Mill, the Wing On, on Lay Road on November 29th. The company was capitalized at $6,000,000, and the building is one of the most complete in the country.

New Race Course A new Race Course was opened by the Chinese north of Yangtszepoo, thus giving Shanghai three Race Courses. Race meetings are very popular with the Chinese as well as with the foreign community, and it has been said that no matter how dull general business may be, the Race Courses are always prosperous.[1]

Ratepayers' Meeting, April 16th At the general meeting of Ratepayers on April 16th, the Council was authorized to enter into a new agreement with the Shanghai Mutual Telephone Company, by which shareholders should be secured an eight per cent. dividend, the Council should be represented on the Board of Directors, surplus earnings should accumulate for the benefit of subscribers, and the automatic telephone should be approved for general use.

---

[1] In recent years another form of racing has been introduced into Shanghai—Greyhound Racing. It has been severely criticized on the ground that it is more of a gambling institution than a sport.

A resolution was also passed allowing the Council to follow one of two alternative plans in regard to the Shanghai Waterworks Company, either to raise money to complete the purchase, or to enter into some agreement with the company similar to the one entered into with the Shanghai Mutual Telephone Company, by which the Council could exercise some control over the operation of a company dealing with a public utility.[1]

Appointment of Traffic Commission
The Council took the important step of appointing a commission to study the whole question of traffic in Shanghai.   As the Settlement grew, the roads became more and more congested.   There were constant accidents and it was apparent that well devised regulations should be put into force.   Motors, trams, buses, ricshas, hand carts, bicycles, wheelbarrows and pedestrians, using the same thoroughfares, presented many serious problems.[2]

New Honan Road Bridge
The building of the Honan Road Bridge was pushed forward, and in its construction beauty was combined with utility, the result from an architectural point of view being very satisfactory.

New Forms of Conveyance
Two new forms of conveyance were sanctioned and introduced during the year.   The first was the pedicab, a combination of bicycle and ricsha.   The passenger occupied the ricsha, and a man, by pedalling a bicycle, pulled it along.   At first the pedicab promised to be popular, but in a short time it was found that it was not as comfortable, safe or cheap as the ricsha pulled by a runner.

The other new conveyance was the bus.   The China

---

[1] Eventually the latter alternative was adopted.
[2] The Commission made its report, with the result that much has been done in the way of introducing traffic signals, and regulating traffic by making some streets one-way roads during certain hours of the day.

General Omnibus Company began to operate in August.
According to the prospectus there was to be no overcrowding and every passenger was to be entitled to a seat.
For a time it furnished a very comfortable way of travelling, but gradually the rules were relaxed, and for some
reason or another overcrowding was allowed so that there
came to be little choice between the bus and the tram.

Sale of the Bowling Alley One of the last of Shanghai's old buildings
disappeared with the sale of its ancient
Skittle Alley at 49 Nanking Road. The
Alley had stood on this site for 70 years. The Bowling
Club in its history had passed through many vicissitudes,
with periods of prosperity and periods of depression. The
land on which it stood belonged to another old institution,
the Fives Court Club, which had already taken steps for
the sale of its property. The Bowling Club continued its
existence in new premises on Hardoon Road.

The Kiangsu-Chekiang War As stated in the opening of this chapter, the
most important event of the year 1924 was
the Kiangsu-Chekiang civil war.

Although we refer to it as a civil war, yet in reality
there was no hostility between the people of these two
provinces. The war was a part of the struggle carried on
between the great political parties, the Fengtien and Anfu
on the one side, and the Chihli on the other.

Agreement of Peace between the Two Provinces A well-known agreement between the rival
generals, Lu Yung-hsiang, Director-General
for the Reorganization of Military Affairs
in Chekiang, and Ho Feng-ling, Defence
Commissioner of Shanghai and Sungkiang, on one side,
and Chi Hsieh-yuan, Tuchun of Kiangsu, on the other, had
been signed in August, 1923, for the preservation of peace
between the two provinces.

As we have stated, after the assassination of General
Hsu Kuo-liang the pact had been endangered by the

appointment of a new Police Commissioner in Shanghai by the Chekiang authorities, but a rupture had been temporarily avoided.

Meanwhile both the authorities of Kiangsu and Chekiang looked upon Shanghai, which geographically is situated in the former province, as a very desirable possession, especially on account of the revenue to be derived from the illicit opium traffic and also from the fact that the Kiangnan Arsenal is on the outskirts of the city.

Cause of Hostilities Generals Tsang Chi-ping and Yang Hua-chao, after being defeated in Fukien, took refuge in Chekiang. When the news reached Marshal Wu Pei-fu of the Chihli Party, who controlled the Yangtze provinces, he insisted they must be expelled, and when this was not done he commanded the Tuchun of Kiangsu to take up arms against Chekiang.

Headed by Chi Hsieh-yuan, the Kiangsu army moved on Shanghai. In order to resist the advance, the Chekiang forces established several lines of defence, one of which extended from Liuho to Minghong.

State of Emergency On account of fighting in the close neighbourhood of the Settlements and the danger of defeated troops attempting to seek refuge within the Settlement boundaries, the Municipal Council declared a state of emergency on September 9th, and mobilized the Volunteer Corps. At the same time, naval parties were landed from the warships in harbour. A cordon of defence was drawn around the Settlements, and the roads leading into them were barricaded.

Taking of Sungkiang and Flight of Generals Lu and Ho For more than a month, the Chekiang army resisted the attacks of the numerically stronger forces of Kiangsu, which had been reinforced by the troops of Wu Pei-fu from Honan and Hupeh and by those of General Sun Chuan-fang from Fukien. When, however, in October,

Sungkiang fell into the hands of Sun Chuan-fang's troops, the position of the Chekiang men became critical, and Generals Lu Yung-hsiang and Ho Feng-ling, fearing treachery among their subordinates, decided to abandon the struggle, and departed for Japan secretly, leaving their troops to shift for themselves.

As soon as the news of the flight of their leaders reached the soldiers at the front, the white flag was raised, and a general retirement on Shanghai began.   On October 14th the Hupeh troops reached Shanghai North Station and occupied Lunghua and the Arsenal.

General
Hsu Shu-cheng
Expelled from
Shanghai
In the meantime there was danger lest General Hsu Shu-cheng, better known as "Little Hsu," who had entered the Settlement, would make an attempt to reorganize the Chekiang troops.   Had he succeeded, there might have been a further struggle on the borders of the Settlements with serious consequences both for the foreign and Chinese communities.   This danger was averted by the prompt action taken by the Municipal Council.   General Hsu was arrested for having entered the Settlement contrary to an order issued by the Council on July 5th, 1921.   Six days later he left Shanghai *en route* for Europe.   The work of the disarmament and evacuation of the defeated Chekiang troops was then carried out.

Although the proclamation of a state of emergency, the landing of foreign naval forces, the barricading of the Settlement roads, the occupation of a section of Chinese territory for strategical purposes, the forcible disarming of Chinese troops, and the expulsion of a general from the Settlement, might have been regarded by the Chinese as infringements of their sovereign rights, yet no protest was made by the people, and the Chinese Ratepayers Association expressed its appreciation of the Council's work for the protection of Chinese lives and property.

Refugees in Shanghai During this period a pitiable and all too familiar sight was the great stream of refugees from the towns and villages in the neighbourhood of Shanghai flowing into the Settlements.

Rich and poor, old and young, all alike were seeking a place of safety from the soldiers. They came by train, by boat, by ricsha, by wheelbarrow, and on foot, bringing with them such portion of their goods and chattels as they could carry.

The Municipal Council erected refugee camps for those who had no place to go to. It is estimated that the number taking refuge in Shanghai was about 200,000.

Various Chinese organizations, guilds, provincial associations, Buddhist societies, and the Chambers of Commerce, gave generous assistance to those who were friendless and without funds. A number of shelters were maintained by these bodies, and the work of feeding and housing the people was well organized.

Thanks to the Defence Force Shanghai was proud of the way in which the Volunteer Corps and the Municipal police acquitted themselves during the trying days of the provincial war, and an inspection of these two bodies held on the Race Course on October 31st, was witnessed by a large number of the foreign residents. Mr. Stirling Fessenden, Chairman of the Council and Civil Commandant of the Shanghai Volunteer Corps, took the salute, and addressed the men, expressing the thanks of the community for their invaluable services during the critical period through which Shanghai had just passed.

Renewal of Civil War Civil war between the two provinces broke out again in December and lasted on into January of the following year. It was due to the following cause:

General Sun Chuan-fang, who had been made Tuchun of Chekiang, was forced to take up arms against General Chen Yao-san, one of the generals who had fled to Japan, with Generals Lu and Ho, when he returned and attempted to resume command over his former troops in Sungkiang.

When General Sun Chuan-fang succeeded in taking Sungkiang, General Chen Yao-san was forced to fall back on Shanghai. Just then General Chi Hsieh-yuan, who had been dismissed from office by the Peking Government, appeared on the scene again. He came suddenly to Shanghai, seized the command of the Kiangsu troops stationed there and joined with General Sun Chuan-fang in eliminating General Chen Yao-san. On January 11th, 1925, his troops occupied Lunghua and the Kiangnan Arsenal, and General Chen's defeated troops withdrew to the banks of the Siccawei Creek, and to the borders of the French Concession where they were disarmed by the French Volunteers and by the police and landing parties from the French men-of-war. Two days later a band of defeated troops, 2,500 in number, attempted to enter the International Settlement. They were disarmed by a company of Volunteers at the Jessfield Railway Station, and were interned in Jessfield Park, and kept under guard by the Chinese Company of the Shanghai Volunteer Corps until they were sent to concentration camps in the Settlement. The whole number of troops interned in the International Settlement and the French Concession amounted to 10,000. Later these interned troops were deported to Shantung.

General Chi Attempts to Take Nanking The victorious generals returned to their respective headquarters, General Sun to Hangchow, and General Chi to Chapei. General Chi then attempted to revolt against Peking and made an advance up the Shanghai-Nanking Railway to attack Nanking, at that time in the hands of the Fengtien forces. Partly owing to treachery, his success, however, was short-lived, and ten days later he was obliged to retreat.

Fengtien Troops Occupy Shanghai
The Government troops sent from the North consisted of Fengtien soldiers and a mixed brigade of Russians. After his defeat, General Chi and his staff departed for Japan on January 28th, following the example set by Generals Lu and Ho in the previous year. This finally brought the war to an end. Ten thousand troops under the personal command of General Chang Chung-chang, the Tuchun of Shantung, occupied Shanghai and took control over the adjoining districts.

Measures for the Protection of the Settlement
Prompt measures had been taken again, by the erection of barricades on the Chapei-Settlement boundary and in the western district, to prevent the entry of fugitive soldiers into the Settlement.

During the critical period, a naval detachment was stationed in Jessfield Park to guard the approaches from the west.

Although there was war in the vicinity of Shanghai, life in the Settlement was not as much affected as might have been expected, the only difference being that foreigners did not venture far beyond the Settlement limits.

Commerce and Trade
The commercial interests of the Settlement were influenced adversely by the civil war, but comparing the Customs revenue for the whole country for the years 1923 and 1924, we find that there had been an increase. The figures were Hk. Tls. 63,504,250 for 1923 and Hk. Tls. 69,595,131 for 1924. This may be more than accounted for, however, by the tariff having been raised to an effective five per cent.

The Salt Gabelle showed a decrease of Tls. 9,001,000, due undoubtedly to the disturbed conditions caused by the war.

Death of Rev. C. E. Darwent
The death of the Rev. C. E. Darwent occurred at Tientsin on October 12th. Before accepting a call to Tientsin, Mr. Darwent had been Pastor of Union Church in Shanghai for twenty years and had endeared himself to all sorts and conditions of men, and had exerted a unique influence in the community. For sixteen years his sermons had been published weekly in the *North-China Daily News*.

Transfer of Russian Consulate to Soviet Government
We close the chapter with a reference to an event that was to have serious consequences upon the Far East. On May 31st, 1924, China recognized the Soviet Government which had agreed to give up her claim to extraterritoriality. The Russian Consulate in Shanghai was handed over to the representatives of the Soviet Government by the former Consul-General, M. Victor Grosse, on July 24th. Inasmuch as there was fear of a demonstration by the "Whites," the transfer was carried out under a strong guard of European and Sikh police. The sinister red flag, bearing the golden sickle and hammer, was flown from the top of the building, and Shanghai became a centre where organized Bolshevist propaganda could be carried on.

Warnings were uttered about the growing influence of Bolshevism, but for the most part they were unheeded.

CHAPTER XXVIII.

A GREAT CRISIS.

We have now followed the history of Shanghai to the close of the year 1924, and have pointed out that at that time there were indications of the approach of a great political, social and industrial upheaval, which might affect the Settlements in many ways. During the years 1925, 1926 and 1927, this upheaval occurred. As it is still in progress, it is too soon to see with any certainty the ultimate results. The historian treats of things that are past, not of those of the present and future, and hence we may consider our task to be finished. We will, however, attempt to give a brief review of recent events, and a statement of the present situation, avoiding, as far as possible, discussion as to their significance, or prediction as to the future.

In the year 1925 the outstanding event, as far as the Settlement was concerned, was the May 30th incident.

Strikes in Japanese Mills Early in the year there were frequent strikes in Japanese mills. A raid upon the Shanghai University situated on Seymour Road, and the seizure of a large amount of Bolshevistic literature, gave reason to believe that the strikes were fomented by a party which had come under Soviet influence.

Death of Dr. Sun Yat-sen On March 12th, 1925, Dr. Sun Yat-sen passed away in Peking. In his political will, which has become the great charter of the Kuomintang, there were phrases which seemed to encourage a closer alliance with Russia, which had proffered friendship to China.

**Strike at
Nagai Wata
Kaisha's Mill**
It was during a strike at one of the Nagai Wata Kaisha's mills that serious trouble arose. An assault was made by some of the Chinese labourers, and a Japanese overseer in charge of the property fired several shots into the crowd. Seven of those attacking were injured, one of whom died the following day.

**Clash between
Students and
Police at
Louza Station**
This incident led to further anti-Japanese agitation and culminated in the unfortunate event of May 30th. On that day parties of students took part in anti-Japanese propaganda in the Settlement, and became greatly incensed when some of them were arrested and taken off to the Louza Police Station. Other students followed into the Police Station, and demanded that either those detained should be released, or that all should be arrested. A crowd soon gathered on Nanking Road in front of the small gate to the Police Station. In the attempt on the part of the police to drive the crowd back, a serious clash occurred. Inspector Everson, who was on duty, believing there was danger of the police being overpowered, and the Louza Station being rushed, ordered his men to fire, with the result that four of the crowd were killed outright and a number wounded. Of the wounded who were sent to the Shantung Road Hospital, four succumbed later. In the days following there were further clashes between the police and mobs. The total Chinese casualties connected with the May 30th incident, as far as could be ascertained, were 24 killed and 36 wounded.

In an incredibly short time the Chinese community in Shanghai was ablaze with indignation.

The emotional excitement over the incident was far greater than over any happening of a similar character in the past, and can only be explained on the ground that the nationalist movement had succeeded in stirring up the people so that they now resented what had been passively submitted to in the past. It seemed outrageous to the Chinese that foreigners who were guests in China should have the power of life or death over the people in whose land they dwelt.

The news of the May 30th incident rapidly spread throughout China, and strengthened the nationalist and anti-foreign movements.

General Strike On May 31st the Chinese General Chamber of Commerce declared a general strike. Shops were closed, and labourers in foreign employ went out on strike. The total number of strikers in the Settlement was 100,000 and in Pootung 15,000.

Council Declares State of Emergency On June 1st, in order to prevent further disturbances, the Council declared a state of emergency. The Shanghai Volunteer Corps was mobilized and Col. W. F. L. Gordon, Commandant of the Corps, was appointed commander of all defence forces in Shanghai. Measures were taken for the continuance of essential services, and for an adequate food supply for the Settlements.

As an evidence that the incident of May 30th served as the spark to fire the train already laid, we have wide use of the following slogans at this time, "Abolish extraterritoriality," "Cancel unequal treaties," "Restore all foreign settlements to China."

Mixed Court Trial Forty-nine persons (some of whom were students) were tried before the Mixed Court for creating trouble in the International Settlement. After thorough investigation from June 4th to 11th they were dismissed upon giving a bond for future good conduct.

Chinese Government Investigates The Chinese Government appointed Admiral Tsai Ting-kan and Mr. Tseng Tsung-chien, Vice-Minister of Foreign Affairs, to proceed to Shanghai to investigate the matter and to settle it on the spot.

At the same time, the Diplomatic Body in Peking also appointed a commission to visit Shanghai and to hold an inquiry.[1]

Chinese Demands Before either of these bodies arrived, the Chinese organizations on June 6th formulated several demands, which with slight amendments were approved by the Chinese General Chamber of Commerce. Among these were the following: Punishment of offenders, compensation for the dead and wounded, an apology, rendition of Mixed Court, all strikers to be reinstated and their wages paid during the strike period, participation of the Chinese in the Municipal Council and Ratepayers' meetings, the Chinese representation on the Council to be in proportion to the amount paid to the Municipal revenue, the qualifications for franchise for the Chinese to be similar to those for foreigners, no roads to be constructed by the Municipal Council beyond Settlement boundaries and those already constructed to be turned over unconditionally to the Chinese Government, withdrawal of the proposed regulations concerning printed matter, increase of wharfage dues, and licensing of exchanges, dismissal of the Secretary of the Municipal Council, Mr. E. S. B. Rowe.

International Judicial Inquiry The Diplomatic Commission made its report which proved to be unacceptable to the Municipal Council. The respective Powers then announced their intention to establish an International Judicial Inquiry into the Shanghai incident. This proposal, however, did not meet with the approval of the Chinese, and on August 17th the Chinese General

---

[1] See *Shanghai: Its Municipality and the Chinese*: A. M. Kotenev, pp. 140–142.

19

Chamber of Commerce forwarded to the British, French, American, Italian, Japanese and Belgian Legations, a protest against this method of procedure.

Chinese Government Refuses to Take Part It appears that the Chinese authorities were aware of the terms of the report of the delegates of the Diplomatic Body, although up to that time they had not been made public, and being on the whole satisfied with them, did not want the matter re-investigated. They gave as their reason " the case has already been very carefully investigated by the Chinese Government and the Diplomatic delegates, and its merits have already been well established. To propose to conduct a judicial inquiry of re-investigation after the lapse of more than three months would seem to ignore the above facts in their entirety and would, it is feared, only serve the purpose of complicating the issue."

Findings of the Judicial Inquiry This Judicial Inquiry, however, was held, the Court consisting of Mr. Justice Finley Johnson (United States), Sir Henry Gollan (Great Britain) and Mr. K. Suga (Japan). No Chinese Judge was present, although the Chinese had been urged to appoint one. Thirteen sessions were held from October 7th to 27th, but no Chinese witnesses were willing to appear and very little new evidence was obtained. Each of the Judges drew up a separate report. Although the reports differed from one another on several points, all exonerated Inspector Everson.

The American Judge criticized the Commissioner of Police, Mr. McEuen, both for his absence from the scene of trouble, and for his not having taken sufficient precautions against serious disturbance.

Action of the Council On December 21st, 1925, the Council informed the Consular Body of the resigna-

tion of Mr. McEuen, and Inspector Everson,[1] renewed its
expression of regret at the loss of life on May 30th, and
requested the Consular Body to forward to the Commissioner of Foreign Affairs a cheque for $75,000 as a mark
of sympathy with the wounded and with the relatives
of those who were killed. Under instructions from the
Waichiaopu, the Commissioner of Foreign Affairs refused
to receive it.

Opinions
of Justice
Finley
Johnson

Mr. Justice Finley Johnson in his report
went behind the immediate causes of the
local disturbance, and pointed out what
appeared to him the deep-seated reasons
for the antagonism between the Chinese and the foreign
communities. In this connection he suggested that the
question of extraterritoriality, and the alleged infringement of China's sovereignty should be considered and
settled. He pointed out also the need of taking up the
revision of the treaties, and called attention to the changed
mentality of the Chinese in regard to liberty and independence.

The Long
Strike

As we have said, the May 30th incident led
to the most serious and prolonged strikes
in the history of Shanghai. Commerce and industry
for a time were at a standstill.

But by June 26th the situation was somewhat
alleviated by the reopening of the Chinese *hongs* and
shops, in accordance with a resolution passed by the
Chinese General Chamber of Commerce. The industrial
strike, however, continued, and shipping was almost
entirely tied up.

The Municipal Council finally resorted to cutting off
electric power from Chinese owned mills and factories.
This was greatly resented by the Chinese employers, and

---

[1] The Chinese criticized the retirement of these two men on
pension.

although attempts were made by them to furnish their own power plants, yet many industries were seriously crippled.

In course of time the strike fund for paying the unemployed labourers became exhausted. There had been considerable dissatisfaction among the workers as to the way the fund was distributed.

Chinese Representation on the Council The constant friction between the Council and the Chinese residents made it perfectly apparent that harmony could only be secured by offering the Chinese representation on the Council.

Experience had shown that the Chinese Advisory Committee was not satisfactory either to the Municipal Council or to the Chinese community and it was felt that a new step must be taken—a step that would radically change the constitution of the International Settlement.

According to the terms of the treaties the Chinese had no legal right to demand representation, but in the course of years a new situation had arisen. A great city had developed of which ninety-five per cent. of the inhabitants were Chinese, and it had become impolitic, to use no stronger word, to attempt to carry on the government without giving the Chinese population some voice in public affairs, and especially in the matter of taxation.

Several attempts had previously been made to bring about a change in this direction, but each time the Rate-payers were unwilling to give their sanction.

Action of the French Municipality The French had acted more wisely, and had entered into an agreement with the Chinese authorities on April 8th, 1914, according to which "Two Chinese notables shall be designated by common accord by the Commissioner of Foreign Affairs and the Consul-General for France for arranging questions touching Chinese residents in the French Settlement with the French Municipal Council." [1]

It was easier for the French to reach a settlement in this matter, inasmuch as their Municipal Council is only an advisory body, and the final authority rests with their Consul-General.

We can see, however, that the policy of meeting the wishes of the Chinese had a good deal to do with the consent of the Chinese authorities to the extension of the French Concession, when at the same time the request for extension of the International Settlement was refused.

There was continued agitation on the part of the Chinese in the International Settlement for representation, and after the May 30th incident it increased in vehemency.

Resolution Passed at Ratepayers' Meeting on April 15th

At the Ratepayers' meeting on April 15th, 1926, the following epoch-making resolution was passed " that in the opinion of this meeting the participation of the Chinese residents in the government of the Settlement is desirable; and that the Council is hereby authorized and instructed to make forthwith representations to the Powers concerned with a view to securing the addition of three Chinese members at an early date."

There was considerable delay in the election of these three Chinese members, due largely to the fact that during the revolutionary period the desire was expressed by a section of the Chinese that "an equal share in the responsibility in the administration of the Municipal affairs and the maintenance of peace and order in the Settlement with the foreign members of the present Municipal Council" should be given to the Chinese.

Later the proposal that there should be three Chinese

---

[1] Later, this number was increased to five.

representatives on the Council was agreed to for the time being, and they were duly elected by the Chinese Rate-payers Association, taking their seats in April, 1928. In addition, six Chinese representatives were elected to seats on the Departmental Committees.

Chinese Political Affairs General Sun Chuan-fang, who at first had reached an understanding with the Peking Government, according to which he was to control Chekiang and a part of Kiangsu, afterward determined to make himself independent, and on October 17th, 1925, declared war on Marshal Chang Tso-lin. At the outbreak of hostilities, the Fengtien troops in Shanghai were withdrawn. In order to obtain war supplies, General Sun reopened the Arsenal at Lunghua, which had been closed at the request of the Chinese residents after the Kiangsu-Chekiang War, and used it for military purposes.

He arrived in Shanghai on May 3rd, 1926, and was installed the following day as Director-General of the Port of Shanghai and Woosung with Dr. V. K. Ting as Associate Director-General and Mayor of Greater Shanghai. Plans were made for organizing a municipality in the environs of the Settlements on a modern basis. Unfortunately Dr. Ting was injured in a serious automobile accident (December 13th, 1926) and was obliged to resign his appointment.

Rendition of the Mixed Court The Chinese delegates who came to Shanghai for the settlement of the May 30th incident made the statement that "the rendition of the Mixed Court or setting a date for doing so" was one of the essential points to a permanent understanding between the Chinese and foreign communities in Shanghai.

An account has already been given of the way in which the Mixed Court passed under the authority of

the Municipal Council at the time of the Revolution of
1911.   The change in the original status of the Mixed
Court had undoubtedly become a sore grievance in the
minds of the Chinese, and demands for rendition became
insistent.

A new situation also arose owing to the fact that
the Russians who had waïved the rights of extraterritoriality and come under the jurisdiction of the Chinese
courts, refused to recognize the jurisdiction of the Mixed
Court and were backed up in this stand by the Soviet
Government.

Negotiations in regard to the matter were first
carried on in Peking between the Diplomatic Body and
the Chinese Government, but no agreement was reached.
Then in April, 1926, the Consular Body at Shanghai
undertook to settle the problem with the local Chinese
authorities.

The Chinese representatives were Dr. V. K. Ting,
and Mr. Hsu Yuan, Commissioner of Foreign Affairs
at Shanghai.   Both acted under instructions from Marshal
Sun Chuan-fang.   After long deliberations, it was decided
that the Court should come completely under the jurisdiction of Chinese Judges, except that, in cases in which a
foreigner having extraterritorial rights or the Municipal
Council is plaintiff or complainant, the Consul of the
nationality concerned or the Senior Consul may send an
official to sit jointly with the Judge in accordance with
the provisions of the treaties.

On January 1st, 1927, Mr. N. Aall, Norwegian
Consul-General and Senior Consul *ad interim,* handed
over to the Commissioner of Foreign Affairs the official
seal of the Mixed Court.

1925
Census   During the year 1925 the Council took a
census of the population of the Interna-

tional Settlement. The figures showed a remarkable growth within a period of five years.

The total number of foreign residents in 1925 was 29,947 as against 23,307 in 1920, and the number of Chinese residents was 810,299 as against 759,839 in 1920. In the French Concession the population was foreigners 7,811 and Chinese 297,072.

An analysis of the figures showed that the Germans had a threefold greater number than in 1920 (indicating a rapid return after repatriation) and that there was a great increase in the Russian population. The Japanese was the largest foreign community, numbering 13,804 as against 10,215 in 1920. The British and Portuguese remained stationary, while the Americans showed a decrease.

Gift of Country Hospital At the Ratepayers' meeting in April, 1926, the Chairman of the Council made an announcement of the generous gift to the Municipality, by an anonymous donor, of the Country Hospital on the Great Western Road. It had accommodation for 125 patients and was to be "for the benefit of the foreign residents of Shanghai without distinction as to nationality or religious belief." The value of the gift was one and a half million taels.

Dr. J. B. Fearn, the Medical Superintendent of the General Hospital, was appointed as the first Resident Medical Superintendent of the Country Hospital. Although in poor health, he devoted himself untiringly to the work of both hospitals and fearing his days were numbered, was especially eager to get the new hospital well organized before his end came. He died, greatly lamented by all who knew him, on June 7th, 1926.

Industrial Troubles Industrial conditions remained very unsettled throughout the period we are describing. Although the long strike had ended, yet strikes continued to break out, showing that labour agitators were at work stirring up trouble. Again we see the sinister influence of Bolshevism. Four Soviet emissaries arrived in Shanghai in August, 1925, and assured the Chinese workers of the sympathetic friendship of Russia. There were strikes in cotton mills, China Merchants Steam Navigation Company, Chinese Telegraph Administration, Commercial Press, Chung Hua Book Company, and the Post Office. To show how serious this was in regard to the productive activity of labour, it was estimated that by the long strike some ten million working days had been lost.

New Buildings　　In spite of the strikes, however, several new large buildings were completed and others were in course of construction. In 1925 the new American Club was formally opened, and the new Race Club Stand on Mohawk Road was finished. The latter is 490 feet in length and is one of the largest in the world. The rows of steps from which the racing is viewed, put end to end, are estimated to be three miles in length.

In 1926 the new premises of the Cercle Sportif Francais, on the site of the former German Country Club, were thrown open.

The foundation stone of the Foreign Y.M.C.A. Building was laid by Captain Robert Dollar, a generous benefactor of Y.M.C.A.'s throughout the world. This building, of a novel style of architecture, recently completed, stands opposite the Race Course on Bubbling Well Road.

Work was begun on the new Sassoon Building on the corner of Nanking Road and The Bund. The entrance to Nanking Road, the main thoroughfare of the Settlement, had always been too narrow, but as this palatial structure is built on a new line, allowing greater width to this important road, this defect has now been remedied.

The site of the British Post Office on the corner of Peking and Museum Roads was sold in 1925 to the Shanghai Land Investment Company. It measured a little over two *mow* and three *fun*,[1] and the price paid for it, Tls. 293,000, shows the increased value of land in this part of the Settlement.

Nationalist Movement   Returning to the account of the Nationalist movement in China, we must briefly refer to the events preceding the taking of Shanghai by the Nationalist Government,[2] and the situation which developed in the Settlement.

Advance from Canton to the North   After the communists had gained control of the government in Canton it practically came under the domination of Borodin and other Russian advisers. A northern expedition was organized under the command of Marshal Chiang Kai-shek, who had formerly been principal of the Whampoa Academy for the training of cadets, and his army set out for the North in July, 1926.

As the Nationalist Army advanced, the soldiers occupied, among other buildings, schools, hospitals and churches, and the missionaries were obliged to evacuate. Attached to each army was a political department, at the head of which was frequently a communist. This department carried on propaganda work in the territory about to be taken over, and thus prepared the way for the coming of the soldiers. The Nationalists received a hearty welcome from the people. In the territory which they occupied they set up a government according to the Soviet form. The political departments were bitterly anti-religious and anti-Christian and took as one of their slogans that "religion was an opiate for the people."

---

[1] A *fun* is one-tenth of a *mow*.
[2] The Government of China now in power has adopted the name of National Government.

Marshal Wu Pei-fu's forces in Central China were repeatedly routed, and the Nationalists by September, 1926, were in possession of Hankow and Hanyang. Wuchang was besieged and although it held out for some time, was finally forced to capitulate. The capital of the Nationalist Government, with Borodin as the chief adviser, was moved to Hankow.

There was considerable anti-foreign spirit connected with the Nationalist movement. It was directed especially against Great Britain, the United States and Japan, as they were considered to be the three great imperialistic and capitalistic powers.

Return of the Hankow and Kiukiang British Concessions Hostility to Great Britain led to rioting in the Hankow British Concession, and finally resulted, by the consent of the British authorities, in its occupation by the Nationalist troops. The return of the British Concessions at Hankow and Kiukiang, according to the Chen-O'Malley agreement, was regarded as a great triumph for the Revolution.

Preparations to Defend Shanghai The fate of the Hankow and Kiukiang British Concessions aroused the people of Shanghai to the danger to which they might be exposed when the Nationalist Army advanced on Shanghai, and brought about the adoption of measures on the part of the Western Governments for the defence of the Settlements. In January, 1927, British, American, Japanese, French, Italian, Dutch and Spanish troops were hurried to the East.

Great Britain alone sent a defence force of 20,000 men, the largest Expeditionary Force she had ever sent as far as China.

Nationalists Enter Shanghai The Nationalist advance on Shanghai began on February 19th, and was opposed by Marshal Sun Chuan-fang, who tried to hold Chekiang, but largely due to treachery among his generals, he was forced to give way.

The same policy was adopted in regard to Shanghai as in other places. Before the arrival of the Nationalist Army, a vigorous propaganda was carried on, and labour troubles fomented. A hundred thousand labourers went out on strike under the direction of the communist party. The local headquarters of this party were in the French Concession, and took orders by wireless from Hankow.

When the Nationalist troops took Shanghai, it was entered by an advance guard of less than 500 men which came up from Minghong, and the main army did not enter until two days later. For a time there was considerable fighting in Chapei and in the native city, but the Nationalists soon asserted their authority.

Before their advent, Shanghai had taken on the appearance of an armed camp. Barbed wire barriers had been constructed around both the International Settlement and the French Concession, and troops were placed at the barriers to hinder the entrance of armed troops. In the International Settlement the British forces occupied outposts some distance away from the boundaries, in the western district. All residents were requested to be indoors between the hours of 10.00 p.m. and 4.00 a.m.

In this way disturbances of a serious nature were prevented, and the Settlements were preserved in safety.

Missionary Refugees Owing to the spread of the Nationalist movement and the fact that there was so much communism connected with it, the missionaries throughout the greater part of the country had been ordered to withdraw from their stations by the consular authorities of their respective governments. At one time there were as many as 800 missionary refugees in Shanghai. The Nanking incident is an evidence that the policy of withdrawal from the interior had been a wise one, and the means of avoiding similar calamities.

Chiang Kai-shek Comes to Shanghai   On March 26th, Marshal Chiang Kai-shek suddenly appeared in Shanghai. For some time the breach between him and Borodin had been widening, and he had assumed an attitude of hostility towards communism. After his arrival in Shanghai, he formed a party in opposition to that in Hankow, took stern measures to suppress the communists, and tried to enlist the support of the moderate element in the Kuomintang.

The raid of the Soviet Embassy at Peking on April 6th, 1927, was a revelation to the Chinese of the plot of Borodin to bring the Kuomintang under the control of the Soviet Government and made them inclined to support the more moderate government of Marshal Chiang Kai-shek.

Attempt to Bring about Union between Nanking and Hankow Factions   Later, after the dismissal of Borodin and Eugene Chen, the Minister of Foreign Affairs from the party in Hankow, an attempt was made to bring about a union between the Nanking and the Hankow factions. In order to facilitate this, Chiang Kai-shek resigned as Generalissimo on August 12th, 1927.

Conferences between the two factions began in Shanghai on September 9th, 1927 and a union was effected. Contrary to expectations, Chiang Kai-shek returned to Shanghai on November 10th, and after a short time was persuaded to resume his office as Generalissimo and take command of the expedition against the Northern militarists. On December 1st, he was married to Miss Mayling Soong, the sister of Mr. T. V. Soong, the Finance Minister of the Nationalist Government.

Severance of Relations with Soviet Russia
On December 14th the Nationalist Government severed relations with Soviet Russia, and ordered the closing up of the Soviet Consulates and commercial agencies in Nationalist territory and the departure of the staffs within a week, and thus the Red flag disappeared from the Russian Consulate in Shanghai.

Friction with Defence Force
Taking into consideration the large foreign force gathered in Shanghai, it is truly remarkable that no serious disorder occurred and that there was so little friction between the troops and populace.

The Chinese authorities made frequent protests against what they considered as infringements of China's sovereign rights. The housing of six aeroplanes on the Shanghai Race Course was not viewed by them with favour, and they objected strenuously to flights over the Settlement and the adjoining country.

In one instance, on August 16th, serious friction took place. A plane was obliged to make a forced landing on the International Race Course at Kiangwan, and the Chinese authorities took occasion to register their opposition by retaining the wings of the machine. When the request for the return of the wings was made and refused, the Commander of the British Defence Force, Major-General Sir John Duncan, gave orders that some rails on the Shanghai-Hangchow-Ningpo Railway to the south of the bridge crossing the Soochow Creek near Jessfield, should be removed, thus hindering the traffic on that line. After some further negotiations, matters were amicably arranged, the missing wings were returned, and the line was restored.

Opening of Public Parks to Chinese
During the year 1927, owing to the seriousness of the political situation, it was impossible for the Municipal Council to do more

than conserve its position. Mr. Stirling Fessenden in a manifesto reiterated the offer of putting three Chinese representatives on the Council.

At the Ratepayers' meeting held on April 13th the following resolution was proposed, "That Jessfield and Hongkew Parks, the Public Gardens, the Bund Lawns and Foreshore, Quinsan Gardens and Brenan Piece be opened to the Chinese on the same terms as foreigners."[1]

Opposition to Increased Rates The Council experienced considerable difficulty when it attempted to collect the Municipal rates which had been increased from 14 to 16 per cent., and the same arguments were advanced as formerly in regard to the illegality of taxation without representation and without consultation with the Chinese authorities. Much bad feeling was aroused, and for a time it was feared that serious trouble might arise. After a few months the agitation ceased, and the Local Commercial Federation issued a statement advising that in the interests of peace and order, the increased rates should be paid, under protest.

Crime in Shanghai At this period of Shanghai's history, armed robberies and kidnapping increased at an alarming rate. It became evident that well-organized criminal gangs were operating in the International Settlement and the outlying districts, and that they were under the direction of men of considerable ability. In order to assist the Council in combating the danger, a secret fund was established, to which many of

---

[1] Action was postponed until the following year, and at the Ratepayers' meeting on April 18th, 1928, a similar resolution was proposed and passed. A small entrance fee was charged both to Chinese and foreigners. The Chinese resort to the parks in large numbers. By opening them to the general public on the same terms, another source of grievance has been removed.

the Chinese residents subscribed. Determined efforts, which have only been partially successful, have been made to cope with the evil.

H. B. M.'s Birthday　By the presence of the British Defence Force in Shanghai on the birthday of H.B.M. King George V., June 3rd, the opportunity was given for a spectacle of a unique nature. This was the Trooping of the Colour at the Race Course by the Second Battalion of the Coldstream Guards. The precision with which the various movements of this elaborate ceremony were carried out elicited great enthusiasm from the spectators. In the evening there was another large gathering to witness the Torchlight Tattoo.

Earthquake in Shanghai　Among other matters of interest to the community in 1927 was an earthquake which occurred on February 3rd. It was the sharpest shock felt in Shanghai for many years. The fact that Shanghai is built on a mud flat has prevented these earth tremors from doing serious damage.

New Synagogue　The erection of the beautiful new Synagogue, Beth Aharon, on Museum Road, and its opening on June 30th attracted a large number of interested spectators. This building of Moorish and Byzantine architecture is one of the most striking in Shanghai, and furnishes the Jewish community with a worthy house of worship.

Consecration of Chinese Bishop　Another Chinese Bishop of the Anglican Communion, the Rt. Rev. Ding Ing-ong, was consecrated in Shanghai on November 1st in All Saints Church, to be Assistant Bishop in the Diocese of Fukien. The service was impressive, and the large congregation witnessed to the growth of the Church in China, and gave hope for the future, at a time when the anti-Christian movement was so much in evidence.

Trade in 1926-1927

Notwithstanding the civil war, the trade of China reached a high figure in 1926. The Customs revenue of Shanghai, excluding famine relief surtax, increased by Hk. Tls. 6,682,443 over 1925. The total revenue of Hk. Tls. 32,705,651 meant that 41.81 per cent. of the total Customs revenue was furnished by Shanghai. As pointed out in the Customs Report for 1927, on account of the general political upheaval in China, there was a marked decline in the revenue for that year. The total amount collected under import duty was Hk. Tls. 34,903,322, a decrease of Hk. Tls. 7,951,705 as compared with 1926. A total of Hk. Tls. 25,461,617 was collected on exports, a decrease on the collection of 1926 of Hk. Tls. 802,170. The percentage of the total revenue furnished by Shanghai was 37.34 per cent. Shipping made a remarkable recovery, and placed Shanghai in the list of the first six or seven principal ports of the world.

A good deal of the increased trade was due to the growth of Japan's commercial interests in China. Japanese manufacturers and merchants enjoy special advantages through cheapness of labour, proximity to China, and a greater intimacy with the customs of the people with whom they deal, and hence are formidable competitors of the merchants of other countries.

Deaths of Prominent Citizens

Some prominent citizens passed away during this period. The first of these was Mr. John Prentice, on April 30th, 1925. He was one of Shanghai's oldest and most respected residents, having lived in the Settlement for more than fifty years. In connection with the Shanghai Dock and Engineering Company, he became one of the most widely known shipbuilders in the Far East. He was interested in all that made for the welfare of the community, and took a prominent part in Settlement affairs.

20

The next to follow was the Rev. G. H. Bondfield, D.D., who had resided in China for over forty years, and had done a fine piece of work in connection with the British and Foreign Bible Society. Retiring from Shanghai on account of ill health, he passed away in Bournemouth, England, in November, 1925. While in Shanghai he had taken a keen interest in the educational work of the Municipality.

The death of Mr. Henry Lester, Shanghai's multi-millionaire, occurred on May 14th, 1926. He came to Shanghai in 1863 or 1864 as an architect and land surveyor. His wealth was almost entirely due to his investments in land in the early days.

According to the terms of his will, large bequests were made to the Trustees of the Holy Trinity Cathedral for replacing and rebuilding the present Cathedral School, Deanery and Church House, and an endowment was left for the School.

The large sum of Tls. 2,000,000 was bequeathed to the Shantung Road Hospital for rebuilding and endowment, the hospital thereafter to be called "The Lester Chinese Hospital."

Tls. 200,000 were left to St. Luke's Hospital.

The following institutions were also benefited by his will: "The Institution for the Chinese Blind," "The Children's Refuge," "The Little Sisters of the Poor," "The Shanghai Missions to Ricshamen," and "St. Joseph's Asylum for the Poor."

An Institute to be known as "The Henry Lester Institute for Medical Education and Research" was to be erected and equipped at a cost of Tls. 400,000, and endowed.

A school to be known as "The Lester School" for 300 scholars or more, both Chinese and foreign, but especially Chinese, was to be erected at a cost of Tls. 500,000, and to be endowed.

Dr. C. J. Davenport, Superintendent of the Shantung Road Hospital, died suddenly on September 4th, 1926. He arrived as a medical missionary in China in 1889, being stationed first in Chungking and then in Wuchang. In 1904 he came to the Shantung Road Hospital and did valuable work in the development of that useful institution.

During the year 1927 there were two deaths that call for special notice. The first was that of Mrs. Mary Houston Allen who died on May 14th. She was the widow of the well-known missionary educator, Dr. Young J. Allen, already mentioned in these pages, and arrived in Shanghai with her husband in 1860. Thus her life in the Settlement extended over a period of nearly 67 years.

The second was that of Dr. Gilbert Reid, the founder of the International Institute, who died on October 7th. He came to China as a missionary in 1882. He was a man of many activities, and took as his special work a mission among the higher class Chinese. Out of this grew the International Institute, established in Shanghai in 1902. His great aim was to promote cordial relations between Chinese and foreigners and to bring about better mutual understanding. The buildings of the Institute on Avenue Joffre were erected by contributions secured in China, England, Europe and America.

Owing to the Great War, and changed political conditions in China, the activities of the Institute in recent years have been considerably curtailed.

CHAPTER XXIX.

EPILOGUE.

Five Turning Points As we have traced the history of the International Settlement from the days of its beginnings, we have seen how it has developed from what might be properly called a trading post, established by agreement with the Chinese Government, into one of the most important commercial and industrial centres in the world.

There have been five great turning points in its history.

The first was the consent given to the residence of Chinese within its borders, resulting in an ever increasing Chinese population with growing commercial and property interests, until it came about that the little community of foreigners had to provide a government for a population, ninety-five per cent. of which were citizens of China.

The second was the conversion of a trading centre into a great manufacturing city which came about after the Sino-Japanese War in 1895. The Settlement took on a new character with the coming of the Industrial Revolution, and began to face the same labour problems with which we are familiar in the West.

The third was the decision to develop the harbour of Shanghai by the establishment of the Whangpoo Conservancy Board, after the Boxer Outbreak, enabling Shanghai to become one of the great shipping ports of the world.

The fourth was the adoption of the policy of neutrality for the International Settlement, making it a place of great political importance, sometimes unfortunately a harbour of safety for political refugees, and a place where all factions could carry on secret meetings relating to the political movements in the country.

The fifth was the revolt of the Chinese residents of the Settlements against paternal government, and a demand for a voice in municipal affairs, caused by student agitation, and the growth of the spirit of nationalism.

Contrast between Earlier and Later Days
As the Settlement has grown, there has been considerable change in the life of the foreign community. Some of the older residents regret the passing away of the "good old days." They recall the time when the foreign community was like one large family, every one knowing every one else, the foreigner living in a lordly manner in a large house with extensive grounds, with a host of servants at his beck and call. He enjoyed many exclusive privileges, in a self-centred community, with little interest in the people around him except as it concerned commercial relations. He had his amusements, his pony racing, paper hunts, boat racing, houseboat excursions into the hinterland and good shooting. He enjoyed his club, and entertainments of an amateur nature, in music and theatricals. He found the climate not too trying, and revelled in the weather of autumn and early winter, and in the spring. He was not overworked and always had time for play. There was plenty of opportunity for physical exercise in riding, cricket, football and tennis, and there was a constant round of social engagements, dinners, card parties and dances.

He did not bother himself greatly in regard to intellectual pursuits, but there was always a number interested in good reading, in the debates of the Literary and Debating Society and in the lectures of the Royal Asiatic Society. He could express his public spirit by joining the Volunteer Corps and the Fire Brigade, or if he were a "taipan," by taking his share in Municipal administration.

It was a well-to-do community with but little poverty. In many ways it might be likened to the life of the southern planter in the United States in pre-civil war days.

Much of this mode of life has passed or is passing. The community is no longer one big family, and is divided into many sections. Life has become more complex, and the fortunes of the foreign community have become inextricably intertwined with those of the Chinese community. Wealth and property have shifted more and more into the hands of the latter. The days of amassing a fortune in a short time have passed, and the competition in business has become keener. The man with the moderate income can no longer disport himself as one of the lords of creation, and spend as lavishly as in the days gone by. He is hemmed in on every side by his fellow Chinese residents and cannot live entirely to himself.

Yet with all the changes and with all the seeming loss of a unique and pleasant sort of existence, there have come compensations. Shanghai has been taken into world affairs and its life has broadened. It has become closely connected with other parts of China and with the rest of the world. It is no longer isolated.

The railway and the steamship enable the resident of Shanghai to travel extensively. Summer resorts in China and Japan are open to his family, and the journey to the homeland has become a more frequent possibility.

He still has his old amusements, and his former opportunities for physical recreation, and new ones in addition. Shanghai is visited by travelling theatrical companies, and by the greatest musical artists of the West.

Every year it is called upon to entertain a host of distinguished visitors.

The social life is just as much in evidence as formerly, and clubs and societies have multiplied.

No longer a small community—but a great city, with its imposing buildings, wide boulevards, teeming population, crowded shipping, large wharves, numerous factories, bustling commerce, and congested traffic, under the government of a well-organized Municipal Administration. One wonders as to its future, but that is not in the purview of the historian. By the admission of a Chinese element into the administration of the Settlement, the Municipality entered on a new era. The future would seem to depend in no small degree on the development of a spirit of co-operation and friendship between foreigners and Chinese, in place of the all too frequent antagonism and mutual suspicion of the past.

Granted this spirit of co-operation, the International Settlement may continue to develop as one of the greatest commercial and industrial centres of the world, of benefit to foreigners and Chinese alike.

ADDENDA.

Since the paragraph in regard to Schools for Chinese Children on page 122 was written, the Council has embarked upon a scheme for the elementary education of Chinese children in the Settlement, two schools having been established in different districts of the Settlement under the direction of a specially qualified Chinese education officer. In contrast to the Public Schools for Chinese, which are referred to in the Chapter on "Education," these new schools do not include English in their curriculum, the idea being to give educational facilities to Chinese children of the middle and poorer classes. This noteworthy decision on the part of the Council was taken in the summer of 1928 and it is pleasing to report that work at the schools was actually started in the autumn of the same year.

*　　　*　　　*

By oversight, no mention has been made of the remarkable work and influence of one of the originators of the first Public School for Chinese—Dr. Timothy Richard.

As General Secretary of the Society for the Diffusion of Christian and General Knowledge founded in 1885 (now the Christian Literature Society), he helped to disseminate among the Chinese modern ideas, and a knowledge of the progress made in the Western World. His Chinese translation of Mackenzie's *Nineteenth Century* was instrumental in bringing about the Reform Movement of 1898. His name was probably more widely known among the Chinese than that of any other foreign missionary.

BIBLIOGRAPHY.

BIBLIOGRAPHY.

CLARKE, J. D.: *A Short History of Shanghai*, 1921.

MONTALTO DE JESUS, C. A.: *Historic Shanghai*, 1909.

LANNING, G. and COULING, S.: *The History of Shanghai*, 1921.

KOTENEV, A. M.: *Shanghai—Its Mixed Court and Council*, 1925.

KOTENEV, A. M.: *Shanghai—Its Municipality and the Chinese*, 1927.

Whangpoo Conservancy Board, General Series No. 8, 1928.

DARWENT, C. E.: *Shanghai—A Handbook for Travellers and Residents*, 1920.

WRIGHT, ARNOLD: *Twentieth Century Impressions of Hongkong and Shanghai*, 1908.

MORSE, H. B.: *The International Relations of the Chinese Empire*, 1918.

Files of the *North-China Herald*.

DENNETT, TYLER: *Americans in Eastern Asia*, 1922.

ARNOLD, JULEAN: *China—A Commercial and Industrial Handbook*, 1926.

POTT, F. L. HAWKS: *A Sketch of Chinese History*, 1923.

MILLARD, THOMAS F.: *China—Where It is To-day and Why*, 1928.

WILLOUGHBY, W. W.: *Foreign Rights and Interests in China*, 1920.

WILLOUGHBY, W. W.: *China at the Conference*, 1922.

WILLIAMS, E. T.: *China Yesterday and To-day*, 1923.

TYAU, M. T. Z.: *Treaty Obligations between China and Other States*, 1917.

The Maritime Customs—Statistical Series.

WANG, Y. P.: *Rise of the Native Press in China*.

TAI, EN-SAI: *Treaty Ports in China*.

The China Year Book, 1928.

Report of General Education Committee convened by Municipal Council, 1912.

Report of General Education Committee convened by Municipal Council, 1922.

DAVENPORT, C. J.: Seventy-seventh Annual Report of the Shantung Road Hospital, 1924.

MORSE, H. B.: *The East India Company Trading to China*, 1927.

Annual Reports, Shanghai Municipal Council.

MACLELLAN, J. W.: *The Story of Shanghai*, 1889.

Official History of Shanghai (in Chinese), 同治上海縣志, 1872.

MAYERS, WILLIAM FREDERICK: *Treaties between the Empire of China and Foreign Powers*, 1901.

Land Regulations and Bye-Laws for the Foreign Settlements of Shanghai, North of the Yangkingpang.

KOO, V. K. W.: *The Status of Aliens in China*, 1912.

MORSE–MACNAIR: *Far Eastern International Relations*, 1928.

NORTON, H. K.: *China and The Powers*, 1927.

Eastern Miscellany, 東方雜誌.

INDEX.

A

N

O